Merry Chris
Love, Sue, Rod,

THE SPITFIRE SMITHS

THE
SPITFIRE SMITHS

A Unique Story of Brothers in Arms

Squadron Leader R.I.A. Smith DFC & Bar

with Christopher Shores

GRUB STREET · LONDON

Published by
Grub Street
4 Rainham Close
London
SW11 6SS

British Library Cataloguing in Publication Data
Smith, R.I.A.
  The Spitfire Smiths: a unique story of brothers in arms
  1. Smith, R.I.A. 2. Smith, Jerry 3. Fighter pilots –
  Canada – Biography 4. World War, 1939-1945 – Aerial
  operations, British 5. World War, 1939-1945 – Personal
  narratives, Canadian
  I. Title II. Shores, Christopher F.
  940.5'44941'0922

ISBN 13: 978-1-906502-11-9

Formatted by Pearl Graphics, Hemel Hempstead

Printed and bound by MPG Ltd, Bodmin, Cornwall

Grub Street only uses FSC
(Forest Stewardship Council) paper for its books.

CONTENTS

INTRODUCTION

I initially met Rod Smith soon after my first book, *Aces High*, was published in 1966. He was one of the first – if not <u>the</u> first – of those fighter pilots included therein to contact me with corrections or amendments. 126 Squadron, with which he had served in Malta, had failed to maintain the unit diary during the summer of 1942, and as an inexperienced young researcher with official access only to squadron records (this being pre-Public Record Office release) I had not been able to ascertain any other avenue of investigation.

Rod, at that time still a successful Canadian lawyer, was visiting England and suggested that I should join him for Sunday breakfast. He was staying at the Dorchester Hotel on London's Park Lane, which in those days was just about the best. As a fairly newly qualified and still quite impecunious chartered surveyor, having just taken on my first mortgage and with two very young children to boot, I was deeply impressed. Indeed, I think my eyes must have stood out like the proverbial 'organ-stops'! After eating, we walked and talked in Hyde Park and Rod was kindness itself. He not only noted and signed the biographical item on himself in the book, but also told me who the other pilots in the squadron had been at that time, and what he thought each of them had achieved.

It was the beginning of a long friendship. Rod came quite frequently to England in those days, and each time would ring me and we would meet. We also corresponded, and following his retirement, Rod often telephoned me and we would talk for long periods about books, projects and aviation generally. When Brian Cull and I were writing *Malta: The Spitfire Year, 1942*, he was very helpful to us, providing copies of his own and his brother Jerry's logbooks, Jerry's diary, and copies of relevant photographs. He was later to provide a most detailed critique of the latter chapters covering the period when he had been on the island. We met at the 1992 50th Anniversary of the siege of Malta, held at the RAF Club, and then again at Duxford for the 60th Anniversary of the first flight of the Spitfire.

Rod's two great friends in England were 'Laddie' Lucas,

with whom I had also become friendly, and 'Johnnie' Johnson, who was, of course, probably the RAF's greatest and most famous fighter pilot. I was well aware how upset Rod was by Laddie's death to cancer, and that he was quite devastated by Johnnie's similar demise all too soon afterwards.

The last time I saw Rod was at the RAF Club when he had come over to attend Johnnie's memorial service. Billy Drake and I were having lunch at the Club at the time I was 'ghosting' the latter's autobiography, and I was able to introduce him to Rod and fellow Malta 'ace' Ian Maclennan, who had accompanied him from Canada. In 2002, not so long after this, my wife and I were about to make our first trip to western Canada where we hoped to spend some time with Rod, when the news of his death in tragic circumstances reached me. This was followed by a call from a family friend to ask if, as an old friend of Rod's and an established aviation author, I would take on the task of completing his unfinished autobiography.

I very gladly agreed to this, and as I was about to be in Canada, was invited to visit Rod's sister, Wendy Noble, in Toronto, to discuss the matter and go through Rod's various papers. These proved to be voluminous, and it took me a little time to rush through them and indicate those which I thought might be important to the project. Wendy then went about having all these files photocopied and shipped to me in England. I had several other books that I was working on at the time to complete, and then I set to with the files.

Rod had written chapters covering his boyhood, some of his training, and his time on Malta. Everything else needed to be put together from his notes and correspondence. For me taking the story up to the end of the war in 1945, and covering the years of his postwar studies and service with the RCAF Auxiliary was the easy part. However, Rod had possessed an acute brain and a considerable knowledge of aerodynamics and ballistics. Particularly following his retirement, he studied the air war deeply and became involved in some lengthy correspondences with a number of notable people. In particular, he entered into a long and sometimes almost acrimonious 'combat' with Wg Cdr R.P. 'Roly' Beamont.

In a letter which he sent to the famous test pilot, Alex Henshaw in 1997, he wrote the following important words:

'I'm glad you liked the "prologue" to my book (which I should call my reputed book, I have been at it so long.) I did many of the key parts of it starting about eight years ago, when I was still practising law. I am now trying to do the parts in between. I realise I was procrastinating by doing the parts more suited to my temperament first. The prologue alone took ages.

I must say I love writing, as well as doing the research (which I feel is 97% done). My book is heavy on the historical side, technical stuff included. It has been a hobby of mine to get to the bottom of superchargers and guns, as well as aircraft, etc, which I am sure can be put simply and clearly in a few lines or paragraphs here and there. Without some technical explanations readers never really know what fighter pilots were up against.'

From this I knew at once that to be true to Rod's memory, I had to include a considerable quantity of his views on these matters. However, he had not actually started writing any of this part of the book, so I have adopted the course of action of taking relevant paragraphs out of letters and drafts which show his knowledge and research on the various matters he considered to be of importance. Readers will quickly become aware, I think, that while Rod was a most courteous and kindly gentleman of the old school, he was also essentially a 'cut the bullshit' man of the first order.

Throughout I have been greatly assisted by Wendy Noble without whose efforts I certainly could not have completed this task in what I hope is an acceptable and readable account of a most special person.

POEM FOR ROD

Give me the wings, magician! So their tune
Mix with the silver trumpets of the moon,
And, beyond music mounting, clean outrun
The golden diaspora of the sun.
There is a secret that the birds are learning
Where the long lanes in heaven have a turning
And no man yet has followed: therefore these
Laugh hauntingly across our usual seas.
I'll not be mocked by curlews in the sky;
Give me the wings, magician, or I die.

Hubert Wolfe

PART ONE

CHAPTER ONE

CAPTIVATION

A biplane droning lazily across the sky in the mid 1920s remains one of the clearest memories of my early childhood. It only aroused my curiosity, but if I had known it was going faster than my father's car could go it would have aroused more than that. Others appearing from time to time began to hint of a wider world than the street where my family lived in Regina, in the middle of the Canadian prairies, where I was born in March of 1922.

In the twenties aircraft, which we called 'aeroplanes' and the Americans called 'airplanes', were scarce. The vast majority of those remaining at the end of the First World War were scrapped, and few new ones were being built. The resulting rarity enhanced an aura of danger inseparable from aviation in the public mind. An aeroplane on the ground would never fail to attract attention; nor would its 'aviator', as a pilot was commonly called then.

The aura of danger was not discouraging to every young boy, of course, but my first exposure to a classic example of it, when I was five, repelled me. I was taken to see *Wings*, a movie about two young pilots in the American Air Service in France in the First World War. Though silent for speech, it pioneered sound effects. It became famous for spectacle but, with the exception of a memorable three minute bit-part by a then unknown Gary Cooper, it was hopelessly melodramatic; it became the stereotype for its kind. Scene after scene was of strikingly marked biplanes chasing each other wildly around the sky, machine guns blazing. One of them would inevitably get hit, stream flames and a long trail of black smoke, and then spiral downwards with ever-increasing speed and howl of engine to a fearful crash below. I was terrified; that men would risk such a fate seemed unimaginable to me.

A few months later I had my first real encounter with an

1

aeroplane however, and the effect was altogether different. I was on a Sunday drive with an uncle along the south-west edge of the city when we came across a biplane on the prairie; at my urging we stopped and walked up to it. Three men were preparing it for flight.

It looked surprisingly fragile; its wheels were like a bicycle's; its wings and fuselage, fastened and braced to each other with struts and wires, were obviously just frameworks covered with cloth treated with something ('dope' I later learned) which made it taut and shiny and smelled curiously attractive.

Two of the men soon put on helmets and goggles and climbed into the craft's two open cockpits. The third swung the propeller round by hand a few times, called out "contact", and received it back. After another swing or two the engine coughed into life with a few puffs of smoke and then settled down to a steady rumbling. The rocker arms and coil springs on top of the engine which operated its valves were exposed to the air, in the fashion of the time. Their curious sequence and blurred up and down motion intrigued me, as did the smell of exhaust and dope combined. The whole ritual was engrossing, and I was getting excited.

In a few minutes chocks in front of the wheels were pulled away, the craft trundled ahead a few yards, turned into wind, and paused. The engine then began to pick up and it moved forward, slowly at first but with ever increasing speed as the noise grew to a thrilling roar. Its tail rose until its fuselage was level. Though the prairie appeared smooth it proved to be quite undulating, and the aircraft began to bounce from one high spot to the next. The last bounce, after which the craft became fully airborne, was surprisingly heavy, and the right wheel suddenly broke away from the struts that held it, though remaining fixed on the axle which ran across to the left wheel. Both axle and right wheel ended up dangling down from the left wheel, which became hopelessly skewed. I could hardly believe what I was seeing.

The craft climbed to a moderate height and flew some distance to the north. I had no great fear for the men in it because I felt it could come to a safe enough stop by sliding along on its belly. The man left on the ground expressed concern to my uncle, though, that because the landing gear was hidden by the lower wing the men in the aircraft might not know to brace themselves for a sudden stop. He said that only another aeroplane flying alongside could signal the damage, and that the only place another one might be found was on a field a couple of miles to the north-west. My uncle volunteered to drive there for help and we set off.

There was another biplane there, almost ready for flight. When my uncle spoke to its pilot it took off and flew towards the first one, now barely in sight to the north, while we drove back and reported success. My excitement was mounting by the minute when my uncle suddenly declared that as we had done all we could, we would now leave and go across town to see the flowers in a conservatory he often visited on Sundays. I was aghast; with all the earnestness a five year old could muster I pleaded with him to remain, and to my enormous relief he acquiesced.

In a few minutes the two craft approached together, and the disabled one began to descend in a curving glide with its engine just ticking over. It straightened out into the wind and as it got closer to the ground it became level and then slightly tail-down. When it touched down it kicked up a surprisingly large cloud of dust, and though its tail cocked up to a disturbingly high angle it managed to slide along on the forward part of its belly for some distance, though not nearly as far as I had thought it would. When the dust settled, however, both men in it climbed out and waved. The terror inspired by *Wings* was gone – I had become captivated by aeroplanes!

From then on I was attracted by all things pertaining to flying. I longed to go up in an aeroplane but was frustrated for years, if only because my father and mother, like most people at that time, were wary of them. I was not deprived of all the pleasures of aviation in the meantime however, for there were many happy and stimulating times and occasions on the way to fulfilment. Though it has been said that to travel hopefully is better than to arrive, I would not go that far.

In the spring of 1928, when I was six, my English-born mother took me there to visit her father and other relatives. We crossed the Atlantic in a liner, taking eight days each way. My only memorable aviation experience there was seeing a huge blue and silver Armstrong Whitworth Argosy trimotor biplane airliner at Croydon, London's airport then. But my most enduring memories of the trip were the two ocean passages and the seaports at each end. I acquired a love of the sea and ships which has never left me; it was only surpassed, and just for about 20 years, by a passion for aeroplanes – single-engine ones.

The following year I took to walking the long distance west across the prairie to Regina's aerodrome, as airports were usually called then. It was becoming established on the field my uncle and I had driven to for help a couple of years earlier. By good fortune it was nearest to the south-west corner of the city, where my family lived. Going out to it became for me what going down to the docks in seaport towns must have been for boys in the days of sail. My longing to be taken up for a ride in an aeroplane was soon superceded by a need to fly one. I became obsessed by the desire to climb into a cockpit of one, make it go charging across the grass, rise into the air, and fly over hill and dale wherever my spirit might lead me.

Over the succeeding years I walked or rode my bicycle to the aerodrome every week or so, and spent countless hours there watching aeroplanes take off and land. Strange as it may seem for a city of fifty thousand people, I was often the drome's only visitor, especially in winter; I could then usually come right up to the aircraft and look into their cockpits, even when they were inside the hangar, without being told to stay outside the fence. The air engineer who did the maintenance there, Bert Langdon, grew to recognise and tolerate me though we rarely exchanged a word and he never knew my name.

For a long time the only aircraft to be seen there regularly were a few de Havilland Gypsy Moth two-seat biplanes of the Regina Flying Club, which could be counted on to perform endless take-off and landing 'circuits' of the aerodrome. They cruised at only 75 miles per hour so I was always hoping to see something more exciting. The Moth was a graceful aircraft, though. On take-off its air-cooled four-cylinder Gypsy engine, also made by de Havilland, gave a smooth but satisfying roar, and when gliding in to land the whistle of the wind past its bracing wires, combined with the gently ticking of its throttled-back engine, was very pleasing.

In 1931 two events, one local and one far away, brought home to me that aviation was on the move.

In mid summer a low wing monoplane – the first one I had ever seen – flew into Regina. It was an American Travelair 'Mystery' racing plane flown by Frank Hawks. White with horizontal red stripes, it was named 'Texaco No.13'. When I caught sight of it flashing low across the city at about 250 mph, three times as fast as any aircraft I had ever seen before, my whole conception of speed changed in an instant.

Two months later, on the south coast of England, a pilot in Britain's Royal Air Force, Flight Lieutenant George Stainforth, broke the world speed record by flying at 407 mph in an all-metal low-wing Supermarine S.6B seaplane. The S.6B had been designed to capture the Schneider Trophy for Britain, which it had just done. Though surprisingly small it was powered by a large but trimly cowled specially modified Rolls-Royce engine. Texaco No.13 had been a striking sight, but the photographs of the S.6B revealed lines of surpassing beauty.

George Stainforth and all he represented seemed to inhabit another world to me.

When I was ten I was given a working model of a stationary steam engine for Christmas. Most of its moving parts were external and I found their motion intriguing. In the *Scout Annual* given to me the same Christmas was a diagram of a motorcycle engine which revealed that its moving parts, though all internal, were much the same as a steam engine's. I soon discovered that the engines of cars and aeroplanes had much the same mechanism. Aero engines then began to interest me in their own right. My captivation was now complete.

My brother Jerry, a year older than I, did not have the intense interest in aviation that I had, but we were fated by a thousand to one chance to become involved in it side by side in the most vital and adventurous period of our lives.

CHAPTER TWO

GENESIS OF
THE ALPINE SMITHS

My Father

My ancestors on my father's side originally came from Daviot in the Highlands of Scotland from where they emigrated to Canada, as did so many Scots during the nineteenth century. They were by no means impoverished crofters, however, and appear to have made the move to seek their fortunes and a better lifestyle. In 1860 my great-uncle, John Smith, had constructed an imposing 'Italianate' Victorian brick house with a central tower. This was located amidst 100 acres of farmland to the north of Brampton, Ontario, and was purchased from Great-Uncle John by his brother, Donald Alpine Smith, who would become my grandfather.

Grandfather Donald married Margaret McGregor, whose family lived in a slightly older house which had also been built by Scottish stone masons and which was also located in some

6

100 acres. This house was situated on a hill overlooking the town of Inglewood in the Caledon Hills – also near Brampton. Both houses still exist and have been beautifully restored and landscaped. Indeed, Grandfather Donald's property has now been designated as 'historic' and is known as 'The Smith House'.

It was into these surroundings that five children were born – four boys and a girl. The first of these – also christened Donald Alpine – was born on 22 September 1880. On completion of his schooling he read Civil Engineering at the University of Toronto (known then as the SPS – School of Practical Science), graduating some time after the turn of the century. Two of his brothers became dentists, while the youngest, Rod, obtained his BA from the same university, and then commenced studying law. Sadly, he developed tuberculosis – that scourge of those days – and would die around 1910, just as the family had been about to send him to Arizona in the hope that the dry, hot climate might help.

Rod was remembered as being a lively individual with a good sense of humour. A surviving high school picture of him indicates that he possessed a quite close family resemblance to myself, and it was after him that I received my name.

Having completed his studies, Dad became a surveyor and moved to Regina to work, as did all his brothers, including Rod who it seems was articled to a law practice there shortly before his death.

Dad opened his own surveying practice, but closed this in 1914 on the outbreak of World War I to enlist in the 5th Battalion of the Regina Regiment, in which he was commissioned. Shipped to England, and then to the Western Front, he was involved in the 2nd Battle of Ypres, where as an engineer he was responsible for going out under fire to map bridges and other targets for the artillery, etc. It was while he was on leave in London, having transferred to the Canadian Army Engineers, that he met the young English girl who he was subsequently to marry.

My Mother
I have a copy of a nineteen page printed tract entitled *Annals of a West Riding Family* written in 1968 by a Wilfred Robertshaw (whom I had never heard of). This begins in 1379, though the first definite identification is of Jeremiah Robertshaw who was born circa 1795-1800 in the Allerton area of Yorkshire (now a rather dismal suburb of Bradford).

My Mother

He married Mary Illingworth who was born about 1802. They had seven children – including twin boys Luther and Calvin in 1831, and Illingworth, their fifth child, in 1838. The eldest had been a daughter, Sebina, who married Julian White.

In 1850 Jeremiah had set up his own woollen mill in which all his sons would subsequently become partners until the business was sold during the 1890s.

It seems that all Jeremiah's sons lived in the same general area, all owning large villa residences typical of mill masters' houses of the Victorian era, and close to the woollen mills the family owned. At least five of these villas were still standing as late as 1960. Following the disposal of the business several of the family members settled in Ilkley.

I also have a copy of a typewritten memorandum dated March 1921, the letterhead of which is *F. White & Co., Bradford*. This concerns a lecture on 'old Allerton' given by a Mr John Smith. Listed are two partners by the name of Robertshaw. I think my family was related to the Whites by Sebina's marriage, rather than just being their business partners. F.White appears to be someone that my mother called 'Uncle Fred' when she and I visited Ilkley in 1928, when I was six. We also visited Lucy White and her sister (Mary, I think) at Millbrook, Ilkley; mother and I called them 'aunt'.

In 1943 I visited Fred's son, Harold White, and his wife at The Briery in Ilkley, a house he may have inherited from Uncle Fred. I saw Aunt Lucy again at Millbrook, (these two addresses having been included in an address book prepared for me by my mother when I went overseas in 1941). At the end of my visit Harold said to me, "Keep in touch with your Uncle Harold". 'Uncle' and 'Aunt' are commonly used among families that are close friends, of course.

My grandfather Jerrold (christened 'Jeremiah', but hated it and changed it, understandably) was born in Allerton on 28 March 1866, and was the younger son of Illingworth Robertshaw, who had married a local girl, Marianne Briggs. He played rugby for Yorkshire but didn't like the wool business; however, he loved acting in the local Little Theatre. So he left the business for the stage at age 25, and was paid out for his share of the partnership. He had his first professional part in 1894, according to the *Who's Who in the Theatre* of the 1930s, but died in late 1940, a few months too soon for me to see him again.

Particularly, he joined The Garrick Theatre Company, his 'Memorandum of Agreement' with Henry Irving, the actor/manager, lists his first assignment as "A Season in London, at Drury Lane or other Theatre, of about twelve weeks, commencing about the end of April 1903." It appears from this that he then played Antonio in *Merchant of Venice*, opposite Irving as Shylock and Ellen Terry as Portia at Drury Lane from 14 July that year. Certainly he fulfilled this role again from 11 October 1905, this time at the Garrick with Arthur Bourchier as Shylock and Violet Vanbrugh as Portia. The company then did a command performance for King Edward VII on 16 November 1905; the family still have Grandfather's admittance to Windsor Castle for "the Performance by The Garrick Theatre Company", which is stamped with a thick red seal, and topped with an embossed coat of arms with crown and initials ERA made of the same material as the seal.

Grandfather also took part in some ten films, and we have a DVD of *Don Quixote* (a rather primitive 1923 silent movie, directed by Maurice Elvey) in which he played the title role with George Robey as an excellent Sancho Panches. Grandfather was reviewed as bringing a certain grace to the film.

Jerrold's wife was his first cousin, Isobel Robertshaw, daughter of Thomas, his father Illingworth's younger brother. She was a fine pianist and teacher, and at one time had Mark Twain's daughter as a pupil. By 1899 she was accompanist to Blanche Marchesi, a noted singer and teacher, daughter of Mathilde Marchesi, the famous singing teacher who gave the final training to the five great sopranos of the nineteenth century, the most famous of whom was Nellie Melba. Blanche was egotistical and very jealous of Melba, and this was shown in the TV film *Melba*, a splendid eight-hour Australian production produced in the late 1980s, I think. Isobel and Blanche eventually became close friends, but Jerrold didn't like Blanche because she was so domineering and he persuaded Isobel to give up accompanying her in about 1908.

Jerrold and Isobel had a son, Illingworth, who was born about 1897. He went to St Paul's day school in London, where he won a prize for Greek. He was a rather sickly boy, and never amounted to much, although he appears to have stood up to First War trench life as a young subaltern surprisingly well. In a letter to his sister dated 5 June 1918, he wrote:

My dear Popsy,
Just a line in answer to your many letters. We are at present in the front line so please don't expect a long letter as I have no news and must go round the posts to see that every thing is alright. It is now 8 pm & I can imagine you & Smithy returning from the pictures or somewhere home to supper and Bridge while here am I sitting down opposite a desperate enemy preparing to keep him back for one more night, miles away from civilisation, home and friends. It is strange is [it] not? I am feeling very fed up as we are here for nearly a fortnight & we've scarcely done a quarter of it yet. I don't mind the day time but now just as the sun is setting & it begins to get dark the feeling is not at all pleasant as one never knows what may happen during the hours of darkness especially at present. As Old Bill says, "it's times like(s) these, Alf, what makes Victoria Station seem an 'ell of a long way off." A saying the British public who hear it every day and laugh do not realize until they're situated like we are at present.

Well, I think this is quite sufficient about the war.

By the way you seem to be having 'some' time with Smithy, you naughty little girl. Enjoy yourself to the utmost but don't either break his heart or let him break yours (if it were possible) will you.

Well I must really close and get round the posts. Tell Ma to buy you or herself [something] with my 25 shillings. I don't want it. Hoping she is getting on alright now. With fondest love to both of you.

From
Illingworth

Illingworth died in Manchester in 1955.

Mother, christened Christine Blanche, was born in London on 25 November 1901 (the Blanche came from Blanche Marchesi, of course, who became her godmother, and whom I visited in her London flat with mother in 1928). However, at some stage in her life she appears to have dropped the

Christine. Her marriage certificate records her only as Blanche, and I note that when she was married in Brighton, my grandfather was not present; she was 'given away' by Uncle Illingworth. Mother was very familiar with Ilkley and the Robertshaws who lived there, but she spent her early life in London, and went to Broadstairs, a girls' school in Hove (on the Sussex coast).

While Jerrold was in Australia in 1910 he wrote two letters home, one to Isobel and one to her closest friend, Christine D'Almaine Robbins ('Tina'), a contralto who was leader of the chorus at the Frankfurt opera house for some years before the First War, and who also sang at Beyreuth. Unfortunately, Jerrold put the letters in the wrong envelopes, and remained in the domestic deep freeze until Isobel died in 1920. I think this may have been the reason why my mother dropped her first name in response to her father's behaviour. He married Tina three or four years later, and she became my step-grandmother, of course. She and Jerrold got on very well and lived at Barn Cottage in Merstham, Surrey, from some time in the 1930s onwards. I used to stay with Aunt Tina, as I called her, during the war, and saw a lot of her brother's family (who also lived there), especially her two nieces, who were about my age. She died in 1950.

Towards the end of the First War mother did war work with Isobel, serving meals at an officers' club in Brighton, where she met my father, then a lieutenant on leave from France in 1918. He was by then a mere 36 or 37. Partly, I think, because my grandparents were by then separated, my grandfather insisted that Donald came home first after the war, from where he would have to return to England to claim his bride in due course. It was in effect a test of their lasting affection for each other to ensure that it was not just a wartime 'fling'.

They were married in Brighton on 15 May 1920, giving their address as the 'Ship Hotel'; due to the distances involved, only Blanche's mother and her brother Illingworth were able to attend the service. Thereafter they set sail for Canada, settling initially in Regina, where Dad had lived and practised from about 1908. As I have said earlier, Dad was a civil engineer, but he mostly practised as a land surveyor, establishing boundaries. The practice prospered until the onset of the Great Depression when nothing much was being built. Dad was therefore very lucky to be offered the position of Controller of Surveys for the Department of Natural

Resources. My parents continued to live in Regina until Dad retired in 1956, and then they moved to Vancouver. Mother was a champion tennis and badminton player. Dad died on 22 March 1964, and Mother on 26 June 1967.

They had produced four children, the first of whom was my brother, Jerrold Alpine, born in 1921. I followed in 1922 (Roderick Illingworth Alpine), and then came my younger brother, Donald Alpine, in 1930. The 'baby' of the family was my sister, Wendy Margaret Alpine, who was born in 1935 when Jerry and I were already entering our teens. Indeed, Dad was 54 when Wendy was born and consequently worked until he was 75 in order to ensure that she could be put through university. I think this was typical of Dad; the only letter which the family still has from my Uncle Rod to his mother (Isobel) before his untimely death, says of him: "Alpine certainly is an optimist – he seems to have fewer things to worry him than almost any person I know of."

Isobel, my maternal grandmother, came to Regina with Mother and Dad, more or less indefinitely, I think, and died there of a stroke in 1920.

Jerrold's sister, Alice Robertshaw, a spinster, visited us in Regina in about 1927. Sadly, she was knocked down by a bicycle when she was getting off a street car with Mother about two blocks from our house. The bicycle rider was young and bolted with his bike, but she died in hospital that evening. Dad always thought the police knew who the boy was, and in fact believed he was the son of the sheriff of Regina, who lived nearby. We only knew the sheriff and his family by sight, but the strange way they seemed to shy away from us thereafter makes me believe it too.

Jerrold also had an elder brother, Sydney, whose son, Ballin, was to become perhaps the family's most illustrious member. Born in Ilkley in 1902, he attended the Royal Naval Colleges at Osborne and Dartmouth, then joining HMS *Centurion* as a midshipman in 1920. A succession of promotions and command appointments culminated in 1953 when he became a rear admiral and was appointed Chief of Staff to the Commander-in-Chief, Portsmouth, in 1953. His final appointment was as Chief of Allied Staff, Mediterranean, in 1955 with the rank of vice-admiral and in 1958 on his retirement from the service, was created a Knight Commander of the Most Excellent Order of the British Empire.

I think Mother said the Robertshaws were also related to the Maufs of Ilkley (or nearby), who were also in the wool business – and perhaps in the partnership. Harold Mauf was awarded the Victoria Cross in the First War and was commanding officer of the local Home Guard during the Second. Harold White told me during my 1943 visit that Harold Mauf was killed during a grenade-throwing practise when a thrower let a grenade slip to the ground after pulling the pin. Harold Mauf immediately dropped on it and smothered it with his body, saving the thrower and others around him. That's leadership and valour combined, I would say.

Mother also told me that one of her grandparents (or great grandparents?) came from Spain, having met a Robertshaw travelling there, who married her and took her to Yorkshire. She was apparently very happy there, liking the relative informality of England and the freedom that English women had.

In 1928 Mother and I visited one Kathleen Eddison and her family in Midlothian, in Scotland, who I also feel was related to us. One of her sons, Jim, I think, was taken prisoner in Singapore or Burma, and survived working on the infamous railway in that area. Mother told me she understood that a Robertshaw ancestor used to drink in a pub with Branwell Bronte (1817-48), the wastrel brother of the famous sisters. Since Haworth is about ten miles by foot trail from Ilkley and a lot more by road, this sounds rather fanciful to me. However, Branwell worked as a clerk for the Leeds and Manchester Railway (until he was fired for 'culpable negligence') so he could have been at or near Ilkley at some time.

CHAPTER THREE

AIRCRAFT – MENACE – RESPONSE

Though unable to fly, I did the next best thing – I read about it continually. Within two or three years I had gone through virtually all the aviation books in the public library. My favourite was a late 1920s flying instruction manual for student pilots of the United States Navy, superbly illustrated; it came as close to telling a 'chairborne' person how to fly as is possible, and I revelled in it. On the historical side I became so fascinated by accounts of pioneer flying, air fighting in the First War, and record long distance flights that I became wistful for the great days past and began to regret I had not been born sooner.

I kept up to date with aviation nevertheless, my interest ever increasing. I pored over the latest issues of the leading British and American aviation magazines. The British ones, *Aeroplane* and *Flight*, were superior technically. Their scope was limited, though, because until the mid thirties almost all British aircraft were old fashioned fabric-covered biplanes, with external strut and wire bracing. They still had fixed-pitch propellers, which had much the same effect as single-gear transmissions would have on cars. Rolls-Royce was producing the finest liquid-cooled Vee-12 engines in the world, however, their Vee arrangement abetted by superior supercharging making them superior for attaining the highest speeds when fitted in streamlined aircraft.

The American magazines took the stance that their country's aircraft and engines were unquestionably the finest in the world. Their claims regarding aircraft and air-cooled radial engines (superior for transport and most bombers but not for fighters) could not be refuted. Fairly early in the thirties they began to come out with streamlined all-metal monoplanes having cantilever (internally braced) wings, monocoque (rounded shell) fuselages, retractable landing gear, landing flaps and controllable pitch propellers with metal blades (sometimes three blades instead of the usual two). A mere glance would show that their aerodynamic drag was much less than typical British aircraft, and that they would therefore be much faster for the same power; the British had actually pioneered or invented most of those features but had largely failed to incorporate them in their own production aircraft.

At the end of January in 1933, on the playground of my school, I became aware of the name Hitler for the first time. A ten-year-old friend and classmate, Walter Martin, began on some impulse to ape and ridicule the man who I found out had become Chancellor of Germany the day before. None of us could have imagined that Walter would live only ten more years, and that his name would appear on a war memorial in the Egyptian desert as an airman with no known grave.

Jerry and I started to take an interest in public affairs about a month before Hitler became Chancellor, which was unusual for boys of eleven and ten. It began by our witnessing parliamentary debate, though not in any world capital or involving any great issues. Regina is the capital of Saskatchewan, a province half as large again as Germany but with fewer than a million people; the provincial parliament buildings, the most impressive in Canada, were only a few minutes walk from where we lived. The annual legislative sessions began in January; Jerry, always questing and aggressive, discovered at the beginning of the 1933 session that young boys were not excluded from the visitor's gallery, even with snow on their moccasins.

When Hitler withdrew Germany from the League of Nations eight months after becoming Chancellor, my father and mother became more apprehensive than most, he having served with the Canadian army in France in the First War and she having endured some bombing in London during it. This probably caused Jerry's and my interest in public affairs to expand to international ones. Watching the debates in the Saskatchewan legislative chamber, which followed British House of Commons procedure, made it easy for us to picture the momentous debates that began to take place in the British House and other parliaments after each of Hitler's menacing moves that led up to the Second World War.

Around that time my father suggested I might enjoy reading Winston Churchill's *My Early Life*, written in 1930. It was the first grown-up's book I had ever read and to my surprise I found it easy to follow and fascinating. Churchill became my first political hero, a timely happenstance. When he warned the British House in late 1934 about the clandestine German air force, I began to wonder whether scenes from *Wings* would be re-enacted in modern form.

In the spring of 1935, Hitler declared that his Luftwaffe had achieved parity with the RAF. Air power became the underlying issue in European politics overnight. Churchill could be impetuous and difficult whether in or out of power, and though his judgement was by no means infallible it was matchless on this issue. For a slowly increasing number of people in the democracies he began to appear as the only politician with enough insight and determination to save Britain and Europe from disaster.

Jerry and I could not understand why Britain and France, the most likely bombing targets for a new German air force, would have allowed it to become so large without intervening under the Treaty; nor could we understand why, later on, a British Conservative government which proposed to triple the size of the RAF was bitterly opposed by the Labour and Liberal opposition and even made many of its own party members uneasy.

We gradually became aware that the answer was pacifism, a movement which had gained a huge following from the revulsion against the terrible slaughter of the First War and had become a key factor in the politics of the thirties. Its most fervent apostles advocated total unilateral disarmament, contending that if you disarmed your own country completely, your example would inspire all others to follow. The lack of common sense and the risk of catastrophe inherent in that proposition began to occur to me, but I was surprised by the number and range of its advocates. When questioned about the risk they became evasive. They did not even appear to flinch when Hitler, within days of unveiling the Luftwaffe, introduced conscription for the German army, another fundamental breach of the Treaty. Though less extreme forms of pacifism were advocated as well, diminished reliance on common sense and obvious risk were inherent in all of them. (A demonstration of the extreme form occurred in Regina in the mid thirties. The leading movie theatre there sometimes put on window displays unrelated to its bill of fare. One comprised some models of naval destroyers, whereupon an association calling itself 'The Peace Group' protested, saying "Destroyers are armaments, and armaments can only lead to war." The protest appeared in a local evening newspaper and the models were removed the next morning.)

Looking back, the pacifist movement's revulsion was shared by countless others, and was fully justified by the leadership of the French and British armies in France in the First War. The policy of their commanders-in-chief had been to keep on the offensive at any cost, and it had soon led to the slaughter there becoming senseless.

Pacifism received ever-increasing support between the wars as aircraft became more developed and their engines more powerful, foreshadowing the practicability of the destruction of whole cities by a single air raid, a concept which kept fermenting in the mind of peoples everywhere until it became by far the greatest war fear. In 1933 Baldwin reinforced it by saying, in reliance from the British Air Ministry, that there really was no defence against bombing: "The bomber will always get through." Hitler exploited the fear ruthlessly. One would have thought the politicians in the democracies, when they became aware of the Luftwaffe and the strength of it, would have striven mightily for development of effective air defence. But most of them, with an eye on the large numbers of pacifists everywhere and the prevalence of the phrase "The people don't want war", chose to ignore the issue (and the maxim that a man cannot have peace if his neighbour will not let him) as long as possible. Pacifist sentiment often came down to: "It mustn't happen, and if we don't even contemplate rearmament it won't." Jerry and I became fascinated as the internal politics of the democracies from the mid thirties onwards developed into struggles between those who had faith in pacifism and those who had none; in effect between those who were against rearmament and all for trusting or at least ignoring Hitler and those who opposed them on both counts.

The rise of the Luftwaffe shifted my interest in aviation to the military side. I thought the simple answer to any enemy bombers that might be developed would be to develop fighters that could destroy them. It disturbed me that Germany was making great technical strides in aviation while Britain, in spite of being practically next door to her in flying terms, seemed to be making almost none.

In fact, however, the first stirrings of an aeronautical technical revolution had occurred in Britain, unheralded, a year or so before Hitler unveiled the Luftwaffe. The harbinger was a medium size twin-engine monoplane commissioned by Lord Rothermere (proprietor of the London *Daily Mail*), from the Bristol Aeroplane Company and completed in the late spring of 1935. Though ordered for his personal use, a parallel intention seems to have been to force the Air Ministry into the nineteen thirties because it incorporated all the advances of the latest American aircraft and he named it 'Britain First'.

When I saw the first photographs of it in *Aeroplane* and *Flight* I realized instantly that Britain might catch up if she had a mind to. Britain First turned out to be 40 mph faster than the latest fighter *projected* for the RAF. When the Air Ministry asked Rothermere for permission to carry out tests on it he went one better – he presented it to the nation. It was eventually modified into a medium bomber which went into production for the RAF as the Blenheim, equipped with one fixed machine gun firing forward for the pilot and a two-machine-gun turret after for a gunner.

A further surprise for the military aviation world occurred that summer when Boeing Aircraft in Seattle rolled out its B-17 four-engine bomber, an all-metal monoplane of course, whose wingspan was just over 100 feet. Because it had five machine-gun positions it was dubbed 'Flying Fortress'.

The relief I had felt on seeing the first photographs of Lord Rothermere's Britain First paled beside my reaction to the first ones I saw of the prototype of the Hawker Hurricane low wing monoplane single-seat fighter which appeared near the end of 1935. I felt in a flash that Britain would be able to put up a terrific fight if Hitler sent the Luftwaffe against her.When I read that the Hurricane was powered by a liquid-cooled Rolls-Royce Merlin V-12 engine of '1000 horsepower plus', that its top speed was '300 miles per hour plus', and that it had no less than eight machine guns, I concluded it could destroy any enemy bomber in seconds. (Most people thought the Merlin was named after the magician of King Arthur's time, not knowing that a merlin was a small falcon and that Rolls-Royce aero engines were always named after birds of prey; ignorance was even better than bliss.)

The Hurricane's aerodynamically clean shape was what caught my eye. It was the work of Sydney Camm, Hawker's chief designer, who had designed biplanes for the RAF that were the most beautiful in the world; the multi-purpose

Hawker Hart series and the Hawker Fury single-seat fighter. The Hurricane was rather humpbacked, as the Hart and Fury biplanes had been, to improve the pilot's forward vision; its undercarriage was retractable of course.

I particularly admired its slender nose which the 'Vee' arrangement of its twelve-cylinder Merlin permitted, in contrast with the open barrel-end form required by the air-cooled radial engines that were predominant in the United States. Its cockpit was enclosed with a sliding transparent canopy to protect its pilot from the part of the slipstream which would tend to eddy inwards aft of the windscreen and would be intensely cold at the great altitudes fighters with modern supercharged engines could reach. The Hurricane had several old fashioned touches, nevertheless; its wing was very thick, had a blunt leading edge, and was fabric covered, as was its fuselage behind its cockpit; also, it had an old fashioned fixed pitch two-bladed propeller but several years later that was replaced with a three-bladed controllable-pitch one and its wing became metal covered.

Early in 1936 the RAF in Britain was divided into three new operational commands; Bomber Command, Fighter Command, and Coastal Command, a functional reorganization which cleared up some overlapping.

In June of each year the RAF would put on a display at Hendon where the prototypes of any new aircraft the Air Ministry had either accepted for production or was considering it were displayed to the public for the first time. In 1936 *Aeroplane* and *Flight* covered that year's display with special issues. The photographs in them showed at a glance that Britain's aeronautical revolution had been complete, and they fascinated me. The prototypes on display that year were remarkable, most of them being monoplanes embodying the latest advances. The air attachés of foreign countries, always present there, must have found the sight astonishing. Besides the prototype Hawker Hurricane and Britain First there were several new bombers, all of whose names were to become household words in Britain and their shapes recognizable to many, not just young boys.

But besides that of the Hurricane there was the prototype of another new single-seat fighter there which must or should have made the German air attaché's heart sink when he saw it. It was, of course, the Supermarine 'Spitfire'. Like the Hurricane it was powered by a Rolls-Royce Merlin with a two-bladed wooden propeller, had eight machine guns, and a top speed announced as "300 mph plus". Designed by R.J.Mitchell, who had been responsible for the Schneider Trophy-winning S.6B seaplane, it was clearly from the same 'stable'. Only two or three truly great designers exist in any country at one time, and 'R.J.' was Britain's finest. Sadly, he had been suffering for three years from cancer which would end his life in one more.

The Spitfire, like the S.6B, was superb of line and no larger than it had to be – much smaller than the Hurricane in fact. Each part of it, beautiful in itself, blended perfectly into the whole. Improved forward vision by humpbacking its fuselage had been sacrificed for more speed. Its wing, all metal like its fuselage, was elliptical in shape, and against aerodynamic opinion then prevailing in Britain was kept thin, with quite a sharp leading edge, for high speed; it was immensely strong nonetheless. Its propeller was later brought up to date when the Hurricane's was. Had I had been told this fighter's name and shape would become the most famous in the world it would not have surprised me. The Spitfire's all-metal monocoque construction, however, made it more difficult to produce than did the older type construction of the Hurricane.

The *Illustrated London News* covered the Hendon Display in 1936 as well. Two photographs in it showed the Spitfire being flown by Supermarine's principal test pilot, Jeffrey Quill. I stuck them on my bedroom wall. Like George Stainforth, Jeffrey Quill seemed almost from another world to me.

Because I had long concluded that for aeroplanes handsome does only as handsome is, I was certain the Spitfire would be beautiful to fly and matchless to fight in. However, because its undercarriage legs looked rather far back and close together for full stability during take-off and landing, it seemed to me that unlike the stouter Hurricane it might be too delicate to operate from the rough temporary aerodromes that I assumed would be used in France, where I also assumed that most of the opening air battles in any war begun by Germany would take place. I was confident however that the Spitfire, operating from established aerodromes in England, would quickly discourage German bombers from attacking that country.

Expansion of the RAF was actually underway when the Hurricane and Spitfire were shown at the 1936 Hendon Display, the Air Ministry on the advice of the Air Council (the

Ministry's supervisory body comprising civil servants, air marshals and civil and service specialists) having ordered 600 and 310 of them respectively a few days before. However, a year and a half to two years could be expected to pass before even trickles of them would reach squadrons.

My first awareness that Germany had not been idle in fighter plane development either was not long after that Hendon Display, when I saw photographs of an early model of the Messerschmitt Me 109, its prototype actually having flown six months before the Hurricane's. It was considerably smaller than the Spitfire let alone the Hurricane, and rather angular, with little bumps marring its lines here and there; its tailplane, instead of being cantilevered like the Spitfire and Hurricane, was braced with external struts. It had only three machine guns, and its first production model had a Vee-12 Junkers Jumo 210 engine of only 700 horsepower which was inverted, an arrangement which allowed a better view over a fighter's nose.

Surprisingly, its undercarriage legs were attached to it at the lower back corners of its engine and therefore had to be splayed outwards to keep its wheels far enough apart for sideways stability during take-off and landing; viewed on the ground from in front it brought to mind a new-born fawn with its legs splayed out, struggling to its feet for the first time. The wheels themselves had to be splayed out too, and they and their tyres to be narrow, in order to fit inside the wheel wells in the wings when retracted. The whole arrangement appeared unsound, making the Spitfire's undercarriage seem downright rugged by comparison. Though I was confident that both British fighters could handle the Me 109 easily, I had to admit that the first photograph I saw of it in the air, with its dubious-looking undercarriage retracted, revealed a lean, mean and purposeful look.

CHAPTER FOUR

INTERLUDE –
ADOLESCENCE –
HITLER RESURGENT

On a summer evening in the mid thirties I went for my first ride in an aeroplane. It chanced to have an exciting prelude. The aircraft was an American Waco single-engine cabin biplane seating four. Its pilot was Charlie Skinner, the best known local commercial pilot. His wife handled the money and I paid her the one dollar charge for a boy, exacting a condition that I would sit in the right front seat beside Charlie.

While we were waiting for another customer or two to come along, a flying club Moth biplane flown by an inexperienced woman member with a passenger glided over us while approaching to land. Instead of assuming the landing attitude a foot or two above the ground, she did it at about fifteen feet. The Moth dropped heavily down about 50 yards from us and smashed off its undercarriage. Neither occupant suffered injury, though the passenger, who to my surprise was Bert Langdon, the club's air engineer, had bumped his forehead fairly hard. (As this was the second crash I had witnessed I wondered if I were a jinx!)

As no other customers had happened along Charlie quickly invited Bert and the woman to join us. She declined but Bert accepted and sat behind Charlie and me. In seconds Charlie started up the Waco's engine with its electric starter, and as there was no wind we took off straight across the field. The roar of the engine, the tail rising and the acceleration thrilled me, as did the ground revealing its clearly laid-out pattern as it fell away. We flew over the parliament buildings, which, with the lake and park around them, showed off to advantage. On returning, the gliding approach with the engine just ticking over and the final trundling of the undercarriage on touch down were very pleasing. My expectation of the joy of flying was confirmed in spades.

I finished public school in 1936, having turned 14, and began first year high school that fall. I had found public school easy enough but in high school, though I stood well up in my class, I discovered to my great distaste that, to do well enough in the Easter examinations to make sure of being excused the finals in June, I had to begin studying at least a week before they began – the longest week of the year it seemed.

I did not enjoy adolescence much. I was six foot three but so thin I felt physically inferior, and therefore inclined to be reticent and often awkward with girls. Winning swimming and running races actually came easily to me, but I had little interest in athletics. I avoided 'contact' sports as much as possible, rugby and hockey particularly. I knew that if a light cruiser took on battleships regularly something would have to give, and as my interest in aircraft and flying was my mainstay, I would not hazard my chances of passing a pilot's medical examination for anything. (When I had been about ten a raised puck in a hockey game hit my left cheekbone about an inch below my eye – a slender margin for the survival of one's hopes and dreams.)

Jerry, a year ahead of me in school throughout, was the quickest learner I ever knew. He always vied for first place with one very clever girl in his high school class. He had limitless energy and would pursue a number of interests in succession, mastering each one to an impressive degree before taking up another. He took Boy Scouts seriously for a couple of years, at 14 becoming troop leader (in reality assistant scoutmaster) of the troop that met at our public school. When he put his hands on his hips and looked you straight in the eye you knew you were being held accountable for something. In spite of an idealistic streak he also had a passion for pranks, becoming the ringleader in our part of town. I and a couple of our friends would often participate but none of us matched his nerve. He became well known to the police for the juvenile crimes of those days, such as pulling street car trolleys off their wires and putting out street lights with slingshots. Halloween was his finest hour, the police being out in force on their bicycles. One Halloween we got separated and I headed for home alone. When passing under the last street light to go I was grabbed by a policeman who said, "We've got him!", but his associate said, "Nah, that's just his brother!" I was thrust aside and they dashed off in pursuit of their main quarry, whom they never ever did catch in the act.

In first year high school I began to build a model aircraft powered by one of the tiny single-cylinder gasoline engines of about one fifth horsepower which had come on the market a year or two before. There were only a handful of 'gas models' in the whole province at that time. They were large and heavy, mine being over six feet in span and weighing more than five pounds. Making one was an expensive undertaking for young fellows and took most of us the whole winter. I did not enjoy building mine. I just wanted to have one to fly. I joined the Saskatchewan Model Aircraft League and spent many happy hours with fellow members discussing our different designs.

In high school my first regular association with Jews began. One of them, Elias Mandel, sat in front of me and became a fine companion. He was short, stocky, and wore thick glasses; having wide interests and a love of reading he was interesting and amusing to boot. He kept a close eye on Hitler's menacing moves and the rearmament of Germany. When later on reading of things Nazis did to Jews I would often conjure up visions of Elias and his family being treated likewise – images hard to dismiss. If anti-Jewry had not been an obsession with Hitler, and he had simply stuck to Germany's real and imagined grievances under the Treaty of Versailles, he would doubtless have avoided much odium among the democracies and caught them even less prepared to stave off his territorial ambitions than they actually were.

In the spring of 1937 my modelling league friends and I began to fly our gas models on the prairie to the south-west of the city where, eleven years before, my uncle and I had seen the biplane break its axle on take-off and then crash land. We could not control models in flight in those days but when properly adjusted to counter some of the propeller torque (twist) they would take off from the ground after a short run and climb in circles, the centres of which would move constantly with whatever wind there was of course. When their fuel tanks emptied they would, free of torque but still adjusted to counter it, glide down in circles the opposite way. Things could go wrong, though, and too often did. I once filled my model's fuel tank too full and a south-westerly breeze took it on a course towards the park surrounding the parliament buildings. A friend with a motorcycle took me on the seat behind him and we sped off to keep the model in sight. It flew over the park and the lake in it, heading towards the city power station a mile or so further on. The power lines and poles radiating out from the station, to say nothing of its high chimney and fenced transformers, can be imagined. The fuel ran out at the worst possible time, and the model glided down toward the whole array in graceful circles. My friend and I watched in horror and amazement as it passed over, under and past all wires and other obstacles, to touch down blithely in what seemed the only safe pathway.

About that time I also thought up and built a wooden framework which sat on my bedroom floor containing, besides a seat for me at the back end, part of a broomstick in the middle and a wooden crossbar at the front end representing an aircraft control column and rudder pedals respectively – both held in neutral positions by wires but movable against coil springs at the ends of the wires; a gramophone winding-up handle on my left in the position of a throttle lever completed the apparatus. It was a crude forerunner of what would one day be incredibly complex 'flight simulators'. I spent many hours simulating take-offs, climbs, dives, turns, spins and recoveries from spins, guided by what I had absorbed from the United States Navy flying instruction manual I mentioned earlier.

During second year high school I began to feel more and more that if I could not become a pilot in my youth I would go through life unfulfilled. And further, that if Germany were to start a war and I were not in the opening air battles (which I felt would be the crucial ones) engaged as a fighter pilot doing my best to vanquish the myth of the bomber's invincibility which was keeping so many peoples and their politicians cowed before Hitler, I would think myself accursed.

Canada's air force, the RCAF as it was then, held little interest for me because its aircraft were so few and antiquated that if war broke out re-equipping it with modern ones and getting them overseas would take so much time that I was sure its pilots would miss the opening air battles. In the mid thirties No. 120 'Auxiliary' RCAF Squadron was formed in Regina, one of six across Canada which were the equivalent of the army's non-permanent active militia. It was equipped with the D.H. Gypsy Moth biplane (supplemented by the later D.H. Tiger Moth biplane), so its pilots would be in no better position for a war than those of the permanent force.

However, I began to notice advertisements by the British

Air Ministry in British magazines which invited young men between seventeen and a half and twenty-four or so, with at least junior matriculation, to apply for pilot training in the RAF and receive five-year 'short service' commissions (in contrast with permanent commissions obtainable only after a two year course at the RAF College at Cranwell in Lincolnshire requiring high fees). I had heard that a few Canadians had done so and been accepted. As that seemed my only chance for fulfilment I resolved that when I matriculated I would cross the ocean and present myself as a candidate.

Saskatchewan high school students normally got their junior matriculation after three years, though most of them carried on another year for their senior. I could therefore expect to get my junior in June of 1939, a couple of months before turning seventeen and a half. I had some hesitation about leaving high school without getting my senior, so I thought I would see how Hitler was behaving then.

In the mid to latter thirties I became aware that two predictions regarding air war in the future had become so thoroughly accepted by most of the air marshals of the RAF Air Staff that they had become doctrines.

The first doctrine was that a formation of bombers could, by relying on its own gunners and therefore with no fighter escort whatsoever, defend itself against enemy fighters in daylight – the 'self-defending bomber formation' doctrine. The second was that the speed of the new monoplane fighters was so high they would not be able to shoot at let alone hit each other, and would therefore be limited to destroying bombers – the 'no more fighter versus fighter combat' doctrine. The first doctrine was much challenged by some officers of the highest rank in all major air forces, and though I was only in my mid teens with no qualifications whatever my intuition told me they were right. I have no recollection of actual controversy over the second doctrine but my intuition told me it was wrong.

The justification for the self-defending bomber doctrine was 'crossfire', a practice whereby every gunner of every bomber in a formation who could bring his one or two machine guns to bear on an enemy fighter that was attacking another bomber in the formation would fire across at it. The larger the formation and the tighter it would be the better of course, because an attacking fighter would come within range of more gunners. But a natural consequence of the self-defending bomber doctrine, it if were valid, would be that fighters like the Hurricane and Spitfire would only be effective against single bombers, or a very few at most. It seemed to me, however, that the eight machine guns of those two fighters, let alone the 20mm cannons which the Me 109 and French fighters were beginning to be equipped with, would defeat the doctrine because I felt that the capacity to deliver overwhelming firepower at any chosen point would carry the day. I also felt that if a fair number of fighters so armed were to attack a bomber formation simultaneously, the crossfire of its gunners would be greatly diluted.

The air marshals received a measure of support for the doctrine in the late thirties, however, when, as planned, hydraulically powered gun turrets replaced manually operated single-gun positions in the nose and tail of the RAF's two heaviest bombers, the Vickers Wellington and the Armstrong Whitworth Whitley (the Wellington's being two-gun turrets in nose and tail, the Whitley's being one-gun in the nose and four-gun in the tail). The gunners in the two-gun and four-gun turrets sat between the guns and aimed them by both traversing their turrets and elevating or depressing the guns in them by power. Though turrets would obviously be more effective than mere gun positions requiring aiming by hand, I still doubted they would be effective against the new heavily armed fighters. (The Luftwaffe seemed to place little reliance on the self-defending bomber formation doctrine; not having developed gun turrets for its principal bombers, the Heinkel 111, the Dornier 17Z, and the newer Junkers 88.)

The second doctrine, no more fighter versus fighter combat, was as new as the Hurricane and Spitfire themselves. In effect it was a declaration that the dogfighting of the First War, which had been practised throughout the balance of the biplane era, had become a thing of the past. (A corollary would be that the ability of the Hurricane and Spitfire to make much tighter turns than the Me 109, due to their obviously greater wing areas and hence lower wing loadings, would bestow no advantage in future air war.) Whether the doctrine originated with the air marshals or by aircraft designers or medical aviation specialists I have never discovered, but in essence it was a conclusion that fighter pilots would no longer be able to manoeuvre well enough at the higher speeds to get an effective shot at enemy fighters nor to withstand the heavier G-loads that would be imposed on them if they tried to.

I thought the doctrine was wrong for several reasons. By the late thirties cars normally travelled along highways at about 50 mph. Relative to one travelling behind another, the car ahead would seem not to be moving, a sitting duck for anyone in the car behind who might be inclined to shoot at it. The same axiom had applied to First War fighters (whose top speeds eventually reached 125 mph) when they were flying straight and level, which they would normally do when their pilots were sure no enemy fighters were on their tails. It would obviously apply to fighters going 300 mph or more, though if the one ahead went into a steep turn or pulled up steeply and the one behind followed or tried to, I could form no idea of what the practical effect of the G-load on their pilots would be.

A still further complication entered into the fighter versus fighter aspect. The pilots of all First War fighters were able to see whether enemy fighters were on their tails or not by simply swivelling their heads around, because the level of the fuselage surfaces behind their cockpits had been no higher than that in front of them. The pilots of the new monoplane fighters could not do that, because the fuselages behind all their cockpits were extended upwards to just above their heads before carrying on back to the tail, a change which prevented their seeing directly behind them.

I had noticed this feature on the Hurricane, the Spitfire and the Me 109, as well as on new French and American monoplane fighters, and was puzzled by it. When I became aware of the no more fighter versus fighter combat doctrine I began to think more about it. I wondered whether the change had been made to protect the pilot's head if his aircraft, lacking the protection the upper wing of a biplane would have given it, were to turn upside down in a take-off or landing accident, or whether it had been made to improve stream-lining. I thought that if it had been made to protect the pilot's head it must have been based on the assumption that the risk to a fighter pilot from turning upside down on the ground was greater than the risk of being shot down by an unseen enemy fighter on his tail, an assumption which seemed dubious to me. But I more or less concluded that if it had been made for streamlining, the similar thinking of so many designers must indicate they knew what they were doing.

I could not help but think, that if the no more fighter versus fighter combat doctrine were to prove false, lack of rear vision would be a dreadful drawback. Since every new fighter was blind directly behind, its pilot would not know if an enemy fighter were on his tail unless he saw it curving in behind him; if it were simply overtaking him from directly behind he would not see it approaching at all unless he kept weaving his aircraft from side to side to have a look, which would slow his progress down of course. Even in the First War pilots used to say that the one that shot you down was usually the one you didn't see. (Rearview mirrors were not yet in evidence on the new fighters; but even car drivers get surprises and no road behind them is as wide or as high as the sky!)

In early 1938 photographs appeared in the British aviation magazines of a new single-engine two-seat fighter being produced for the RAF. It was the Boulton Paul 'Defiant'; powered by the same engine as the Hurricane and Spitfire, the Rolls-Royce Merlin. Though a little longer than the Hurricane it was actually a cleaner design, except that behind the pilot's cockpit was a four-gun turret for the gunner which was faired in as well as it could be but obviously added much drag as well as weight. It struck me instantly that it was ill conceived, and I did not hesitate to differ (perhaps rather precociously!) from the air marshals once more.

The main justification advanced for the Defiant was the surprising success in combat of the First War two-seat 'Bristol Fighter' against enemy single-seat fighters. The Bristol, as was usual for its day, had had one or two machine guns on a simple mounting ring around the edge of its gunner's cockpit behind the pilot, an arrangement having far less drag, relatively, than the Defiant's turret. But it also had a fixed forward-firing machine gun for the pilot, and it had been with that gun that the great majority of the Bristol Fighter's victories had been obtained. For some inexplicable reason the Defiant had no gun for the pilot. Though the Bristol Fighter was heavier than the single-seat fighters of its day and had a larger wing area incurring more drag, it had a proportionately more powerful engine making it competitive in speed while its greater wing area allowed it to turn as tightly as they. My intuition almost yelled at me that if war came Defiants would be easy prey for Me 109s.

Though it may seem that as a young fellow with no qualifications I was amazingly brash in choosing to differ from the powers that be on some doctrinal issues, I nonetheless thought then and I still do that at that time there was no finer air force in the world than the RAF. No human being is infallible, however, so no organization can be either.

The annexation of Austria, followed by that of Czechoslovakia's Sudetenland in September of 1938, led to the Munich Agreement being entered into – many considering this a complete abdication of responsibility by the British, French and Soviet Union governments.

Indeed, much of the world remained skeptical of Munich to say the least, my parents and Jerry and I among them. All appeasers are pacifists, but many of them are inclined to make concessions involving sacrifices of principles – in this case staving off a threat to one's own country by conceding territory of another country to whom an obligation to defend was owed.

Munich incidentally brought home to me that if war did come and I failed to pass the pilots' medical I would feel it my duty to join the army – not a happy thought for a fellow who fancied taking to the air daily from a club-like atmosphere and who disliked physical discomfort.

In February of 1939 a 26-year-old amateur English pilot of superb skill and determination, Alex Henshaw, whose exploits I had followed in *Aeroplane* and *Flight* through the thirties (including winning the race for the coveted King's Cup in 1938) set records for the fastest times from England to Cape Town, the return trip, and the round trip, with no radio aid available. Those three records stand today for propeller-driven aircraft, and were made in a trim and beautiful Percival Mew Gull low wing monoplane so small it could fit in a fair sized living room. I am far from alone in considering his feat to have been more dangerous than Lindbergh's Atlantic flight. He spurned the longer safer route down the east side of Africa, choosing the more direct one across the Sahara desert and down the west coast, where failure to find just one of the crude, far apart and fog-bedevilled aerodromes needed for refuelling would have meant virtually certain death. He arrived back home in four and a half days, tired almost to the point of unconsciousness, bloodied by protrusions in a tight little cockpit, made tighter by fuel tanks tailored around him. More was to be heard of him in the not too distant future.

When Hitler invaded the rest of Czechoslovakia in March of 1939 his statement that he did not wish peoples in the Reich other than Germans was exposed as a blatant lie. Britain's and

France's guarantee of Poland's security followed immediately in the light of this provocation. But when on 22 August 1939 the Non-Aggression Pact between Germany and the Soviet Union was announced, it came like a bombshell everywhere, as the two countries were implacable enemies who knew they would end up fighting each other sooner or later, pact or no pact.

As I now had my junior matriculation and would reach the minimum age for applying for an RAF short service commission (seventeen and a half) in less than three weeks, I could only wonder what changes war would make to that and in travelling to Britain. I knew my father would never fund any travel until those aspects became clear, at the very least, and I was bitterly disappointed that I would miss the opening air battles in any event, Hitler having been too hasty for me. Taking my senior matriculation year, or beginning it at least, seemed the only practical course for the moment.

CHAPTER FIVE

PHONEY WAR – REAL WAR – JOINING UP

The 1939 high school year commenced on Friday, 1 September. I was awakened before dawn by a newspaper boy on the street yelling, "Extra. Extra – Polish cities bombed!" A sense of foreboding stole over me but I eventually went back to sleep. When I finally awoke I wondered if it had been a dream but my father's solemn face told me it had not. School commencement was subdued, almost hushed.

On that very day German U-boats began to torpedo Allied ships and kept it up, but when no bombing of cities occurred or fighting along the French-German border on that and succeeding days, puzzlement and then relief began to spread among Britons and French, and countless Germans too, no doubt. The troops in France's vaunted Maginot Line remained in it, except for the occasional reconnaissance of a mile or two into no-man's land, as did Germany's troops in their new Siegfried Line opposite. This relatively passive state, soon called the 'Phoney War', continued on for eight months; Hitler, with Poland under his belt, wanted late spring weather for attacking France; Britain wanted all the breathing space it could get to make up for its frightful lack of preparedness; France seemed to want nothing except inaction.

The RAF despatched early to France several squadrons of Fairey Battle light bombers, followed by Blenheim medium bombers, Hurricanes, and Westland Lysander army co-operation aircraft, increasing their numbers as time went by. The opposing air forces along the French-German border limited themselves to occasional reconnaissance sorties across it.

A few days after the war began my family's lunch was interrupted by the sound of an aircraft engine unlike any I had heard before. I knew the RCAF had acquired half a dozen Hawker Hurricanes from Britain early in the year and that

32

they were then stationed in Calgary, some 400 miles west of Regina, so on a hunch I dashed out the door; sure enough, overhead was a Hurricane making a wide circle, a second one not far behind it. At last I had set eyes on one of the two fighters I was certain would save the world's future.

Without so much as a word over my shoulder I leapt onto my bicycle and pedalled furiously out to the aerodrome. When I saw the two Hurricanes being refuelled a few yards across the aerodrome fence I was struck by how much larger they looked in real life than in photographs and how thick and blunt their wings were. I could only suppose, though, that 1030 horsepower was enough for the job. When they took off they headed east, bound for Halifax in stages it turned out. Their take-offs were disappointingly slow and quiet to me, their propellers obviously below top revolutions, a state I correctly assumed was due to the fixed pitch propellers they were still fitted with, but would much increase when they levelled off and picked up speed.

The next eight months were to experience what became known as the 'Phoney War', during which little would occur other than some aerial operations which rapidly disproved the RAF's belief in the 'self-defending bomber'. In fact such formations as were sent out to attack naval targets, were slaughtered whenever intercepted by defending fighters.

The propaganda put out by Britain, and virtually copied in Canada, was to me one of the Phoney War's most surprising aspects. Press and radio in Germany were totally controlled by Joseph Goebbels, of course, his output being so often ludicrous I usually ignored it; as he had long propounded the 'Big Lie' principle, however, he was honest about his deceit at least. In Britain, though, the game had to be sophisticated. The outright lie was considered bad form there, so other forms of deceit such as nondisclosure in whole or in part and deliberate exaggeration or minimising were resorted to in order that the public would hear what the government wanted it to hear and thought it would like to hear, and even more importantly it later seemed, to keep it from knowing what the government did not want it to hear. The press was not tightly controlled there but, after its fashion, it reflected the government line by telling the public what the press itself thought the public wanted to hear.

In mid October a prominent British industrialist, Lord Riverdale, arrived in Ottawa to negotiate an agreement among Britain, Canada, Australia and New Zealand for training aircrew from those countries in Canada on a very large scale. The negotiations dragged on and on, leaving me on tenterhooks about my prospects of becoming a pilot.

In late October the British aviation magazines contained photographs and a sectioned drawing of the Messerschmitt 109E, the latest model of the Luftwaffe's standard fighter. An inverted Vee-12 Daimler-Benz DB 601 engine of 1100 horsepower with a three-bladed controllable-pitch propeller replaced the original 700 horsepower Junkers Jumo 210. Its previous three machine guns were replaced by two 20mm cannon, one in each wing outside the propeller arc, and two machine guns on top of the engine synchronised to fire through the propeller. Two small radiators under the wing, one on each side, replaced the rather awkward-looking single one under the engine of the earlier models. Though the new model still had external tailplane struts, and a few little bumps, it looked even meaner and more purposeful than its predecessors.

Regina's 120 Auxiliary Squadron, having been called to active service at the beginning of the war, was transferred to Vancouver in November, though some of its pilots had earlier been posted to another auxiliary squadron then stationed at Rockliffe near Ottawa. We were saddened when one of those posted, Pete Johnstone, was killed in mid November when his Tiger Moth collided with one flown by his closest friend, Jack Morrison, also posted from Regina's 120, while they were doing formation aerobatics. Jack had managed to bail out. A fine pair, I had seen them doing formation aerobatics over Regina's aerodrome on special days flawlessly, and they had acted as judges in our annual gas model competitions. I was to see Jack again.

Late in November the British magazines contained photographs of a new long-range twin-engine two-seat German fighter, the Messerschmitt 110. It was slender and aerodynamically clean; and its engines were Daimler-Benz DB 601s, the same as the one in the new Me 109E. It had two 20mm cannon and four machine guns in its nose, fixed to fire ahead (a high concentration for that time) and one free machine gun for the gunner, who sat behind the pilot. It was designed to be as fast as single-engine fighters and to escort formations of bombers deep into enemy territory in daylight. Hermann Goering was deeply smitten by it, calling it 'zerstörer' (destroyer) and predicting that squadrons equipped with it would become the elite of the fighter arm of his

Luftwaffe. Though I was sure the Me 110 would prove to be very effective against unescorted bombers, I felt confident that no twin-engine fighter could stand up to a single-engine fighter in daylight, even if it were just as fast, because its greater size and weight would make it less agile and accordingly more cumbersome than a single-engine one. Though I seemed to be favouring my intuition over the mighty once more, I could not smother my thoughts.

On 17 December the announcement came from Ottawa I had awaited so eagerly – agreement on the training of aircrew in Canada had been reached. Named British Commonwealth Air Training Plan, it was often called the Empire Air Training Scheme, though commonly referred to as the air training scheme. Its scope was huge, projecting an eventual monthly output of some 1,500 pilots, observers (later called navigators), air gunners and wireless operators. Most pilot trainees were to receive elementary flying training in their own countries and come to Canada for advanced training (though the RAF would carry on fully training a sizeable proportion of its aircrew in Britain). The graduates of the scheme were to serve in RAF squadrons, though the agreement did stipulate that the Canadian government would have the right to form a number of purely RCAF squadrons in Britain when the scheme had got under way; the language of that stipulation was far from clear, however.

The RCAF was to run the scheme, and it therefore planned to form about 70 new schools as soon as possible to train the aircrew, as well as schools for the many thousands of groundcrew and other non-flying personnel who would be required to man the scheme. As it had only half a dozen aerodromes of its own, and about 700 pilots and 6,700 non-flying personnel when the war began (including those in auxiliary squadrons), and it intended to send two of its own army co-operation squadrons and one fighter squadron to Britain in the next few months in any event, the challenge was colossal.

All aircrew trainees (who could be as old as 32) were now to enter the air forces of their respective countries at the lowest rank, aircraftsman 2nd class (AC2). After a month's initial ground training at an initial training school (ITS) they would be selected for training as pilots, observers, or air gunners. They would be promoted leading aircraftsman (LAC) on being sent to their respective air training schools, and to sergeant on graduation, though some graduates would be selected for commissioning as pilot officers. The change made me regret I had not been born soon enough to have entered the RAF under the short service commission system and be trained as one of a small group of pilots at an unhurried pace in a sort of country club atmosphere. But I now resolved, of course, to go down to the new local RCAF recruiting office when I turned 18 on 11 March, less than three months away, and apply for aircrew training, hoping against the odds to be selected as a pilot at the ITS stage of course. First and foremost though, I hoped I would be able to pass the stiff aircrew medical and get my name on the ever growing waiting list.

As 1939 turned into 1940, I counted the days to 11 March. When it arrived I got an appointment to attend on the commanding officer of the local RCAF recruiting office a few days hence; promisingly, he was a friend of my father's who had served in the army in the First War, and in recent years had been a director of the Saskatchewan Model Aircraft League. On the appointed day, a dull cold one, I was ushered into his presence. He greeted me warmly and after a few minutes chat turned me over to a panel of several local doctors. The dreaded pilots medical was now upon me, reputed to be passable only by supermen, a status my thinness convinced me I lacked. In fact, build had virtually nothing to do with it – simply having nothing wrong turned out to be the key. I finished with the eye doctor, an old family friend who told me I had passed everything, and my name was added to the aircrew waiting list. Once outside, indescribable relief and elation made the dull cold day seem rosy and warm.

Jerry, now nearly 19 and taking first year civil engineering at Saskatchewan's university, had decided he would apply to join the RCAF as an aircrew trainee too but he put it off to the end of his academic year, and therefore went on the list a couple of months behind me.

Thereafter the war ceased to be phoney. On 9 April 1940 the Germans invaded Denmark and Norway. A month later their 'Blitzkrieg' into France and the Low Countries followed. Almost at once Chamberlain was replaced as prime minister of the UK by Winston Churchill and a National Government was formed. Nonetheless, by the end of May the Dunkirk evacuation was already underway.

When I was shaving on the morning of 18 June 1940 my father called up to me and I went to the top of the stairs. With an unaccustomed look approaching agony he said, "France has quit!" It was the most shocking news I ever remember. France, our terribly tried but nonetheless true ally in the First War, had been made by our propaganda to seem infallible throughout the Phoney War, and though being gravely pressed thereafter, still fundamentally sound. There is no truer saying than that truth is the first casualty of war. I must admit I had become suspicious of our propaganda ever since the self-defending-bomber-formation doctrine had gone into the trash can, a suspicion reinforced when the no-more-fighter-versus-fighter doctrine proved to be rubbish within a day or two after the fighting in France began.

My suspicion of our propaganda developed into a loathing (the enemy's continuing merely to amuse me). I also developed varying degrees of contempt for those of our people who were more than willing to accept our propaganda, their willingness obviously being inversely proportional to their respect for truth; many of them considered anyone questioning ours to be disloyal. I actually felt some relief when it was exposed for what it was, because it was becoming apparent that the British people under Churchill's straightforward leadership – "I have nothing to offer but blood, toil, tears and sweat", and "we shall never surrender" – could face the truth without being shaken. I do not suggest a "Woe, all is lost" note should have been tolerated for a moment, merely that people dislike being deceived and will accept bad news staunchly if they have confidence in the leadership, notwithstanding that propagandists seem to consider them to be perpetually on the verge of nervous breakdowns. Abraham Lincoln once said: "Let the people know the facts and the country will be safe."

I was excused the final examinations in June, thank heaven, and I waited impatiently for my call-up. Two new units of the Empire Air Training Scheme appeared in Regina that summer. One was an initial training school (ITS), where aircrew enlistees spent a month on average being taught drill, learning air force fundamentals, writing examinations and, finally, being selected for training as either pilots, observers, or air gunners and posted to training schools accordingly. The other unit was an air observer school established at the city's aerodrome and equipped with Avro Ansons. The Anson was an uninspiring low powered fabric-covered twin-engine coastal reconnaissance monoplane made in Britain which had been relegated to the training not only of observers but of pilots destined for twin-engine aircraft.

After some attacks on shipping in the English Channel by the
Luftwaffe in July the Battle of Britain began in earnest in mid
August, and my longing to be in it was again almost
unbearable. The Battle has had huge historical coverage, of
course, and was too involved to dwell on here except in the
barest outline, with a couple of interesting details thrown in.
The Luftwaffe's bombers and fighters came over in daylight in
groups often totalling several hundred, as had been done in
France, but they concentrated on Fighter Command's
aerodromes hoping to wipe out or nullify its Hurricanes and
Spitfires. Though heavy losses were suffered on both sides
Fighter Command was virtually on the ropes in three weeks,
but Hitler then foolishly ordered that the attacks be switched
to London, allowing Fighter Command to recover and win
what many historians rate as the most critical victory of the
second millenium.

Our propagandists made the victory seem easy as far as the
quality of the Luftwaffe's aircraft and aircrew was concerned
but nonetheless difficult because of facing its larger numbers.
Their main theme seemed to be: "All our chaps and all our
aircraft are wonderful and the enemy's are dreadful." History
has, as usual, revealed a far more interesting and infinitely
more complex story, though opinions vary on many aspects of
course. What can be said for certain is that the victory
demanded enormous courage from Fighter Command pilots,
as well as particularly far-seeing and outstanding gifts and
skills from other disciplines in preparation for it of course.

Contrary to our propaganda the Luftwaffe exhibited skill
and bravery. Though its Me 110 confirmed it was out of place
in a daylight battle against single-engine fighters, the Me 109
proved once again to be the principal foe of the RAF and the
only truly deadly foe for its fighters.

Only a few of Fighter Command's Defiants actually fought,
but quickly proved their turret-for-a-gunner-but-no-guns-for-
the-pilot concept to be hopeless. An Me 109 pilot was asked
by an American war correspondent how he rated his Me 109
against the British fighters. He said, "The Spitfire was good,
the Hurricane was not as good, and the Defiant was terrible."
Defiants were tried on other duties but excelled in none.
Postwar research shows them to have been a staggering waste
of effort and material, because the number of them produced
by mid 1940 was about equal to half the number of

Hurricanes and Spitfires engaged in the Battle of Britain daily (though the latter two types were virtually replenished once over throughout the Battle). Moreover, the number of Defiants still on order in mid 1940 (though quickly cancelled) was about equal to the number already built.

I have long concluded that the ability to see in advance the falsity of doctrines and concepts such as the self-defending bomber formation, no more fighter versus fighter and the two-seat turret fighter (especially with no forward-firing guns for the pilot) was an inherent personal gift of visualisation independent of professionsl experience or status. I believe I was blessed with that gift to a high degree, though I never reached a position to provide the benefit of it. I am sure it was akin to the gift of judging aircraft designs, and perhaps akin to designing fine aircraft one's self, both being examples of visualisation.

When the Battle of Britain was at its climax in mid September I received a registered letter telling me to report to the recruiting centre in Regina at the end of the month to be sworn in as a member of the RCAF – at long last. Twenty or so others turned up with me. An officer swore us in on the bible one at a time, first asking: "Are you a British subject or an American citizen?" A fair number of Americans were joining the RCAF, and because of isolationist propaganda in the then-neutral United States they were excused from taking the oath of allegiance ["to His Majesty"] for fear of jeopardising their US citizenship. We were told to prepare to board a train the next morning bound for a manning depot in Brandon, Manitoba, 200 miles east.

CHAPTER SIX

TRAINING

We duly arrived at Brandon the next day, 1 October.

Time spent in a manning depot is never a highlight of a serviceman's career. This one was a huge place, originally built for showing and selling livestock. It had now been converted to receive, house and feed many hundreds of men, to equip them with uniforms, give them shots in the arm and elementary drill, sort them out for trade or aircrew training according to their enlistment, and send them in drafts to appropriate schools – in the case of aircrew enlistees to an initial training school (ITS).

A single concrete floor filled with narrow double-decker metal bunks took up most of the building. The place was spotlessly clean, the sanitation good, and the food satisfactory. The mass of men and the transitory function of the place gave it a highly impersonal flavour – nothing like the country club atmosphere I could have expected had I been born two years earlier and been successful in applying for a short service commission in the RAF.

We inmates began to talk with our surrounding bunkmates of course, the aircrew enlistees being together. I was particularly interested in talking with the small but growing number of Americans. Some had been among the very large number of their fellow countrymen who had failed to be included in the small number of flight cadets accepted annually for flight training at Randolph Field, the US Army Air Corps' famous flying training school. All were driven by a strong desire to fly, of course; most were well informed, and disapproving of the isolationism which had become such a powerful political force in their country.

Isolationism, the refusal to be drawn into foreign wars, was the rigid policy of most of President Roosevelt's Republican opponents as well as the wish of most Democrats, though they were not heavily undermined by pacifism as so many Britons had been. They regarded their navy as their impregnable defence against any foreign attack so they did not oppose keeping it that way, but they thought increasingly that the army was an unnecessary expenditure, obviously feeling that the great oceans on each side of them allowed them to choose non-involvement with impunity. Their influence proved effective in keeping their army and its air corps too small and poorly equipped in such threatening times.

At the manning depot we aircrew enlistees became aware of a hazard which made us anxious. A practise had begun whereby considerable numbers of us were drafted away to serve for two or three months as security guards for aerodromes before being posted to an ITS. The selection seemed wholly haphazard and therefore unfair because most of us wanted to be trained and sent overseas as fast as possible. I soon learned that being put on or left off draft lists was one of the inescapable hazards of the service – 'list hazard' I call it in hindsight. In any event, and to my great relief, in about ten days I found myself included in a draft of 200 men posted direct to the ITS in Regina to begin the one month course there. I had got by the first list hazard.

The ITS in Regina occupied three appropriated buildings spread along the south side of a broad avenue which formed part of the northern boundary of the park surrounding the provincial parliament buildings and their adjacent lake; this is where my gas model had ventured over before landing safely by the city power house a couple of years before. The centre of the ITS, comprising its headquarters and lecture rooms, was the rather gracious Regina College building – which happened to be south across the avenue from the high school I had just left! Just east of it was the provincial teachers' training school, whose lecture rooms had been converted to dormitories and its big hall to the trainees' dining room. Just west of the college was the Darke Hall, a family donation for plays and concerts, which had become 'station sick quarters'. The whole setting for the ITS was therefore the most pleasant, academic and park-like that Regina could muster.

At ITS we exercised and drilled every day, and were given lectures on King's Regulations, armament, and maths, the last a much needed brush-up for men who had left high school or university some years before, not just come across the avenue like me. We could leave the premises at the end of the day, so I could visit my family and see old friends regularly.

A deep anxiety began to be felt by all trainees at an ITS. Its source was the selection for aircrew positions that awaited us at the end of the course, after we had written examinations. The great majority of us wished fervently to be selected as pilots, not observers or air gunners, if only for the anticipated joy of flying an aeroplane – I say 'anticipated' because before the war most people had never been up in one, and I expect most trainees hadn't either. The greater glamour attaching to pilots in the public mind in those days was no doubt an inducement to some, but in fact the advantages of a pilot's status in the service were very real though barely glimpsed by most trainees at the ITS stage. Only a pilot could be the captain of a service aircraft, so his skill and judgement was more of a controlling factor in his own destiny than any other crew position. Furthermore, only pilots could be appointed as commanding officers and flight commanders of squadrons.

Each ITS student spent an hour in the cockpit of a Link Trainer, guided and being tested by an instructor who stood beside it. A Link Trainer was a fully instrumented flight simulator with flying controls, the whole apparatus tilting and turning in response to them. Its actual purpose was to teach trained and partly trained pilots to fly on instruments alone, under a hinged hood which was normally kept closed over the cockpit. The hood of the ones at ITS had been removed, however, which converted them into 'visual' Link Trainers to give the instructor some idea of a trainee's co-ordination. I doubt they were of much value at an ITS, as their motion was rather clumsy, but I was glad I had built my own crude flight simulator three years earlier because the instructor told me I had done very well.

After about two weeks ten of us came down with flu and were sent to sick quarters. Though they were comfortable and pleasant and my father and mother could visit me, I was much afraid of the effect on my future because the written examinations were to be held in about ten days. I was discharged from sick quarters just in time to write them, and the other nine were not. However, I had given a urine sample on being discharged and was soon told that albumin had been found in it, so I was beset with another anxiety. I was sent to a local urologist who thought it was a temporary aftermath of my flu and that drinking lots of water for several days would clear it up. To my great relief it did. I had got by another hazard.

When the examination marks came out three drafts of 35 men each, of which I was not one, were picked for three elementary flying schools in western Canada. This greatly increased the anxiety among those of us left behind because drafts were normally sent to whichever type of school had just graduated a class, and it was therefore more likely that an observer or air gunner school would graduate a class before another elementary flying school did.

However, about ten days later most of those of us left out of the first three drafts were enormously relieved. By what seemed a miracle three more drafts of 35 men each were picked for three other elementary schools. Two of them were in Ontario, one at Fort William and the other at Toronto. But a bitter disappointment faced the nine trainees who had been in sick quarters with me. They were all drafted to take the air gunners course at a bombing and gunnery school, because they had missed writing the exams I could only assume.

I myself was left in limbo, not being on one of the drafts, but I was told to report to a squadron leader in administration. When I entered his office he said, "Are you aware of your medical category?" I told him my urine had cleared up so I was fit now. He said, "I know, that's not what I'm talking about. But your category is only A1B; it's not A3B as well because you're over six feet tall. That means you can never be an air gunner." I had never heard more welcome words in my life. (I had noticed almost everyone had category A3B as well as A1B but somehow had not become aware of the significance of it.) The squadron leader went on: "We are going to include you in the draft to the elementary flying school at Fort William, but you should know that if you fail there you will revert to general duties, things like opening hangar doors and sweeping floors." I said, "I've never failed anything yet, sir," (which makes me cringe to this day). He said, "Well, this could be different." I left his office almost on air. I had somehow scraped by another hazard. He had made a good point though; it would be dreadful to fail at elementary and not be able to become an air gunner, or an observer either in fact.

It was often stated for public consumption that aircrew selection was based on temperament and aptitude. That was sheer nonsense, though no trainees were sent to air observer schools who had not done fairly well on the maths exam.

I had begun to make a few friends among my classmates at ITS but we always knew we could be parted at the end of the course and never see one another again. When I boarded the train east to Fort William I scarcely recognised any of my new classmates, but I was so glad to be among them. We had all been promoted to the rank of leading aircraftsman (LAC) and could sport white flashes in our wedge caps to indicate we were undergoing training for aircrew.

We arrived at Fort William in mid November, just before the snow settled in. It and its twin city Port Arthur were on Thunder Bay, on the north-west shoreline of Lake Superior, the largest of the five Great Lakes which straddle most of the border between Ontario and the United States. The two cities, of modest size and hemmed in by endless rolling bushland to the north, constituted the western terminus of the Great Lakes-St.Lawrence River waterway. (They have since become amalgamated under the name Thunder Bay.)

Fort William's aerodrome, its grass surface already withering, was on the outskirts, close to the bush and some fairly high hills, one or two called 'Mount' this or that. When we arrived it was a thrill to see the line of school aircraft by the hangar. They were De Havilland Tiger Moth biplanes, their engine cowlings black and their fabric doped yellow all over to identify them as air force trainers; they sported the red, white and blue roundels that originated with the Royal Flying Corps in the First War. The living quarters all belonged to the air force. Though the air force ran the ground school, the flying was run by a private contractor, Thunder Bay Air Training Company, employing civilian flying instructors and groundcrew – an arrangement which had become common for Britain's re-armament.

The elementary course was six weeks, subject to the weather. All flying training schools had a senior and a junior course going at the same time, our draft of 35 becoming the junior. The bunks of both classes were mixed together and we naturally got much information from the 'surviving' seniors; almost a third of their class had already failed flying, 'washed out' it was called, most before soloing. Being washed out was the most dreadful end to a student pilot's career and was usually devastating to his self esteem, at least for some time, even though it was no reflection on his character. Those washed out were sent back to the manning depot, those not over six feet 'remustering' as observers or air gunners.

On our arrival at the school we were addressed by its commanding officer, Squadron Leader Johnson, who told us in no uncertain terms what was expected of us. If he was a friendly soul at heart he hid it well. He warned us not to spend our time 'stabbing at women', among other things. He was, surprisingly for his position, an Englishman noted for his part in prewar British civil aviation trials to launch a small four-engine seaplane upon ocean crossings, too heavily laden with fuel to take off by itself, from a framework on top of an otherwise unladen four-engine flyingboat, the two separating at cruising height. The school's adjutant was Flight Lieutenant Chesson, a level-headed fellow and a fine pilot. He and Johnson would help out the civilian flying staff by 'check flying' some of the students for their required twenty-hour and fifty-hour flying tests, and for 'wash-out tests' of students whose instructors had doubts about their ability to become satisfactory pilots.

We were soon issued with parachutes and flying gear and sent over to the hangar, the senior class having left for ground school. A substantial lean-to on the airfield side of the hangar was divided in two by a wall, one part as a lounge for instructors and the other for students. A wicket-like opening in the wall allowed the instructors to summon students, the keenest of whom always kept an eye on the wicket.

Eventually a man around 30 appeared at the wicket and called my name out. He introduced himself as my instructor and told me to bring my parachute to one of the Tiger Moths on the line. Tiger Moths were a development of the Gypsy Moth, and had become the foremost elementary trainer in the Empire. Like the later Gypsy Moths its engine, made by de Havilland too, was the slightly more powerful Gypsy Major delivering 130 hp, still four-cylinder but inverted for a better view over the nose. It gave the Tiger Moth a top speed of 110 mph. The RCAF's Tiger Moths were made by de Havilland's factory in Toronto and differed from the RAF's in some details; instead of small windscreens in front of fully open cockpits, they had large sliding hoods for the Canadian winter. Communication between instructor and student was by the old Royal Flying Corps method of flexible voice tubes leading into ear pieces in their helmets, a system which had become universal in small trainers.

My instructor told me to get into the rear cockpit, the normal one for students in elementary trainers of those days, and showed me how to strap myself in. Civil aircraft (and those of the US Army Air Corps, surprisingly) simply had lap belts, but from the First War on all Royal Air Force aircraft were equipped with the Sutton harness, which also had two of its straps going over the pilot's shoulders to prevent his head from going forward during landing and take-off accidents and forced landings. The number of injuries it saved was huge, lives too sometimes.

My instructor then showed me the controls and explained what each was for and what it did. All of this I knew very well, but fortunately I had enough sense to keep my mouth shut. He got into the front cockpit, and with a groundcrew man to swing the propeller, went through the same starting drill with the ignition switches that my uncle and I had witnessed when we came across the biplane on the prairie near Regina when I was five years old. When the Tiger's engine started the combination of exhaust and doped fabric gave off the same intriguing smell.

My instructor taxied us to the downwind side of the aerodrome and when two or three others ahead of us had taken off he turned into the wind and opened the throttle fully. As we gathered speed he held the control column forward to get the tail up to the level position, easing back to centre position as it rose; after running level for some distance we became airborne. When we were comfortably clear of the ground he throttled back a little and climbed a few thousand feet with the airspeed indicator reading 65 mph. (Each type of aircraft has its own recommended air speeds for routine manoeuvres, as well as recommended engine rpms for them and for cruising.) When he levelled off and throttled back to cruising rpm I noticed the speed settled at 85 mph. It felt wonderful to be airborne in an air force aircraft at last.

After some flight familiarisation the first lesson began, which was feeling the effect of the controls. The US Navy flying manual I admired so much had made it clear that the position and angle of the horizon as it was appearing to a pilot was his basic guide to what his aircraft was actually doing at the moment. The manual was illustrated with fine photographs taken from the cockpit showing how the horizon would appear to be level with the aircraft's nose and parallel to its wings when the aircraft was flying straight and level, and how it would appear when doing each routine manoeuvre.

With my crude home-made flight simulator I had had to picture in my mind how the horizon would change its position and angle with every movement of its 'controls', so it was now immensely satisfying, with my right hand on a real control column and my feet on real rudder pedals, to make a real horizon appear to move as required and expected, and to find that the controls in actual flight felt much as I thought they would. All too soon for me we rejoined the aerodrome circuit and landed, after which my instructor told me I had a nice light touch on the controls; this pleased me because the US Navy manual had cautioned against heavy handedness. According to my logbook the flight lasted only 35 minutes.

Our second flight, two days later, was a short one too. Its sole lesson was flying straight and level, which required continuous synchronizing of the control column and rudder pedals to keep the nose of the aircraft on a fixed point on the horizon and its wings parallel with it. It took a little getting used to, especially with the Tiger Moth because it tended to wander a bit, but I soon got the hang of it.

Further lessons covered climbing, gliding, medium turns and stalling, the last being particularly interesting and vital. It will be mentioned frequently enough hereafter that some explanation is in order. An aircraft stalls when its airspeed becomes so low, either intentionally or inadvertently, that the flow of air over the top of the wing, smoothly curved in normal flight, becomes turbulent, at which point the lift of the wing ceases and the aircraft falls nose first into a dive, quite gently when they are done intentionally as when practising them is intended.

To practise stalls the aircraft is flown straight and level and the pilot simply closes the throttle and raises the nose, or even just keeps it level, to prevent the aircraft from entering a glide. It stalls when the airspeed decreases to what is called normal stalling speed, which in the Tiger Moth was 48 mph. (If the aircraft is in a different attitude, or is subject to some G-loading, the stalling speed would be higher.) At the point of stall the aircraft's nose drops down into a dive at a moderate angle and its speed then builds up to above the normal stalling speed. To recover the pilot simply moves the control column forward momentarily, eases the aircraft gently out of the dive, opens the throttle and carries on normally. Stalling is perfectly natural and is only dangerous if it is allowed to occur too low to recover from the resulting dive (or spin). In fact every normal landing is just a stall, ideally made to occur with the mainwheels and the tailwheel about a foot off the ground – a 'three pointer' (though later aircraft with nosewheels are stalled for landing with the nosewheel higher off the ground than the mainwheels).

None of my subsequent flights was much longer than the first one, my instructor seeming not to like staying in the air as long as the others, who usually stayed up an hour at the least. He had the usual number of other students on his roster of course, but he was also prone to lingering over cigarettes in the instructors' lounge, which I and they found frustrating. Twenty-five hours dual instruction and twenty-five hours solo were required to complete the course, so we were falling behind and getting worried about it.

I found ground school at elementary to be quite easy because I had read so much about the subjects taught. Most of the class were in their early to middle twenties, I at eighteen about the youngest, so most of those I became friendly with were several years older notwithstanding that I was quite immature (as I look back on it). I usually found older men more interesting than those around my own age. The closest friend I made there was John Towse, a few years older then I; he was an American, level-headed, interesting, and well read on aviation.

John had the same instructor I had, and we began to share our concerns about him, our chief one being falling behind the others, not only in hours flown but in advancing through lessons. Admittedly weather good enough for flying had been on the scarce side but it had been the same for all, and most of the other students were into landings and take-offs (the most critical lessons) by their third hour; at the beginning of our fifth we had done neither, and the average time to first solo was only nine to ten hours.

I was beginning to feel I may have survived list and health hazards only to fall victim to instructor allocation – another form of hazard. Our worries increased sharply when a couple of our instructor's students were washed out during their fifth hours. Then early in December, by which time I had received only five hours and twenty minutes instruction, I got a marvellous surprise; another instructor, experienced and with a fine reputation, appeared at the wicket and called out my name. He introduced himself and said, "I'm your instructor now, put your parachute in number 06." His name was Wesley Pollock. Serene and quiet spoken, he inspired confidence. He let me do the take-off, only the second one I had done, and then he put me through the things I had learned from my first instructor. The flight only lasted 20 minutes because darkness was coming on, but he let me do the landing, again only the second one I had done but the first where my hands alone were on the controls. When we were walking to the hangar I said to him, "I'm getting worried because I now have almost six hours and that landing I just did was only my second one." He said, "Oh, you don't need to worry, your flying is all right." Those words were as welcome as the squadron leader's at ITS who told me I could never be an air gunner.

All further instruction was delightful, Pollock's taking over having made a huge difference. In the next two hours and forty minutes I was taught to do spins and recover from them, but most of that time was spent on take-off and landing circuits, which I found quite straightforward.

Spinning was exciting. An aircraft will spin if it is allowed to stall while it is turning or just yawing. Like a stall a spin is perfectly natural. Almost all single-engine aircraft can easily recover from spins, but multi-engine aircraft could have trouble. To practise spins a stall is entered into in the usual way and the moment the nose begins to fall either full left or full right rudder is applied and held, the control column being held fully back. If left rudder is applied the left wing falls (and vice-versa of course) and the whole aircraft begins to rotate downwards to the left in a corkscrew motion at a rapid rate, with its nose not far off the vertical. Its descent speed would not be far above its normal stalling speed because only the left wing would be stalled; the right wing, moving faster than the left one because it is on the outside of the corkscrew, would not be stalled. The early layman's name for this seeming phenomenon was 'the falling leaf', which it resembles from the ground. When recovery is desired, the control column is moved forward a little ahead of centre and then full opposite rudder applied. Rotation usually stops quickly, the rudder is centralized, and the aircraft eased gently out of the resulting dive.

During take-off and landing adherence to an aerodrome's circuit, the pattern around it that aircraft follow after take-off and before landing in order to avoid colliding with others, becomes a regular but almost unconscious part of a pilot's life. Except when climbing after take-off and descending to land, an altitude 1,000 feet higher than the aerodrome is maintained, and all turns are made to the left. Viewed from well above, the pattern of the circuit for take-off and landing practise, for example, is a rectangle whose long sides are parallel to the take-off and landing path (which is commonly an into-wind runway) with rounded corners for the four turns.

Finally, late in the afternoon of 8 December 1940, after we had taxied back to the downwind side of the aerodrome for another circuit, I heard a clinking sound in my earphones which could only be Pollock disconnecting his voice tube. He got out of his cockpit, turned around to fasten up his Sutton harness so the loose straps could not interfere with the controls, gave me a smile and said, "Do a couple of circuits." With a total of eight hours and thirty minutes of dual instruction under my belt I turned into wind and took off on my first solo with enormous pleasure and relief.

During my next couple of hours solo I suddenly found I did not have to think of each movement required for taking off – it was becoming instinctive, the first stage to becoming a pilot I think. Landing always required close attention, however, because the landing approach at elementary schools was always made after a left hand turn during a glide that had begun at circuit height. If a pilot found his approach would leave him short of the field ('undershooting') he would have to open the throttle for a few seconds. If he were too high and was not certain he could come to a stop before the far boundary ('overshooting') he would have to open up fully and 'go round again'. If he had judged his glide correctly he would then have to judge his height and falling off in speed during final approach, levelling off, and raising the nose for the three-point touchdown position. If he levelled off too high and let his speed fall off too much he would stall and fall heavily to the ground, possibly smashing off his undercarriage as the flying club woman had done in Regina while I was waiting to go up for my first ride.

At this point Rod's narrative relating to his period of training ended. Having joined 2 Elementary Flying Training School (EFTS) on 17 November and soloed in Tiger Moth 4013 on 8 December, he continued his training here for another month. Passing out successfully, he was then posted to 2 Service Flying Training School (SFTS) at Uplands, which was located close to Ottawa, and still in Ontario. Arriving here on 11 January 1941, he found it equipped with North American Yale and Harvard advanced trainers, and he soloed in one of the former (aircraft no.3438) two days after arrival. Training on these aircraft indicated that the pupils were probably destined for fighters, since those chosen to become bomber or coastal pilots were generally posted to an SFTS equipped with twin-engine types.

Both the Yale and the Harvard were modern low wing monoplanes of metal construction with considerably higher performance than the Tiger Moth. The Yale, which was never as numerous an aircraft in the Allied forces as was the Harvard, featured a fixed undercarriage, while its 'bigger brother' the Harvard had fully retractable mainwheels – one more thing for the student to remember, but a preparation for the move to operational service types which would soon come.

Rod 'passed out' on 7 March 1941, receiving the coveted 'wings' – the pilot's flying badge, to be worn thereafter on the left breast of his tunic; as one of those with the highest pass marks, he was also commissioned at this stage as a pilot officer with effect from 18 March. His logbook carried the assessment at this stage that he was 'Average as a Pilot'.

Following a spell of leave, he was posted to the United Kingdom, embarking on 14 April and arriving on 1 May. While many Commonwealth pilots found that they were kept waiting for some weeks before receiving operational training, his posting in this respect was quick in coming through. On 12 May 1941 he arrived at 58 Operational Training Unit (OTU) at Grangemouth, which is located in Scotland, just to the east-north-east of Edinburgh. This was a Spitfire training unit which had commenced operating as such only during the preceding January. Rod's initial flight here was in one of the unit's two-seater Miles Master advanced trainers, 8365, on 16 May. His first flight in the Spitfire followed just two days later, recorded in his logbook as 6620. Rod did not record the initial letters prefacing the registration number of the aircraft he flew at this time. However, a process of elimination indicates that the Master was probably T8365, and the Spitfire was R6620, both of which did indeed serve with 58 OTU.

Taught the rudiments of fighter operations by tour-expired Battle of Britain pilots, he was deemed combat-ready by 23 June, when he was posted to 412 Squadron at Digby. Here Rod resumes the narrative.

CHAPTER SEVEN

OPERATIONAL

I joined 412 Squadron on 30 June 1941, the day it was formed. It was then based at Digby, in Lincolnshire, about 100 miles north of London, in 12 Group of Fighter Command. The squadron was a day fighter squadron and was equipped with Mark II Spitfires, which had eight machine guns.

Because 412 was a new squadron it had to work up before being sent on operations, the most significant of which in those days were sweeps over north-east France. Our working up to the sweep stage took almost three months, which I believe was longer than usual. I am sure the reason for this was the general inexperience among our 20 or so pilots. More than three quarters of us were, like myself, straight out of flying schools in Canada. More importantly, although our CO, one of our two flight commanders and one of our deputy flight commanders, had had some operational experience, none of them could be called an experienced fighter pilot, with the possible exception of the CO (Sqn Ldr C.W.Trevena).

It was Canadian government policy, as a counter to having a large number of Canadian aircrew in RAF squadrons, to have a considerable number of RCAF squadrons having all Canadian aircrew (and eventually all-Canadian groundcrew) notwithstanding that at that time there were hardly any RCAF officers with enough hard experience to give a squadron the leadership it needed.

To work up we did endless flying practise. We usually flew two or three times a day, staying up about an hour each time. We flew in formation a great deal, both in small sections of two to four aircraft and as a full squadron of 12. We practised dogfighting in pairs, and we fired our guns at drogues towed by another aircraft.

We spent most of the time between flights lolling around a fair sized well-windowed dispersal hut on the perimeter of the aerodrome, a good distance from the permanent hangars and other buildings. Our 18 aircraft were spaced some yards apart on each side of the hut, some of them in earth revetments. On one wall of the hut was a very large map covering a good part of England and on other walls were aircraft identification posters and charts. There were lockers there for flying gear, some chairs, a few cots, a coal stove for winter time, a table with two or three telephones on it, and a telephone orderly. In dispersal huts just like it all the fighter pilots in Britain spent most of their daylight hours, talking 'shop' most of the time.

Although in those early days nearly three quarters of all pilots joining their first squadrons joined as sergeant pilots, and the rest as pilot officers, it was easy for us to get to know each other well because of the endless time we spent together at dispersal. In spite of our squadron's inexperience, we were enormously pleased to have had the luck to find ourselves in any fighter squadron in Britain. Three quarters of our service flying school classmates had been kept behind in Canada to become instructors or staff pilots in the expanding Empire Air Training Scheme, and were doomed to serve as such for at least two years – a dreadful fate in such stirring times. France had fallen the previous June, Russia had only been in the war a few days before 412 was formed, and Pearl Harbor was an unknown name.

Digby was only eight minutes flying time from the east coast and we therefore did a lot of convoy patrols, which were very boring. We went on three sweeps over France while we were at Digby however, but for each of them we first had to fly to an aerodrome south-east of London, in 11 Group, to refuel and form an ad hoc '12 Group Wing' totalling 36 aircraft. Some highly-experienced RAF wing leader would then lead us on a sweep over the part of France opposite, following which we then had to land to refuel for the trip back to Digby. One of our pilots claimed an Me 109E on the third sweep. We didn't lose any pilots in the first three.

We did, however, see Me 109Es above us on the first sweep and 109Fs on the following two. If we had been experienced we would have been more than a match for the former, but not for the latter. 109Fs could fly a lot faster and higher than our Spitfire IIs, though we could turn tighter. They would make passes at us from behind and usually out of the sun, where it was hard to see them. To avoid getting hit we would turn sharply across their path whenever we could see them coming. Because of the foolish prewar prediction that World War II fighters would be too fast to dogfight, the Spitfire and every other fighter, British or German, was blind directly behind. Inexperienced 412 was lucky not to have lost any aircraft on those three sweeps.

In mid October 1941 the squadron re-equipped with Mark V Spitfires, which had two 20mm cannon and four machine guns. They also had sufficient performance to narrow, by about half, the speed and height gap between the 109F and the Spitfire II we had cast off. The squadron then moved to Wellingore, a village about four miles south-west of Digby. Our aerodrome was a grass field about 800 yards square, a part of Heath Farm, a short distance south-east of the village. The officers' mess was in Wellingore Grange, a pleasant rambling seventeenth century house, across from the village church on a beautiful leafy lane at the south side of the village. The sergeants' mess was in a small portion of Wellingore Hall, a large imposing building on the same lane, just east of the church. The groundcrew, or 'the airmen' as we usually called them, lived in the remainder of the Hall.

At the end of October our CO left and returned to Canada. He was succeeded by our senior flight commander, Kit Bushell, a very fine man but with little operational experience. Kit had been transferred to 412 from an army co-operation squadron, so his experience was therefore limited to our three sweeps. At twenty-seven he was our oldest pilot and a natural leader. His greatest ambition had been to lead a fighter squadron, and he loved it.

On 8 November the squadron went on its last sweep of the year, which dealt us a grievous blow. We flew down to West Malling, a small aerodrome in 11 Group, to take part in a sweep over France with two other 12 Group squadrons that also flew down. One of them was 616, a highly experienced RAF squadron. The wing was led by a relatively old RAF wing commander we had never heard of, and we were surprised to see that he didn't have the DFC ribbon – unheard of for a wing leader. One of 616's flight commanders caught my eye. He had a seasoned look about him and he did have the DFC ribbon. He seemed to be the only pilot there who knew what to expect on a sweep and what to do about it. I found out later he was 'Johnnie' Johnson.

We were briefed to proceed 75 miles east to a point about five miles north of Dunkirk, and then southward and patrol on an east-west line just south of Dunkirk at about 22,000 feet. We were to give withdrawal cover to 12 Blenheim bombers which were to be escorted by one or two other Spitfire wings to bomb locomotive shops at Lille, about 50 miles south-east of Dunkirk.

We took off about half past ten. When we got airborne we could see that ground haze was forming. When we got to the east coast of Kent we saw that the sea was covered with thick fog. The sky above was clear and we realized that to the Me 109Fs we expected to see above us we would stand out like ants on a white carpet.

We arrived at our turning point north of Dunkirk a bit early. Instead of just accepting this and making the planned turn south to our patrol line, our wing leader began a three-quarter circle to the left. This was no doubt intended as a partial orbit to kill time but he made the circle much too tight for a wing of 36 aircraft. The sections of the various squadrons soon became mixed up because most of the section leaders could not keep track of their own squadron leaders' sections. Most sections of four eventually broke up into pairs and singles and all flew round and round in a continuous and pointless left hand orbit. The wing disintegrated into a great milling beehive, because we could not tell which was the wing leader's aircraft. The beehive never even crossed the French coast, it simply remained over the sea just north of Dunkirk.

109Fs soon began to attack us from above. They would shoot down one of our aircraft from time to time. Fairly early in the orbit I saw a Spitfire shot down which I am sure was Kit Bushell's. Although I was by then alone I am confident I had kept position on him fairly well in spite of the tight orbit. I saw a 109 approaching his section from the south and above, and I turned sharply towards it. Before I could get within range the 109 closed in behind Kit's aircraft, fired at it and knocked some small pieces off it. I couldn't warn Kit because the radio telephone was hopelessly jammed with other pilots' transmissions. I saw him coming away from his aircraft with his parachute streaming behind him. The 109 broke away southwards in a shallow dive towards Dunkirk and I chased after it. It pulled steadily away, so when it got over Dunkirk I turned back and rejoined the beehive.

A little while later a voice on the R/T calmly said, "I guess I'm too old for this boys." We were sure it was our wing leader. He never returned.

In the middle of the shambles a few radial-engine enemy fighters appeared on the scene. This was astonishing because all Me 109s had inline engines. The newcomers were Focke-Wulf 190s, of course, though I myself never caught sight of one of them. Several times, though, I did hear interference on the R/T that had the unmistakable frequency of a machine gun. I broke to one side or the other each time, but saw nothing behind me. (The 190 was soon to become famous as the nemesis of the Spitfire V. The following spring I read an intelligence report saying that the synchronisation gear of the two Mauser cannon in the wing roots of the 190 had been interfering with R/T, which would thereby give warning that there was one very close by; the report added that a condenser had now been fitted to prevent that.)

Eventually, the Blenheims came out below us heading north-west, intact, and we were able to head back to the Kentish coast. When we reached it the ground haze had thickened greatly and we were very low on fuel. Most of the wing landed at Manston, which was sensible because it was almost on the coast. I managed to make my way back to West Malling, landing with zero on my fuel gauge. No other 412 pilots got back there but landings at other aerodromes were quickly telephoned in. I was particularly cheered on hearing that my friend, John Magee, had landed safely at Hawkinge, on the south coast of Kent.

412 had lost three pilots including Kit, more than any other squadron; nothing was ever heard of any of the three again. Two other squadrons had lost their COs. Fifteen Spitfires were lost out of the two or three wings which had taken part in the whole operation, which is close to a record for that type of action. Pilots in other squadrons claimed to have destroyed five enemy aircraft and to have probably destroyed three more. I learned many years after the war that it had been Adolf Galland's famous Jagdgeschwader 26 pilots we had been mixed up with, so our hapless squadron's pilots had been pitted up against the enemy's best. I also learned that our lost wing leader had never flown on operations before. He should therefore never have been allowed to lead 36 aircraft in action, to start with at least. Nonetheless, he had wanted to 'have a crack'. Hand it to him for spirit, if not to Fighter Command for having him lead us.

Our surviving pilots gathered the next morning in an upper room in Wellingore Hall with Hart Massey, our intelligence officer, for interrogation. John Magee had not only survived what had been his first operational flight, he had actually fired at an enemy aircraft, though he saw no results. He told us that when he mentioned to a pilot at Hawkinge that he had fired his guns but seen no damage, the fellow had disgusted him by saying, "Oh, put in a claim, put in a claim!" He made a combat report which, though making no claim, did contain the line: "Foolishly I dived to the attack." I don't know whether Hart let it stay in, or even filed it. John and I left the room together and at the door he said to me, "Gee, I'd like to have a score!"

A day or two later we got a new CO, Jack Morrison, who had been a flight commander in another RCAF squadron. He was, like Kit, a very fine man. In 1939, soon after the war began, he had collided with his closest friend while doing formation aerobatics near Ottawa. They had joined 120 RCAF (Auxiliary) Squadron in Regina several years before the war. Jack had managed to bale out but his friend was killed. In 1940 he had taken some part in the Battle of Britain. I sensed that his heart wasn't in flying anymore, but he always led us on anything out of the ordinary. The squadron made no more sweeps in 1941, but we continued to do convoy patrols and the usual endless practises of various kinds.

Editorial Note

The operation which took place on 8 November 1941 was codenamed 'Circus 110' by the RAF. The various escorting squadrons of Spitfires were indeed intercepted by fighters of JG 26, the pilots of which claimed 12 Spitfires shot down between 1250-1320; seven of these claims were made by the Jagdgeschwader's II Gruppe, led by Hauptmann Joachim Muencheberg, this being the part of the unit which had recently re-equipped with FW 190s, and which appears to have been mainly responsible for attacking the wing of which 412 Squadron formed a part. Claims by the pilots of this wing's squadrons actually totalled four destroyed, one probable and four damaged; in fact JG 26 losses were limited to two FW 190s, with one pilot killed and one wounded. Amongst the successful Luftwaffe pilots, Oberstleutnant Galland, Hauptmann Josef Priller (I Gruppe) and Muencheberg each claimed two Spitfires shot down.

While Circus 110 actually cost Fighter Command 11 Spitfires, with six pilots killed and three prisoners of war, other operations on this date brought six more losses of aircraft, with two more pilots killed and two PoW. The other two commanding officers lost were from Polish squadrons 315 and 316, both of them surviving as prisoners. The ill-fated wing leader was Wg Cdr D.R.Scott, AFC, who at the age of 33 had been appointed wing leader of the Kirton-in-Lindsey Wing; he led the formation of Spitfire Vbs in an older Mark II, P8701. The losses sustained by 412 Squadron were:

Sqn Ldr C.Bushell in W3959
Plt Off K.R.E.Denkman in W3952
Sgt O.F.Pickell in AD270, all of whom were killed.

John Magee

I have mentioned John Magee, who had joined 412 Squadron in mid September 1941 as a pilot officer, three months after he turned nineteen. He was tall, handsome and slender, and had a small moustache. I remember that when he was introduced to me in front of the fireplace in the officers' mess ante room, his eyes somehow conveyed a fine spirit.

His father was an American of Irish background, and his mother was English. Both were missionaries, he Episcopal and she Church of England. They had met and married in China, and spent thirty years there. John was born there but went to prep school and then Rugby School in England. His mother and father came to Washington, D.C. in the late thirties, when his father was about to retire. His father's last appointment was as assistant rector to the St. John's Episcopal church which was on La Fayette Square across from the White House and was known as the 'President's Church'.

In the summer of 1939 John was holidaying in Washington, having passed into the sixth form at Rugby. When the war broke out at the end of the summer the American government would not allow him and other American students to return to England.

When he turned eighteen the following June he went to Canada and joined the RCAF, getting his wings and being sent to Britain. After training at an operational training unit (OTU) at Llandow in Wales he was posted to 412 Squadron. At that time although I was only nineteen, I had been made a deputy flight commander shortly after the squadron formed, mainly because I had received my wings and been made a pilot officer a few days before the only four of the other inexperienced pilots who had been made pilot officers too.

John was a skilful pilot. His formation flying was tight and his practise dogfighting was gutsy, which I have always thought were the two early signs of the right stuff. John was inclined to be impractical at times, however. One day when the wind was strong he took off downwind towards the hangars at Digby at the very moment that the Duke of Kent arrived to visit us. John provided a memorable diversion by barely clearing the hangars. He also once forgot to connect his oxygen tube to the aircraft's supply tube and passed out at 22,000 feet. He came to in a high speed dive, just in time to pull out. He once allowed a wing to drop on landing, damaging it, and was so distraught he taxied into a parked aircraft, hitting one of its wingtips with one of his own. His flight commander, then Kit Bushell, was not amused. I am inclined to think John would have got over that stage though, if he had lived a few months longer.

He loved squadron life, and had many happy times at Wellingore. His casual arrival in the mess or our dispersal hut always gave a lift to us because his company was so pleasing. He was remarkably articulate, precocious and interesting; he had great integrity and high personal standards. He spoke with an accent which owed something to England, New England, and Canada.

The famous Lincoln Cathedral sits on the only hill for many miles around and is surpassingly beautiful. It was a fine landmark for us because its towers usually stood above the frequent haze and fog there. When the evenings drew in at Wellingore we often went into Lincoln to see a movie. When we got there we would first have a drink in the Saracen's Head, a large and far from cozy pub near the southern gate in the wall surrounding the hill which the cathedral sat on.

Lincoln was in the heart of the bomber squadron country so the pub always had lots of bomber crewmen in it. I always felt a bit sorry for them. It was not just because of their steady losses; we fighter pilots were not noted for our longevity in the first half of the war. It was because of their seeming anonymity in their large numbers. In fighter squadrons we knew every pilot, but I doubt whether bomber crews could get to know all their fellow aircrewmen. In his book *Full Circle*, Johnnie Johnson, the great RAF wing leader, expressed the same thought about the infantry in the First War by quoting from

Wilfred Owen's *Anthem for Doomed Youth*:

> What passing-bells for those who die as cattle?
> Only the monstrous anger of the guns.
> Only the stuttering rifles rapid rattle
> Can patter out their hasty prisons.

I have since been persuaded, however, that most bomber crewmen felt that they sortied with many friends.

One night in early November, when we were lounging around our bar in the Grange, one of our pilots mentioned that during a walk that afternoon he had seen a sheep stuck in the edge of a pond about a mile away. It was a cold foggy night and the thought of it made us feel uncomfortable. We began to look at each other and then Kit said, "Let's try and get it out." We put on our flying jackets and went off. Though the fog was thickening we found the poor animal, which bleated as we came near. I was tallest so Kit, John and one or two others gripped the bottom edge of my flying jacket and held me suspended over the sheep like the arm of a crane. I put my arms under the water and around its chest, and they pulled hard. The sheep gave a loud bleat as it came loose and out onto the bank. It loped stiffly but happily away in the dark.

On another evening a service vehicle which was to take us into Lincoln to see a movie was u/s (unserviceable), a not uncommon state, so John and I then went across the lane to Wellingore Hall where Charlie Chaplin's *Great Dictator* was being shown on 16mm film. When we were well into it the projector began to act up and finally quit. We were fed up, and as we left John laughingly said, "Everything in this country is u/s!"

On the morning of 11 December 1941, we were detailed to take part in a wing formation practise with an RAF squadron from Kirton-in-Lindsey, a few miles north of Lincoln. There was a 3,000 foot thick overcast, its base at about 1,200 feet. 412 was to join the Kirton squadron high above the overcast and the Kirton wing leader was to lead them both. 412 took off from Wellingore in a northerly direction in line abreast, led by one of our flight commanders.

As soon as we got airborne some white vapour began to stream back from my engine cowling up near the propeller and I realized that my engine coolant filler cap had not been screwed down. I left the squadron just before it entered the overcast and landed quickly. It took only a moment to have the cap fastened down but it was then too late to rejoin the squadron.

About an hour later I saw the squadron approaching the aerodrome from the south-east, under the cloud. Its formation was rather ragged while it made a circuit of the aerodrome before landing. Before it touched down sector operations control telephoned to say that a Spitfire had crashed between Wellingore and Cranwell, which was about four miles south-east of Wellingore. Cranwell was the RAF college, but early in the war it had become an ordinary service flying school equipped with Airspeed Oxfords, twin-engined trainers made of wood. I took off straight away, even before the last of the squadron aircraft had landed, and turned towards Cranwell. I soon spotted a crashed Spitfire burning in a farmer's field, just north of a wood, a mile or two north of Cranwell. Its wing was broken in half, with one half lying underside-up across the fuselage showing the roundel on its pale blue surface and its classic elliptical shape. It looked like a beautiful broken bird.

I returned quickly to Wellingore and landed. I learned that the Spitfire had collided with an Oxford and that John had not returned with the squadron. Hart Massey and I got into his four-seater MG and drove down a road leading south-east. We found the crash, a little bit to the west of the road, and at the same time saw an ambulance heading away from us towards Cranwell.

We left the car and walked across the field to within about 80 feet of the wreckage. It was John's Spitfire. We did not go closer because ammunition was exploding in the fire. We stood there for several minutes. The cloud ceiling had begun to clear and patches of sunshine appeared here and there. When we turned to leave we noticed a hole in the ground about 100 feet east of the crash. We walked over to it and saw it was the imprint of the back of John's trunk about a foot deep in the soft soil, the imprint of his head and elbows being about half that deep. His legs must have been doubled above him. Nothing remained there except a large pool of blood in the bottom of the hole. The wreckage of the Oxford was in some trees about half a mile to the east, and we walked over to it. Its pilot was an eighteen-year-old student, who had been killed and his body removed. We went sadly back to Wellingore. (John's and the student's mothers corresponded for years afterwards.)

What had happened was surprising. When the wing formation practise ended the wing leader told the 412 leader to return home. When 412 got back to within a few miles of

Wellingore, it was still above the overcast cloud layer but the leader noticed one small hole going right down through it. As was usual in those days he preferred to lead the squadron down through a hole instead of doing a slower and more stately instrument let-down in the cloud itself. When sweeps or wing practises were coming to an end pilots often had only a few minutes of fuel left and were anxious to get their wheels on the ground. So the leader ordered the squadron into line astern and dived down through the hole. They formed into a single file behind him accordingly, about 100 yards apart. Their speed built up to over 400 mph. The controls became heavy at that speed except for the elevators, which remained sensitive, the Spitfire being remarkable for its ability to pull out of a steep dive very quickly.

Unfortunately the hole happened to be over Cranwell's northern flying circuit and the Oxford happened to pass underneath it just as the squadron was coming out of it. 400 mph is about 600 feet a second. It was no wonder that the Oxford, at slow circuit speed, was not avoided once it had the misfortune to cross the path of 11 fast-diving Spitfires.

John's burial service took place in a graveyard that is a nearby continuation of one beside the church at Scopwick, a small village about a mile from Digby. I was an honorary pallbearer and I remember clearly that when the air force ensign was removed from the single oak coffin, the brass plaque on the latter read:

P/O John Gillespie Magee
R.C.A.F.
Died December 11, 1941
Age 19 years

We never saw anyone like John again.

Jack Morrison wrote the usual letter to John's father and mother. I recollect that a line of the letter he received in reply read: "Words can't tell you how much we miss John." A copy of John's soon to become famous poem, *High Flight*, was enclosed. He had written it at his OTU in Wales about a week before he joined the squadron, but had never mentioned it. Jack read out the last line – "Put out my hand and touched the face of God" – with a trace of a smile. I sensed he thought it was a bit far out, and I rather thought so too at the time. I cannot remember John ever quoting poetry or even hinting that he liked it, let alone wrote it. I can only assume he thought barbarians like the rest of us might think him sissified.

Years after the war I learned that John had won the Rugby School poetry prize in 1938, thirty-four years after Rupert Brooke had won it. I also read some poems John had written at Rugby from age thirteen to sixteen, and had had published privately while at a New England school in the latter part of 1939. They seem remarkable to me for a boy of those years. *High Flight* lives on, in my experience being recited at the funerals of most pilots.

A monograph on Rupert Brooke by Sir Edward Marsh in *Encyclopedia Britannica* implies that a poet takes years to mature. Sir Edward appraised the poems Rupert Brooke had written from age eighteen until his death at twenty-seven, saying of him:

> In the earlier poems he is still a boy... He writes with gusto, and a sense of verbal and metrical beauty, Neither quite under control... he is too lavish with the token coins of poetry... there is hardly a poem without some memorable phrase or passage... The later section shows a great advance... in his rapture there is still an immaturity or exuberance and bravado... Finally the fragments written on his last voyage... hold more surely than anything else he wrote the promise of a great poet.

It struck me those words might well have been apt for John.

I have been back to England a number of times since the war but I never returned to any squadron haunts until 1984. On a beautiful morning in early May of that year I drove down a quiet road from Lincoln to Wellingore with a woman friend. She was a one-year-old Westphalian when John died, but a dozen years later she moved to Canada with her family and eventually came across *High Flight* in one of her school books.

The south side of Wellingore was just the same, quieter if anything. We turned into the leafy lane where the Grange, the church and Wellingore Hall were. All were as serene and beautiful as I remembered them.

We drove the short distance south to where the aerodrome had been, and found it was a farm again. We then drove east towards Digby and came to the graveyard where John was buried. Its general aspect was pleasingly natural as before, in large part because of some ageing trees along its southern boundary and a few rustic buildings beyond them. We entered through the lych-gate, on its east side. First are older graves of villagers and then of several RAF pilots from the twenties and thirties. Many graves of wartime RAF and RCAF aircrew lie just beyond, each marked with the simple form of air force tombstone which replaced the wartime white wooden cross.

John's grave is on the south side, among several other 412 Squadron pilots, all of whom were killed in collisions. I recognised his name first, and noticed that the first and last lines of *High Flight* were inscribed below it. To my surprise tears suddenly came to my eyes, and I turned away and pretended to look for other names so that my friend wouldn't notice.

John Brookhouse

I also remember my first meeting with this John; he was tall and firm featured, with a pleasant, intelligent, rather thoughtful expression, and he looked you straight in the eye.

As I have already mentioned, in those early days nearly three quarters of all pilots joining their first squadrons did so as sergeants. For some reason I never fathomed John was not commissioned when he received his wings on graduation from service flying school in Canada, and he therefore joined the squadron as a sergeant pilot. This seemed unusually incongruous in John's case, since commissions were usually given to those in the third of the graduating class who had obtained the highest marks in flying tests and ground school examinations. I wasn't in John's graduating class but I recollect hearing that he had stood up to it well. If this is true he never showed any disappointment he may have felt. It seemed likely to me that he would command a squadron some day if he lived long enough, but long life didn't come easily in the first half of the air war.

When a new pilot joined a fighter squadron and began formation flying and practise dogfighting, the other pilots could soon tell if he was going to be one of the best, or about average, or not up to par. John easily established himself as one of the best. Furthermore, because he had great integrity and a kind of quiet dignity, and was down to earth and had a fine sense of humour, he became liked and respected.

Two of John's and my close friends in 412 were Chuck Charlesworth, a fine pilot like John, who became an architect after the war, and Hart Massey, our intelligence officer, who, though critically wounded in Holland on New Year's day, 1945, also became an architect.

John and Chuck were commissioned fairly early in 1942 and were welcome additions to the officers' mess. Although few pilots had cars in those days, John and Chuck bought a

Morris Minor from Jack Morrison for £40 and managed to get about in it quite a bit.

Other close friends of John's and mine were Art Young and Barry Needham. Art and Jack Morrison were shot down on a sweep the following spring, Jack dying of wounds in a French hospital. Art was also wounded and became a PoW. He suffered from blackouts thereafter and died in the 1960s. The CO who succeeded Jack (Sqn Ldr R.C.Weston) had little operational experience. Barry was shot down in Normandy two years later and became a PoW. He eventually took over his father's weekly newspaper in Yorkton, Saskatchewan.

At the end of the winter John and I happened to be on leave at the same time. By arrangement we met in London one morning and took a train to Dover. We wished to go for a run in the English Channel on a high-speed Royal Navy motor boat. We went down to Dover harbour, found out that a motor gunboat was going out on a test for an hour or so, and were invited aboard. It was a beautiful morning but there was some low fog on the sea, which was probably just as well. We had a fine ride, although somewhat bumpy now and again, until one of the three engines shut down for some reason and we had to reduce speed. All through the trip we kept wondering what would happen if a Focke-Wulf 190 found us and let go at us with its four 20mm cannons and two machine guns!

In the spring of 1942 we began to go on sweeps over France again, but it was tiresome having to refuel at an 11 Group aerodrome before and after each sweep. Our greatest wish had always been to have the entire squadron posted to an 11 Group aerodrome so that we could have our own groundcrew with us and do daily sweeps in the normal course. At the end of April we were finally posted to one, but it turned out to be Martlesham Heath, very near the coast of Suffolk and the one aerodrome in 11 Group where operations consisted almost entirely of convoy patrols. It was some consolation that no squadron was left there very long, but it was nonetheless irksome and to us as it was a continuing reflection of the inexperience of our squadron, especially of its leadership.

John and I rented a sailing dinghy on the nearby River Deben a few times. Chuck Charlesworth joined us once or twice. I remember that we discussed the doldrums the squadron was in and wondered how long it might take us to get to a normal 11 Group station. A few days later Chuck, who had applied to go to the Middle East four times because he was fed up with the situation, was finally posted there.

John and I went to the railway station in Ipswich to see him off. It was the last time John ever saw him, and the last time I saw him for two years.

At the end of May I was suddenly posted to Malta. John came to the railway station to see me off. We did not know we were seeing each other for the last time, but the thought certainly crossed my mind in that perilous year of 1942.

At the end of October of the same year 'Dusty' Davidson, another friend of John's and mine in 412 Squadron, came out to join my squadron in Malta. Dusty and I had shared a room at Wellingore and I was very pleased to see him again. However, he told me straight out the sad news that John had been killed and he related the circumstances. He said that in June, not long after I had gone, 412 had been posted to Merston, an ideal 11 Group aerodrome almost on the south coast, a bit to the east of Portsmouth. From there they had done sweeps in the normal course and had begun to get some real experience. On 19 August they were briefed to make a low level sweep behind Dieppe while the famous raid on that port was taking place. Unhappily, the tail of John's aircraft was shot off by Flak and he crashed straight into the ground without a chance to survive.

Fairly early in November I went to hospital with a virulent form of jaundice which was endemic in the Mediterranean. A few days later a few of the squadron pilots came to see me and gave me more sad news. They told me that Dusty was missing after attacking an Me 110 over the sea near the island of Pantelleria. He reported that his oil pressure had gone and concluded by saying: "I guess I've had it." Although they searched for him he was never found.

Another event which occurred just before I left 412 Squadron related to a crash by another pilot, Flt Sgt Allan Porter, on 15 April 1942. Allan crashed because our new CO (Weston) had kept us up too long on an afternoon practise with the Kirton-in-Lindsey wing leader, the latter having brought a squadron with him from there. The wing leader was a few minutes late to the rendezvous, over Kirton, and then after a very long exercise, asked our CO if five minutes more would be OK. Our CO, ever anxious to please a senior officer, consented without hesitation, but I felt an uneasy foreboding. When the wing leader finally dismissed us, at 20,000 feet over Kirton, our CO, instead of diving for Heath Farm, kept us at that height until we were directly over it, and then brought us down in a long slow spiral. I broke away at about 10,000 feet, dived quickly and landed. I had zero fuel when I reached B Flight dispersal in the south-east corner of the field; my logbook shows an hour and forty minute trip. I then saw the squadron approaching to land from the west in fours (two fours and a three actually!) and I noticed that the propellers of two of the aircraft were windmilling. The wheels of one of them were slowly coming back up and its pilot, a sergeant, was fortunate enough to belly-land short, but Allan ploughed through the hedge near the south-east corner of the field and into a blockhouse. He could not see this because it was hidden by the boundary hedge and was painted much the same colour. It was a sickening sight as I ran over there. The only way I could tell it was Allan was that his curly blond hair showed above his totally bloody, chopped-up and unrecognisable face, and his battledress tunic had the flight sergeant's stripes and crown on it. He was in hospital a long time, but his terribly smashed face did eventually heal for the most part. However, the doctors wouldn't pass him for high flying because of the very bad concussion he had suffered. He was therefore sent back to Canada and for the rest of the war flew Tiger Moths with student wireless operators in the back seat.

After we landed our own wing leader, 'Cowboy' Blatchford, came over to our mess from Digby and had tea with us. Our CO sat at the head of the table with Cowboy on his right and me on his left. The CO was very quiet and appeared uncomfortable, but Cowboy began to expound on how stupid the two crashed pilots had been. This displeased me very much and I said straight out that they had been kept out too long. Cowboy said, "Well you knew enough to break away early." I replied that because the fuel gauges in Spitfires read low at altitude no pilot could tell how much fuel he actually had, that I had a lot more experience than the two unfortunate NCO pilots, and as a deputy flight commander I had a lot more confidence about breaking away. The CO stared at his plate and looked even more uncomfortable, and Cowboy scowled at me. The two NCOs had their logbooks endorsed, at Cowboy's insistence I suspect.

I think Cowboy always liked me actually, and I always liked him too, although he wasn't a Jamie Rankin, but I am sure he thought I spoke out of turn a bit too readily. The CO was a nice man; he and I never actually had a word out of place, but I didn't think he was strong enough, as may be gathered. He immediately developed a phobia about empty tanks (not entirely unjustified where British and German fighter planes are concerned) but it became quite inhibiting to us and even embarrassing. Shortly after the unfortunate Kirton fiasco we went on a sweep over France as part of another ad hoc 12 Group Wing. After about 40 minutes our CO announced to the wing leader, who I think was 'Jamie' Jameson from Wittering, that our squadron was running low on fuel. The leader of an RAF squadron with us said, "He must have a game of golf on!" Jamie sounded a bit surprised, no doubt because we had all taken off together, but he let us go home early. We had bags of fuel when we landed.

I left the squadron six weeks later to go to Malta, and a month or two after that our CO went to RCAF Headquarters Overseas, at Lincoln's Inn Fields, to ask to be sent back to Canada. Even that limp outfit didn't like it, as he had put very few hours in that were actually against the enemy. He was posted back, but he lost his acting rank and so went back as a flight lieutenant. Nevertherless, he was taken on in the regular force after the war and retired as an air commodore. I think the fact that his father's brother was a big tycoon in this relatively small country never hurt his career.

Towards the end of April my brother Jerry telephoned me one morning to tell me to come and see him if I could in a hotel in Glasgow where he was staying for a few days with a nice WAAF officer from his station at Eglinton, Londonderry. I took off immediately for Renfrew aerodrome, which was virtually on the bank of the Clyde. In his hotel room he told me that he was waiting to go aboard the US carrier *Wasp*, which was then being loaded with tropical Spitfire Vs for an unknown destination. He said he had left his squadron, 152, because he had hit a tree with his Spitfire during an army co-operation exercise and had been offered the chance to take a timely no-name posting 'overseas' by his new and likeable CO, Bird-Wilson. As he had been court-martialled the previous fall for hitting a signal pole with a 152 Squadron Spitfire during a visit to me at Wellingore, he took up B-W's kind offer.

Incidentally, when I had landed at Renfrew I had my first glimpse of tropical Spitfire Vs. I shall never forget it. Their ghastly air filters appalled me, and the 90 gallon 'slipper' tanks that most of them had on did not help. Some of them were VCs, with their 'universal' wings sporting four cannon; a more ludicrous get-up I had never seen. I pitied the poor bastards who would have to fly them! However, after Hurricanes they probably thought they were angels from heaven.

Another lasting sight that morning was the *Wasp* at dockside only a stone's throw from the aerodrome, with Spitfires being loaded on her and some Grumman Wildcats parked on her flight deck forward. Sadly, she was sunk the following September; while in 'Torpedo Junction' south-east of Guadalcanal she picked up three of a fan of six 'long lance' torpedoes fired from the Japanese submarine *I-19* at 1,000 yards. What *I-19* never realised was that there was another task force about six miles beyond *Wasp*, and that one of her torpedoes hit and sank the destroyer *O'Brien* while another hit the battleship *North Carolina* and put her out of action for two months! *I-19* went down with all hands a year later but some of her crew who had in the meantime transferred still recall the sinking and have had a 'reunion' with some of the crews of the American ships involved.

CHAPTER EIGHT

JERRY

As I described earlier, my older brother, Jerry, had joined the RCAF a few weeks after myself, his training following a quite different path than my own. His initial posting had been to 1 ITS in Toronto, where he arrived for kitting, etc on 13 January 1941, and where he too was held for some weeks – though not as long as I had been at Fort William. On 21 February he arrived at 10 EFTS at Mount Hope, Ontario, where he commenced his initial flying training not on Tiger Moths, but on Fleet Finches, first soloing in Finch 4691 on 7 March 1941.

With this milestone under his belt he moved on to 9 SFTS at Summerside on Prince Edward Island on 3 May 1941, and here he undertook his advanced training on Harvards, soloing on one of these ten days later. Like me, he was one of the lucky few to receive a commission on completion of his time at Summerside in mid July. Following this came the wait for passage to Britain, but early in September he was able to sign in at 57 OTU at Hawarden (pronounced 'Harden'), which is located in north Cheshire, near the cathedral city of Chester. Here he was to make his first flight in a Spitfire, coded PW-D, on 13th of the month. Just one week later he was posted to 152 Squadron at Swanton Morley, another of 12 Group's aerodromes, this one in Norfolk.

152 had done well during the Battle of Britain, and could

be considered a very experienced unit. Jerry's CO here was Johnny Darwen, a career officer who had returned from India at the end of 1940 to take part in the European war. He had brought with him his new nineteen-year-old bride, but tragically she had been killed while in his arms dancing when the Café de Paris in London was hit by a bomb during March 1941. Having attended a 'refresher' course on Spitfires at the same Hawarden OTU, he had been attached to 66 Squadron to gain experience as a supernumerary, taking command of 152 in June. With him had come another ex-66 Squadron pilot, Flt Lt 'Bogle' Bodie, DFC, a tough and successful fighter pilot who was to be Jerry's first flight commander.

Like 412 Squadron, 152 was equipped with the Mark IIa Spitfire at this time, but unlike ourselves, 152 was considered fully experienced and operational. Inside a week of joining the unit, despite his very limited hours on Spitfires, Jerry was involved in his initial operational sortie on 27 November when he took part in an escort to Beaufort torpedo-bombers making an anti-shipping raid off the Dutch coast during which a 1,200 ton tanker was claimed sunk.

At the end of the year, on 30 December, the squadron flew south to take part in Operation Veracity II, a substantial daylight bombing raid on the battlecruisers *Scharnhorst* and *Gneisenau*, and the cruiser *Prinz Eugen*, in Brest harbour. The raid was intercepted by fighters of Jagdgeschwader 2, which shot down three four-engined Halifax bombers and three of the escorting Spitfires. Jerry, flying Spitfire T8659 as part of the top cover, saw one of the big bombers go into the sea in flames after being attacked by four Me 109s, then giving chase to a 109E, which he followed down from 17,000 feet to 7,000. Just as he opened fire he saw the tail come off his target – not, however, due to his shooting – and at that moment another Messerschmitt which had been on his tail, shot past his nose. The escorting Spitfire pilots claimed eight of the attackers shot down with an additional six as probables – two of the latter claimed by 152 Squadron.

Operations for 152 came to a sudden halt when it was posted to Northern Ireland on 15 January 1942 where six days later 'Bogle' Bodie spun into the ground and was killed while undertaking aerobatics. It was here that Jerry's 'misdemeanours' occurred, and where Harold Bird-Wilson took over command from John Darwen during March.

Jerry kept a diary from the time of his overseas posting, which my mother had typed up after the war, which I now quote from, written in his style.

1942

April 25th Posting came through for four people from our
   Flight of which I was one.

April 26th Began to pack preparatory to leaving. God, how I
   hate to leave 152 Squadron. The grandest bunch of chaps
   I ever hope to meet. Had last party at Sergeants mess.

April 27th I hate to even think of Desert Sand. Spent part of
   morning getting clearance sheets and finished packing.
   Transport arrived and we went into Londonderry and got to
   port. Shot up dispersal as we passed the boys on readiness
   and tossed out a note. They escorted us in Spits shooting up
   the Transport at intervals.

Arrived at Paisley after midnight and went out to Abbotswick –
   finally getting rooms and so to bed.

April 28th Woke up at 11 am. Drew out tropical kit from the
   stores and learned that we shall have to take off from an
   Aircraft Carrier. Some fun. Phoned Rod but could not get in
   touch with him.

April 29th Did packing. All we can take with us is tropical kit
   and 10 pounds personal baggage. The rest will be sent on.

April 30th Had good sleep and woke up feeling rested for a
   change. Phoned Rod and he is trying to get down tomorrow.

May 1st Got up early and went out to the drome. We learned
   that we are to report with all ready at 7.30 pm. Rod arrived
   about 3 pm. We chatted for more than an hour, then Rod
   departed for Wellingore flying a Spit. We packed stuff on to a
   bus and drove to an Aircraft Carrier – USS *Wasp*. Beautifully
   clean ship and quarters very comfortable. Wingco, just back
   from Malta, gave us the 'gen', which was rather frightening,
   though exciting.

May 2nd Started down the Clyde but stopped at Greenock for
   the night.

May 3rd Started again very early in the morning. Passed
   Eglinton about noon. Hoped some of 152 would shoot us up
   but no luck. Ireland looked beautiful; in the sunshine.

May 4th Headed south and west all day. At night we were 100
   miles or so south-west of Ireland. The boys did a spot of flying
   today – an amazing sight. The groundcrews are absolutely on
   their toes.

May 5th Very comfortable and lazy existence. Spent day
   drinking coffee and Coca Cola and eating toast.

May 6th Approaching Gibraltar today. Waiting to see HMS
   Eagle but it did not turn up at rendezvous. Low clouds today.
   The Americans did some flying. An enemy plane was reported
   in the vicinity but no sign of it.

May 7th Aircraft operating from carrier during most of the day.

Passed through Straits of Gibraltar about midnight. Could see the lights of Spain and Morocco. The *Repulse* and several Destroyers joined us later.

May 8th Spent day going through Mediterranean with Aircraft Carrier *Eagle* behind. *Repulse* in front and good escort. Will be glad to be off. Fear of subs great. Ran up Aircraft and tested jettisonable tanks at night.

May 9th 580 miles from Malta. We took off today. One of our lads went in off the end and ship cut him in two. He never came up. I took off and found wing tank out of commission, so after others had finished I landed back on the Carrier – the first Spit ever to do it. The Americans made a terrific fuss and presented me with Navy Wings and a cake. Had grand time that night but they wouldn't let me take off when trouble remedied.

[Thereby hangs a tale, as I shall describe later. *RIAS*]

May 10th Passed through Gibraltar at midnight. Took off in same Spit with six Swordfish and landed at Gib. Most magnificent scenery and plenty of fresh fruit.

May 11th Learned that one of our Spits landed in Africa; one crashed near Malta and the rest went into action half an hour after landing and shot down 30 Jerries. Good show. Slept last night at North Camp. Spent most of the afternoon testing cannon on my kite. Went up four times. Moved kit down to Rock Hotel; in room with Australian. Wonderful view and rooms and accommodation good. Weather perfect. Had a meeting at 10 am and leave to report on board *Eagle* on Sunday.

May 12th Slept in until 11.30. Spent afternoon climbing to the top of the rock. Magnificient natural defence, plus many manmade traps, etc. This rock is probably the nearest to being impregnable of any fortress in the world. Went to the Show tonight 'Mr and Mrs Smith'. Quite good but rather weak toward the end. Got to bed about 11.

May 13th Weather not so good so did not get sun bathing. Learned that in three days the boys in Malta got 99 Jerries, confirmed and probable. Why in hell didn't I get there for the fun. Am stuffing myself with oranges and bananas.

May 14th Slept in until 11.30. A friend and I went round by taxi to Cot Beach and had wizard sun bathe and swim. Water cold but refreshing and weather perfect – not a cloud in the sky. Came back. Had tea in Town. Went to Wizard of Oz, then back to Rock. Dressed for dinner then went for a walk to south end of Rock. Came back to Hotel and talked with some Canadian Catalina boys and so to bed.

May 15th Had breakfast in bed at 9.30. Perfect day. Am rather sunburned after yesterday's effort. Went swimming in the afternoon. Ate rather more than my share of oranges.

German spring offensive seems to be opening up in Russia.

May 16th Breakfast in bed at 9.30. Ho hum. Wandered down town about 11. Got another advance in pay (all next month's money spent!). Watched some Hurricanes and Swordfish shooting up the harbour.

May 17th Down to the Dock at 10 am. Got on HMS *Eagle*. Left harbour at one and headed east. Lovely clear day. Ack ack defences tested on drogue. What a row.

May 18th Waited until 1 pm when ship tried to gain enough speed for the take off but failed. About 2.30 first nine took off without incident though some rather shaky. Then we took off about three. Perfectly clear day. Could see far into Africa. Flew nearly 400 miles along the coast then cut off across Pantelleria. At one point could see Tunis, Sicily, Malta and far down the Coast to Tripoli. Landed in Malta in the middle of a raid but all safe. Stayed on drome till dusk then were taken by bus to Nashar; we were billeted in the Palace.

May 19th Got up late. Went to drome at Luqa. Small raid by high flying Eyeties. Located some of kit at Nashar. Meals here awful. Watched Wizard "beat up" of Takali by Junkers 88's. Nothing hit by bombs. Ack ack looked wonderful in different coloured streamers. Am now in 601 Squadron.

May 20th Got up at 4.00 am. Went up to Luqa. Spent day doing cannon tests on Spitfire. Failed to get them to work properly. Back to Nashar at dusk in time to see 88's bombing Takali again. Some bombing during day – mostly Eyeties.

May 21st Up late. Wandered into Valetta later and looked over the appalling damage. Got back to Nashar quite late and so to bed.

May 22nd On readiness at 5 am. Went practise flying at 6 with Flight Commander and a Sergeant Pilot for one hour. Was scrambled about 10.30. Some 109's bombed the drome but we didn't see them. One of the boys from Takali shot down one. Another cannon test and as usual failure. Amazingly we were released at 1 pm and went to St. Paul's Bay for swim. I became ill and went to Hospital at 10 pm. Dysentry of 'Malta Dog'.

May 23rd Feeling better today. Played chess, read story of San Michaele for the second time. Watched a Macchi firing at a Spit. Spit pilot didn't even know it but was unhit. Three 109's and one Eytie bomber shot down. Leaned later that Spit pilot was my CO. [This was Sqn Ldr John Bisdee, DFC.]

May 24th Played chess – read – wrote home and slept. What an existence.

May 25th Still in Hospital. Will probably stay until Saturday. A little bombing down today but nothing hit.

May 27th Colonel's big inspection today. Bags of bull when the old boy passed by. Thank God I am not in the army. A bomb hit the gymnasium a few hundred yards away last night. Could hear it whistling down. Rather a shock to us. Went for a walk.

May 28th Up and about today. Am reading 'Jamaica Inn' just now. Reminds me a bit of 'Hatter's Castle'. Will be able to go out for quite a while today. Went to Luqa to collect kit. More stuff missing. Went for a walk to Rabat and got back about 10. Slept well for a change.

May 29th Thousandth day of the war. Germans and Russians having bloody great battle near Kharkov. German offensive in Libya starting today. Went up to Luqa to check up on missing stuff stolen by our Maltese batmen. Failed to find culprits. Went into Valetta – bought a bit of clothing then back to Rabat and from there to hospital. Very tired.

May 30th Went before Medical Board today and got seven days sick leave. Missed the ambulance at 2 pm and had to hitch hike to St. Paul's Bay. The Rest Home is a wizard spot – marvellous swimming – meals good and all very comfortable.

May 31st Swam and sun-bathed most of the day. Finished off new log book. Had a raid tonight and some bombs very near.

June 1st Went for swim before brekker. Started for Luqa at 9 am. Went to Valetta for a while and then to St. Julien, our new quarters. Very good mess and had a good tea. Hitch hiked to St.Paul's again. Had a good swim and so to bed.

June 2nd Swim after breakfast. Hitch hiked to Valetta and then to Luqa. Weather perfect. Still no word from Home or the United Kingdom. Spent day swimming and sun-bathing. Quite a bit of cloud today and a little rain. Bathing is wizard. Went to a flick at night. Very poor and one of the worst I've seen but still a change. Went to bed but couldn't sleep for insect bites. Quite a raid tonight. About 25 fires between here and Takali – several bombs rather close.

June 4th Raining part of the day – very cold and cloudy. No swimming today, thank you. Caught a bit of a cold last night and Malta Dog is beginning to bite again. More bites – very miserable with these sand flies and mosquitos.

June 5th Rain in morning. Packed kit and prepared to leave for St. Julien. Transport arrived about 3. Went via Nashar and killed a dog en route. Didn't want to appear too much like Mussolini dashing through the streets of Rome, so stopped. The Malts however, were almost apologetic for having a dog in the way, so we weren't delayed. Went into Valetta later. Ordered a tropical battle dress and a peaked cap – on the Government, I hope.

June 6th Waited for the MO to come and pronounce me fit for action but he had come and gone before I knew it. Went into Valetta. Collected £5 – tropical allowance. Saw a flick and watched a good raid.

June 7th Got up at 5 – after not sleeping a wink. Beastly bites. Up in the air early. Tried to chase a 109 but not high enough.

June 8th Usual swimming and bathing. Went into Valetta, was fitted with battle dress.

June 9th Readiness 6 am to 9 pm. What a time. Chased a couple of 109's about one third of the way to Sicily. Had a dog-fight. Had a couple of squirts but didn't observe hits. Shot up St.Julien on the way back and went to bed early.

June 10th Went into Valetta saw 'Another Thin Man'. Had seen it before but enjoyed it.

June 11th Readiness 6 am to 9 pm. What a bind.

June 12th Went into Valetta. Got battle dress – saw show on way back. Had swim before dinner and went to bed early.

June 13th Went up for a couple of air tests, preparing for long range convoy patrol. Put an aircraft on its nose when starboard wheel sank in a rock filled bomb hole. Propeller changed and a tyre. Could have been worse. Everyone keyed up for battle expected.

June 14th Hung about the pens nearly all day. Got off readiness about 9 pm and had a talk by AOC about Convoy due in tomorrow.

[This was a major relief convoy which was fighting its way through to the Island under the codename Operation 'Harpoon' CS].

June 15th What a day. Went out to Convoy just off Pantelleria. Bill's wireless out of commission so I led the section. Patrolled for 15 minutes, then Junkers 87's and Me 109's arrived. I went through flak after an 87 and saw a huge piece break off. Had a dog-fight with a 109 and it left trailing smoke heading for Pantelleria. Was hit by flak on first trip but got back a few minutes before engine would have packed in. One of ours missing. Went out again about 5.20 pm. Over Convoy for an hour when 88's and 109's bombed it. Damaged an 88, shot at a 109 and shot down another 88. Its rear gunner shot me up and as I headed back for Convoy I caught fire. I bailed out and was picked up in 15 minutes by Destroyer *Blankney*. Destroyer beside us struck a mine and survivors came aboard our ship. Got into Grand Harbour about 6 am. Three hours sleep.

June 16th Raid on harbour by four 88's but was sound asleep, thank Goodness. Got off ship about 10 am. Caught a lorry and went up to St. Julien. Had lunch there, took cart and went around to Luqa, getting helmet, goggles, parachute, etc. Made out combat report. Kept the dinghy. Got back and had tea about 6. Went to bed. Usual raid about 11 pm. Bombs dropped at Luqa and over the harbour. Ships being unloaded all night. Another small tanker arrived.

June 17th Convoy from Cairo turned back and our Convoy

from the West lost four merchant vessels out of six and two
Destroyers. Big Naval battle off Greece – Italians lost six
Battleships and two Cruisers. Our East Convoy lost heavily.
Scrambled. Couldn't find an 88. Saw two 109's. Off at 1 pm.
Back to St.Julien. Had lunch and swim. Played in the water
with my dinghy. Saw a show 'The Lady Vanishes'. Got to bed
early.

[The information that Jerry had about the naval engagement
was clearly wrong! In fact no battleships or cruisers were lost by
the Italians on this occasion. CS]

June 18th Dead tired. Up at 4.45 on early readiness. Went up
for one and a quarter hours waiting for reconnaissance 109's
to come over the Island but they didn't appear. My 87
probable may be confirmed destroyed. [It wasn't. CS]. Had a
swim about 10 pm. Army bloke kicked us out. Said it was
contrary to regulations – and they wonder why we are losing
in Libya.

June 19th Went up at 9.30. Made up log book then in for a
swim. Went into Valetta.

June 20th On readiness all day and didn't have one blinking
scramble. Had swim in dark before dinner. Got hauled up by
the Army as it was contrary to their anti-invasion exercises –
trust the blooming Army.

June 21st Learned that Squadron is to go to Middle East –
flying out – a shaky do. Ten to go tomorrow and another ten
later. Went dancing.

June 22nd The Malta Dog has bitten again. Violent spasms and
brought everything but my heart up. Went back to bed after
some tea. The rest went down to the drome early, 7 am and
tested long range tanks. They got back about 7 pm and I went
over and had some soup and tea, Sollum has fallen. If we
don't hurry up we shan't have even Egypt to go to.

June 23rd Nine of Squadron finally got away. Later learned all
reached Egypt safely despite rumour that one had gone in the
drink. Tested new system of twin Hurricane tanks under
fuselage and found it absolutely useless. Average cruising
speed about 137 miles per hour.

June 24th Had mail from United Kingdom. More postings from
my old Squadron. Convoy has been unloaded and there have
been few raids. Spent day sun-bathing and swimming. Later
saw 'Paris Honeymoon' in Valetta.

June 25th All day on beach. Went to bed early. We are back on
readiness now operating as a separate squadron. Rommel's
troops advancing about 120 miles into Egypt now so we
shan't be going until (and if) he is driven back. The fools for
letting him get the better of us. No excuses of unpreparedness
now.

June 26th On readiness for first time in ages. Delayed action bombs going off all day after heavy night raid. Four Ju 88's shot down by Beaufighters. Scrambled to 24,000 ft; had no oxygen and came down; blacked out at 1,000 ft after staying up for better part of an hour. Enemy aircraft came over in bunches of 24 fighters, 12 and five bombers.

June 27th Swam all morning and part of afternoon. Went to Club, danced for hours; got to bed late.

June 28th Up early for readiness. Feel a bit fagged. Squadron moved to Takali at 2 pm. Flew over; not very pleased about the move.

June 29th Sun-bathed and swam most of the day. Packed things in evening preparatory to moving to Rabat.

June 30th Became ill during the night. Went up at 5 am in the bus to Takali and from there to sick quarters on a motorcycle. Doc proclaimed it Sandfly fever. Got a bed and took Aspirin. Bombed during the night. Two within 200 ft, one delayed action went off early in the morning – a bit shaky. Germans within 70 miles of Alexandria.

July 1st Got up and had a spot of breakfast. Went to St. Julien. Moved stuff over to mess. Went to bed, felt a bit ill and pains on right side. Uncomfortable night; several bombs dropped near here and guns banging away. Also party in the bar next to our rooms so very little sleep.

July 2nd Three of us are staying behind. Remainder of Squadron posted to Middle East. Am in 126 Squadron now. A good Squadron and I am not sorry to stay although the old 601 gang were a mighty good lot. We lost five Spits and two pilots yesterday. Activity on increase – I hope.

July 3rd Feeling better but not in the pink yet. Had short swim before lunch. The boys didn't get away last night. Luqa badly bombed. Tommy bailed out and was in the mess for lunch. Engine trouble and picked up 12 miles out in sea. [This was Plt Off F.D.Thomas]. The boys [of 601 Squadron] left for the drome in a bus at 8 pm and left tonight in Whitleys. Not much bombing tonight.

July 4th Eyeties came over about 10 am. Four bombers, one turned back, the others were all shot down. One came down in flames near the drome. About 7 pm five BR 20's came over with large Fighter escort of Macchis. I had squirts at three Macchis, one of which was firing at a Spit. Was fired at several times, once by bombers, when I raked across them with only one cannon firing. All of our chaps got down safely but only one bomber was probably shot down and one damaged. Pretty poor show, but fun while it lasted. Felt a bit ill. To bed without supper.

[This was a day for bad aircraft identification as well! The morning raid was actually made by three Savoia S 84bis bombers of 4 Gruppo BT. Two were shot down and the third got back, although it was badly damaged. Its gunners claimed one Spitfire shot down and the escorting Macchi C 202 pilots claimed three more; two Spitfires actually suffered some damage. The afternoon raid was by five Cant Z.1007bis bombers of 33 Gruppo BT, the escort including 20 Macchis and ten Reggiane Re 2001s. Two of the bombers were damaged, but the escorting fighter pilots claimed five Spitfires shot down, three probables and two damaged, the bomber gunners adding a sixth claimed shot down and one more damaged. As Jerry said, none were actually lost! CS]

July 5th Stayed in bed till 1. Got up and sun-bathed. Went to flicks. Saw 'Balalaika'. Very good.

July 6th About 10 am received call to readiness. Waited in mess until 2 pm then went down to pens. Scrambled almost immediately but had to return – undercart wouldn't retract. Three 88's bombed the drome, very low and bombs dropped very close. Two were hit and went into the sea just off Grand Harbour. Felt very sick again and ate little supper.

July 7th Spent day on beach. Three raids in morning. Wallace McLeod shot down and crashlanded. Another bailed out and is OK. Some bombers shot down. Some went back to United Kingdom – lucky blighters. I saw Doc today and he said I had a cold in lower chest. Gave me some liniment and advised much sun-bathing.

[Wally McLeod, a fellow Canadian, was the second highest-scoring pilot on the island during the defence. He later commanded an RCAF squadron during the Normandy invasion, becoming the RCAF's top-scorer with 21 victories before being shot down and killed in September 1944. CS].

July 8th Scrambled twice in morning. Too late the first time to get at Bombers. The second time engine packed in and I force landed on drome. Passed 88's and 109's on way down as they bombed Luqa. Two shot down.

July 9th Stood on porch watching raid and we saw a long spiral at about 2,000 ft – a 109 had been shot up. Pilot bailed out. The aircraft came streaking down and crashed straight into a rock about 300 yards from us. We could see the markings clearly. Got tail wheel as souvenir. Increase bombing activity.

[This would appear to have occurred actually one day later than recorded in Jerry's diary, and would seem to have been Lt Hans-Jurgen Frodien of Stab II./JG 53 who probably fell to another Canadian, Malta's greatest 'ace', George Beurling. CS].

July 10th On readiness. Rip Jones and I jumped seven 88's and shot down one each. Rip was being fired at by a 109 while firing at the bomber. I wonder he didn't 'buy it'. Larger raids coming in these days and far too many fighters. Had great dog fight with 109's and Macchis off Gozo. Was shot up thrice. Once in head-on attacks at Fighters, once by Bombers, was hit in oil tank by 88 I got and force landed at Halfar while Luqa was being bombed.

July 11th Swam and bathed all day. Saw 'Rulers of the Sea' in evening. Went up to Rocky Vale for a while. Two big raids came in and very few intercepted. Must change our form. Battle in Egypt dragging along. Don't know how we stand.

July 12th Had pot at 109 which I claimed as damaged. Later one was confirmed as destroyed.

July 13th Swam and sun-bathed. Watched two big raids come in and none shot down. A Sergeant of 185 Squadron has shot down nine Fighters in four days. Good show.

[I'm not sure who Jerry was referring to, as no 185 Squadron sergeant seems to have claimed nine fighters in four days. It may have been the Australian, J.W.'Slim' Yarra, who between 15 May and 11 July had claimed ten fighters in six days of actual flying. CS].

July 14th Had smack at 109 today; damaged him. Later learned that two went into sea, so he may be confirmed as destroyed. [So far as I have been able to discover, it was not].

July 15th Got up about 8 am. Went on readiness at 8.30. Very dull day, windy and dusty. New Spits arrived in the morning and was amazed to find THAT ROD LANDED HERE. He was in AOC's car when I saw him and we had a short chat before he left for the mess. Released early; picked Rod up at mess and went to St. Julien. Had swim and went to Show.

The following year our mother met a US naval officer who had been aboard the carrier *Wasp* when Jerry had landed back aboard. In September of that year he wrote to her accordingly:

I'm so glad you wrote to me about Jerrold as his exploit aboard the *Wasp* was one of the most thrilling I've seen in this war; and I had a grandstand seat for it, as it were – I was standing just where he set his plane down.

You see his plane was fitted with an auxiliary gas tank because of the distance he had to fly, and when this tank dropped off, Jerrold knew he couldn't go on. Our Admiral (Captain at that time) had to make up his mind in a hurry whether to take a chance on letting him try to land on the deck – an explosion was a possibility. But Capt Reeves is a man of decision and he ordered the decks cleared and everything readied for Jerrold.

The first time he came in he measured off the distance, and if he wasn't scared of a crash, I was. He got up speed and came in the second time for a perfect landing and stopped right in front of me, about 10 feet short of the end of the deck. You must remember that he had no hook and we couldn't put up the barrier for fear he would crash into it and hurt himself. I tell you, his feat was thrilling, exciting, marvellous.

The *Wasp* crew went wild – they gave your son a tremendous ovation. That evening in the wardroom our Air Officer decorated Jerrold and made him an American airman. It was a wonderful evening. One of the moving spirits was the movie star, Douglas Fairbanks Jr., then a Lieutenant, junior grade in the *Wasp*. He had the time of his life making a real celebration of the heroic and dashing deed. I sat at dinner with Jerrold that night who was quite excited as well he might be. Our band played in his honor; toasts were drunk (in Coca Cola); two of the mess boys marched in carrying the British and American flags; and another mess boy ended the procession bringing in a big cake. The Air Officer pinned our wings on your son, there were speeches and the most spontaneous Anglo-American feeling you could imagine.

After we left Malta, your son flew off at Gibraltar. I can't begin to tell you what a wonderful boy I thought he was. It grieves me to know that his luck didn't hold ... I can say this: I feel strongly that Malta's holding out due to the reinforcements we were able to get in, was the turning point of the war. If it had to be, your son couldn't have been in a spot where he could have contributed more vitally. His spirit gave both the British and American naval and air forces new courage and determination to carry on. Those were critical, tense, dangerous days and his spectacular feat heartened us and made us feel that together as allies we could do anything. No single death I know of contributed so much to morale. You can be very proud.

M.M.Witherspoon, Captain, USN.

Further, the Air Officer who Capt Witherspoon mentions, was Lt Cdr David McCampell, himself a fighter pilot undertaking a period of deck duty. This same officer would later command Air Group 15, flying Grumman Hellcats aboard the USS *Essex* in the Pacific. He would end the war as the top-scoring naval 'ace' with 34 victories, including nine in a single sortie, for which he received the USA's highest award, the Medal of Honor.

In later years I met Dave at one of the symposiums I attended in the US, and later (May 1990) he wrote down for me his memories of Jerry's eventful landing:

At the time I was Senior LSO (Landing Signals Officer) aboard the *Wasp* and signaled Smith to land on board after he indicated that was his desire. I was able to get him down slow and low enough to give him the 'cut' signal on his second pass. We were able to give him the whole run of the deck since all our planes were in the air. He landed, and applied his brakes and stopped six ft from the ---------- [Unreadable in original] of the flight deck, and ----- [unreadable] to greet him, as he got out of the plane, to congratulate him on a good and safe landing and at the same time took my hat off to him. I then said to him, that you must have a lot of time on the Spitfire to pull this ----- [unreadable]. His reply was that he had only 128 hours of flying time and that he had flown a Spit ---- [unreadable] before. He obviously had trained in Hurricanes.

That night in the wardroom for dinner we introduced him to the assembled officers and presented him with a pair of Navy wings. We dropped him off at Gibraltar on our way out of the Mediterranean. We were given to understand that he was sent on to Malta shortly thereafter and some time later we were notified that he had been shot down.

CHAPTER NINE

MALTA

To my surprise I had received notice of my own posting 'overseas' at the end of May. I arrived in Gibraltar in late June, and on 15 July I found myself taking off from the old carrier HMS *Eagle* in a tropical Spitfire V bound for Luqa, the principal aerodrome on Malta, where I arrived as Jerry recorded in his diary.

Since that time never a day goes by without some memories of Malta going through my head. The most persistent are of the heat and dust on the aerodrome. The most vivid are of yellow-nosed 109s spouting puffs of smoke from the spinners on their down-swept noses, of 88s in formation putting out tracer that looked like coils of thrown rope, and streams of mingled white and black smoke and whitish flame coming from the engines of the stricken ones.

I remember other things too; the feeling of never having enough to eat; wondering after every show if Jerry had survived it; the perverse effect of the air raid sirens on me at night, when I found the warnings pleasantly stimulating and the all-clears rather saddening; the very kindly Maltese women who staffed our house at St. Julian's Bay and who used to cross themselves when they were behind us and thought we couldn't see them doing it; never being able to have a bath, cold water taking too much energy from us in our nearly starved condition; the half dozen lovely teenage Maltese girls in surprisingly up to date bathing suits who always came to swim with us at the private beach in front of our house and who told us that if they failed to get married by eighteen they would then be too old; the ragged, sunburned 'erks' who had no way of ever getting clean but managed never to seem downhearted; the silent and cool pre-dawn nine-mile ride to Luqa in our small rickety old windowless bus, contrasting with the talkative ride home in the war, dusk and the never spoken relief at having survived another day ... and the black Labrador dog who hung around our tented telephone desk at the aerodrome and seemed to live for nothing else but to chase and retrieve the hot cores of spent Very pistol cartridges fired for scrambles, which turned his mouth whitish grey as a result, but who put his tail between his legs and went for cover when he began to hear the approaching enemy aircraft and the ack-ack, apparently never connecting them with the cartridges.

From the start, I looked forward to the day when I would leave the island. I began to feel that my life after Malta would seem different and I believe it has in some indefinable way. I am very glad I went there but I often think with sadness of those who didn't come back.

Returning to my journey out to Malta, I too had occasion to spend a little time in Gibraltar en route – though my own experience here differed somewhat from his, due in no small part to a character called 'Smokey' Lowery. I first met Smokey on the troopship *Narkunda*, which landed us at Gibraltar on 27 June 1942. The carrier *Eagle* was there, destined to take us north of Algiers on 15 July with our tropical Spitfire Vs so that we could fly off her flight deck to Malta.

Smokey was a Tenneseean, quite sophomoric, and fixated on Hemingway. I wish I could have known that Lawrence Durrell would view Hemingway's stuff as 'sentimental crap'.

A few days after we arrived in Gibraltar we noticed some posters in the streets advertising a bullfight on 'Julio 12' in La Linea, the Spanish town at the north end of the low sandy isthmus that connects Gibraltar with Spain. Inspired by Lowery (himself inspired by Hemingway's *Death in the Afternoon*) four or five of us, including Tony Bruce who had been included on the draft that had sailed from Birkenhead on the *Narkunda*, got tickets, and also twelve-hour visas for Spain which in true British style were available to officers only.

A little before noon on the appointed day, which was oppressively hot, we fortified ourselves with a drink or two, took the rank tabs off the shoulders of our shirts to demilitarize us, and made our way on foot to a gate in a high fence which ran along the north side of Gibraltar's aerodrome at the south end of the isthmus. We found ourselves on a raised causeway which ran about half a mile north to a white blockhouse which was La Linea's south portal. Lower down in the sand on each side of us were a number of slit trenches Spanish soldiers were lounging in. Their demeanor wasn't unfriendly but their helmets looked German and Lowery said their rifles were Mausers.

When we approached the blockhouse we noticed a table a few yards in front of it at which sat a portly Spanish major looking through binoculars, and a clerk with a notepad and pencil. The major was focusing on an RAF aircraft approaching to land on the runway at Gib. We had been warned that any military information gleaned from Gib would reach Rome in twenty minutes. We recognised the aircraft as a Bisley, a hapless development of the hapless Blenheim, As we passed by the table the major said to the clerk, "Blenheim". We yelled "Bisley!" and burst out laughing. The major looked as if he thought we had a touch of the midday sun, which may have been true because we had left our service caps behind of course.

After presenting our visas in the blockhouse and passing into an adjoining street we were approached by a short swarthy man who introduced himself as 'Charlie' and offered to be our guide. His English was good and Lowery took him on.

As the bullfight was not until half past four Lowery asked Charlie to take us somewhere for coffee, and we were led along streets of dingy white houses to a central plaza. Though the plaza was fairly picturesque and had a few trees the general aspect of the town was of poverty, even squalor. The inhabitants seemed listless and despondent and one in every three or four begged from us. A cigarette butt thrown down was pounced on as a great prize.

A rather ominous note was lent by the presence here and there of Franco's political police, the 'Guardia Civil', equivalent of the German Gestapo. Its constabulary wore green uniforms with black belts, black boots and three-cornered shiny black hats, giving them a sinister almost eighteenth century look.

Charlie brought us to a sidewalk café in the plaza where we sat in shade and drank coffee from tall glass goblets. A little girl about twelve years old, who was carrying on her shoulder a tiny naked baby that had flies crawling over it, came up to our table and held out her hand. Charlie warned us off beggars, prophesying inundation for any weakness, but this was too much and we gave the girl some coins.

We discussed what to do before the bullfight. Lowery, likely fired up by Hemingway again, declared that Latin women were the world's greatest lovers and was all in favour of our going to a brothel. I did not share his enthusiasm; the heat and squalor of the town, to say nothing of the prospect of arriving in Malta with something considerably worse than athlete's foot, made the idea unappealing to me. Lowery's leadership carried the day though, probably because none of us wanted to seem too squeamish in carnal matters or be left alone in the town.

We therefore set out for a brothel, guided by Charlie. What little traffic there was in the town seemed to be horse-drawn, but presently an offical-looking black limousine drove by in the back of which a well-dressed, well-fed man with sleeked-back shiny dark hair was lounging with a big cigar. A little while later we saw a thin unshaven poorly dressed man reach down into the gutter and pick up a fish skeleton which had turned dark grey in the hot sun. There was a piece of flesh left on the backbone no bigger than the tip of one's little finger. The man looked at it for some time and then dropped it back into the gutter. La Linea was exposing me to real poverty, as well as the contrast between rich and poor in Latin countries which I found disturbing as well as depressing.

We duly arrived at the brothel, a large superior house surrounded by a few trees and a high wall with substantial gates. Its clientele obviously did not share the general poverty. We were ushered into a large central hall rising the full height of the house and topped by a skylight which let in a pleasantly suffused light and not too much heat.

A grand staircase descended into the hall from the balcony of the floor above. An imposing bar stood opposite to the foot of the staircase, doubtless not part of the original layout. To my surprise, around the walls were portraits of saints with their hearts out on their chests.

We were greeted graciously in Spanish by a short stout woman whom I correctly took to be the madam. We were offered sherry and stood sipping it in front of the bar for about half an hour, chatting in a leisurely manner. The pace in a Spanish brothel seemed not to be hurried. Lowery appeared downright buoyant but I was in a quandary; visions of spirochettes danced through my head. I kept wondering what I would do when we paired up with the senoras de la casa, and what I would say afterwards.

Tony Bruce and I leaned over the bar chatting to each other until we heard some rustling and the patter of feet. We turned round to behold a sight that will be with me to the end of my days. Seven or eight smiling women flaunting white chiffon and shiny black hair were tripping barefoot down the grand staircase towards us. What was so unforgettable was their faces, which looked as if someone had fired a sawed-off shotgun at them, whitewashed the result, and then painted red circles on their cheeks.

Tony and I spun back around in a flash and leaned over the bar again, trying to look as if we had just dropped in for a noon drink. My quandary was resolved, though the women began to mingle among us; I felt one of my buttocks being pinched but I kept staring unwaveringly at a row of bottles behind the barman. A hush fell over the assembly. I expected to hear Lowery ask Charlie to tell the madam as tactfully as possible that we would like to be on our way when we had finished our sherry but in a loud clear voice he exclaimed: "You'll have to do better than that, Charlie!" The women did not have to understand English to know that they had been summarily found wanting. The details of our departure have mercifully faded from my memory, but I do remember thinking that the bill for the sherry must have included a substantial amount for demurrage. We did not waste time haggling though, and found ourselves out on the hot streets again.

And the bullfight? Well, after that episode, I really cannot recall much about it!

I did get in a local flight while still at Gibraltar, spending thirty minutes flying around from North Front aerodrome in Spitfire BR117 on 11 July. A couple of days later we sailed on *Eagle* and at dawn on 15th I was the second to take off, becoming airborne within a 500 ft run. With the first batch of eight, we undertook the 710-mile trip in three and a quarter hours, making landfall at Tunisia and passing over Tunis safely. We changed tanks in sight of Pantelleria, and I landed with BR140 still having lots of petrol left.

As soon as I was on the ground at Luqa I was directed to a pen on the south side of the aerodrome, where the erks pounced on my aircraft to refuel it and strip out the four useless Browning .303s. [This seems to have been an unusual event, since accounts of combat over Malta recorded subsequently by a number of other pilots, specifically mention on occasion using the machine guns only when pressing the wrong firing button, or when the cannons ran out of ammunition. CS]. A minute or two later a tan-coloured American Ford drove up sporting a pennant from a staff on its radiator cap. A famous hawk-faced air marshal got out from the right front seat, and I saluted him. He offered his hand and said, "I'm Park, I'm AOC here, how was your trip?"

I was thrilled to meet the man who had commanded the bulk of the day-to-day fighting in the Battle of Britain, of course. I told him everything had gone well and he said, "Bring your gear, I'll give you a lift across the aerodrome." I got into the back seat and we set off straight across the aerodrome towards what passed for a control tower at Luqa. At the half way point, to my great surprise, we came across Jerry walking in the opposite direction with a parachute over his shoulder. Almost involuntarily I said, "Stop the car" and the driver obeyed rather hesitantly. Jerry spotted me and got into the back seat. I introduced him to Park as: "my brother, sir, Pilot Officer Smith". Park acknowledged him gracefully and we went on, pulling up at the control tower where Jerry and I got out. For the life of me I could not remember Jerry's Christian name for several minutes. (Not remembering people's names was a lifelong failing which prevented my aspiring to become prime minister of Canada!)

At the control tower I found that I had been posted to 126 Squadron, Jerry's unit, and so would be destined to fly with him as well as live with him at the house which was Luqa's officer fighter pilots' mess on St. Julian's Bay, a nine-mile drive from the aerodrome. Up to the day Jerry went missing, all my Malta flying was done as his number two, at our joint request. He usually flew as a subsection leader, but sometimes led the second section. (Malta fighter squadrons were only two thirds size then, putting up only two sections of four instead of three.)

I quickly discovered that Jerry had a passion for going after the bombers – heavily-escorted Ju 88s – a passion I soon shared in full. As his diary extracts have shown, he had made two trips over a mid-June convoy from Gibraltar in which only two of the six merchant ships survived to reach Malta. On the first trip, near Pantelleria, he got a Ju 87 probable and damaged a 109, saw two of our merchantmen sinking, and caught an interesting glimpse of naval history – the curving wash of some Italian cruisers well north of the convoy doing one of their famous 180 degree turns. His oil cooler got a tiny hole from the convoy's ack-ack but he managed to get the aircraft all the way back to a wheels-down forced landing at Luqa. On his second trip that day he damaged a Ju 88, overshot it, got behind another one, shot it down in flames, picked up a bullet from it in his radiator, caught fire and bailed out. He was picked up and brought in by the destroyer *Blankney*.

Top left: Grandfather Donald Alpine Smith.

Top right: Grandmother Margaret Smith (née McGregor).

Bottom left: Maternal grandfather, the classical actor Jerrold Robertshaw.

Bottom right: A painting of maternal grandmother, Isobel Robertshaw.

Right: Father and his English bride, Blanche 'Poppet' Robertshaw.

Bottom left: A pair of rascals! Jerry (left) and Rod ready for mischief.

Bottom right: Jerry (left) and Rod as teenagers.

Opposite page, top: The complete Alpine Smith family shortly before the outbreak of war in 1939. From left to right, at the back are Rod, Jerry, Father and Mother. In front are younger brother Don, and the baby of the family, Wendy.

Opposite page, bottom: Rod with a Tiger Moth at 2 EFTS, Fort William, Ontario.

Top: Unlike Rod, Jerry undertook his initial training on the Fleet Finch; he is seen with one of these aircraft at 10 EFTS, Mount Hope, Ontario.

Middle left: Advanced training at 2 SFTS, Uplands, Ontario; Rod is seen here with a North American Harvard.

Middle right: Jerrold Alpine Smith prior to completing flight training, while still an LAC.

Bottom left: Formal portrait of Roderick Illingworth Alpine Smith on completion of flight training, sporting his new 'wings'.

Bottom right: Very much the future fighter pilot! Rod in his Harvard "looking the part".

Top: No 6 Course at 58 OTU, Grangemouth, Scotland, in June 1941. Several of those present were to become notable fighter pilots.
Back row, left to right: Sgts Welby, Spence-Ross, Smithyan, J.A.Plagis, Corine, G.Elcombe, Munro, Long, Murchie, J.G.Magee, Bayly, Belcher, J.C.Gilbert, Arrowsmith, Ellis.
Centre row: Sgts M.R.Sharun, McCarthy, Smith, Booth, Grimsdick, Paveley, Rowkind, Howard, Holden, Kenwood, Vilandre.
Front row: Plt Offs Bishop, Williams, Marsh, R.I.A.Smith, R.W.McNair, Johnston, R.H.C.Sly, Shearn, Jones, Coker, Sgts Halse, Bassett, Charlesworth.

Bottom: No 26 Course at 57 OTU, Hawarden, Cheshire, in September 1941.
Back row: left to right: Sgts Cassell, Fox, Halama, Martin, Janata, Mowat, Norman, Riddell, Hamilton.
Third row: Sgts Shelley, E.L.Mahar, E.S.Dicks-Sherwood, Blaikie, Browne, Reid, E.G.Shea, Williams, Cordova, Duff.
Second row: Sgts Brown, Barr, Norsey, Hilton, Omdahl, Robb, Redman, Harvey, Hubbard.
Front row: Plt Off McLaren, Flg Off Aldridge, Plt Offs McDonald, J.A.Smith, Jones, Guerin, Hamilton, I.H.R.Shand, Harrison, Buckley.

Top left: Pilots of 412 Squadron at Wellingore in April 1942 with a Spitfire VB. Sitting on the propeller spinner is Sgt 'Stew' Pearce; with him is Flt Sgt Lloyd 'Pipsqueak' Powell. On the wing are Sgt 'Tommy' Thompson (left) and Plt Off Rod Smith; in front of them are Sgt Kenn Robb (left) and Sgt Joe Richards.

Top right: 412 Squadron pilots at Wellingore, April 1942. Left to right: Barry Needham, Joe Gould, Joe Richards and John Brookhouse.

Middle: The Spitfire VB in which Flt Sgt Allan Porter crash-landed on 15 April 1942 after running out of fuel.

Bottom: Rod Smith (left) and Bill Haggard discuss the planned route of a flight in front of one of 412 Squadron's Spitfire VBs.

Top: A trio of 412 Squadron's Spitfire VBs prepare to take off.

Middle: A group of 412 Squadron pilots during the winter of 1941/42. From the left are Rod Smith, Art Williams, Harry Bott, George Lacey and a visitor from 401 Squadron, Don Blakeslee. Blakeslee, a US citizen, later transferred to the USAAF, gaining considerable fame as the leader of the 4th Fighter Group and becoming a leading 'ace' with 14 and one shared victories credited to him.

Bottom left: Jerry in the cockpit of a Spitfire VB of 152 Squadron.

Bottom right: Jerry with a girlfriend meet the pigeons of Trafalgar Square while on leave in London.

Top: Jerry with his Spitfire after successfully landing back aboard USS *Wasp* with a faulty fuel tank.

Bottom: Jerry (left) is congratulated on his successful landing by the deck-landing officer, Lt David McCampbell. The latter would later command an air group in the Pacific, becoming the US Navy's top-scoring fighter pilot of the war with 34 victories.

Top: The executive officer of USS *Wasp* pins US Navy 'wings' to Jerry's tunic in appreciation of the skill shown in his landing on the carrier.

Middle: Jerry (centre, with both RAF and US Navy 'wings' on his left breast) at a dinner in honour of his deck landing, given by the aircraft carrier's senior officers. He is reading a telegram of congratulation.

Bottom: Jerry prepares to take off from USS *Wasp* for the second time, as a flight of US Navy F4F Wildcats pass overhead on defensive patrol. Note the four cannons with which this delivery of Spitfire VCs were fitted, and the large 'slipper' tank carrying additional fuel, fitted beneath the belly of his aircraft.

Inset: Off he goes from the clear deck of the carrier.

Top left: Jerry relaxing after arrival on Malta. This is probably the last photograph taken of him before he was reported Missing in Action.

Top centre: Rod on leave in Canada following his service on Malta and his period as an instructor after his return to the UK.

Top right: The combat veteran, with the DFC ribbon beneath his wings badge.

Middle: Rod with Wendy, Mother and younger brother Don while on leave in Canada during 1943.

Bottom: Celebration as Rod (pipe in mouth) when commanding officer of 401 Squadron, ends his second tour of operations. On his right, tankard in hand, is Flt Lt 'Snooks' Everard, who was just about to be promoted to take over the unit after Rod's departure. On his left is Wg Cdr B. Dal Russel, wing leader of 126 Wing, of which 401 Squadron formed a part.

Top left: Rod on graduation from Osgoode Hall, Toronto, as a barrister in 1955.

Top centre: Rod in his prime – still a pipe smoker and beer drinker

Top right: Rod deskbound and hard at work as a successful lawyer.

Middle: At one of the early reunions. Left to right: J.A. Omer Levesque (who claimed four victories during WWII, subsequently adding a claim for a MiG 15 over Korea), Dan Browne (4 victories), 'Johnnie' Johnson (34 and seven shared victories), George Keefer (12 victories), unknown and J.G. Larry Robillard (seven victories).

Bottom: Getting somewhat older, but still attending the reunions. Left to right: Dan Browne, Johnnie Johnson, unidentified, Larry Robillard and Rod.

Top: At a fighter pilots' symposium in the USA in 1988, amongst a galaxy of 'aces'. Left to right: Rod (RCAF, 13 and one shared victories); Johannes 'Macki' Steinhoff (Luftwaffe, 178 victories); Geoffrey Page (RAF, ten and five shared victories); the moderator; Johnnie Johnson (RAF, 34 and seven shared victories); Hugh Godefroy (RCAF, seven victories); Adolf Galland (Luftwaffe, 103 victories); Guenther Rall (Luftwaffe, 275 victories); Peter Brothers (RAF, 16 victories); Dan Browne (RCAF, four victories).

Middle: Formal portrait of the group of British, Canadian and German fighter pilots prior to dinner. Left to right: Godefroy, Page, Steinhoff, Peter Townsend (RAF, nine and two shared victories), Galland, unknown, moderator, unknown, Johnson, Rall, Brothers, Browne, Smith, unknown.

Bottom left: Rod with US aces Paul S. Bechtel (left) and Rex T. Barber (both five victories) during a meeting of the American Fighter Aces Association at Mesa, Arizona, on 25 February 1991. Both flew in the Pacific area, Barber taking part in the famous mission when Admiral Yamamoto was shot down, while Bechtel, although a US Army pilot, claimed his final victory while flying on attachment to a US Marine unit.

Bottom right: Rod with J.F. 'Stocky' Edwards, who by the 1990s was the highest-scoring living Canadian fighter pilot. Nearly all Stocky's claims were made in North Africa and Italy. By the war's end his personal tally stood at 15 and three shared.

Top: Rod with his motor cruiser, *Kestrel III*.

Inset: Rod the sailor during the 1990s.

Bottom: Rod reunited with a group of his classmates from his legal studies at Osgoode Hall, and other friends. The event was the 40th wedding anniversary of Robert Stevens. Left to right, are: Rod, Donald McFarlane, Jim Southey, John Stevens (himself an ex-RCAF pilot), Robert Stevens, Edward Huycke, Michael Hickey and Jim McQuat.

Top: Rod and Danny Browne being filmed with a Spitfire during the Normandy D-Day 50th Anniversary celebrations in 1994.

Bottom left: Billy Mills in uniform.

Bottom right: Rod with an unidentified lady friend.

Top left: Preparing for a formal dinner with Margarete Zillich.

Top right: Elizabeth Tyler McLennan – known to Rod as Judy, or Jude – but now answering to Tyler.

Bottom: With Robin Fleming and fellow Malta fighter pilot, Gordon Farquharson (three and one shared victories) in Normandy, 1994.

Top left: Sandralee Jackson.

Top right: With sister Wendy during a visit to Malta.

Bottom: Rod in the sitting room of his Vancouver apartment with his beloved Siamese cat, 'Boofuls'.

On a scramble on 10 July he got another 88, was hit three times (by 88s, and some 109s head-on!) and, Luqa bombed, force-landed wheels-down at Halfar with a bullet in his oil tank.

Our first readiness together occurred on 16th, the day after my arrival, but although we flew, we saw nothing. Jerry noted that next day we swam and sunbathed in the morning (days on readiness alternating with days off immediate duty). In the afternoon we went to see Smithy – another 126 Squadron Smith, this one an Australian, Don Smith, who had been shot down and quite badly wounded on 14 July, the day before my arrival. We then went to watch a performance of 'Thief of Baghdad' which we enjoyed despite some very corny acting.

Following a swim and early lunch we came to readiness at 1 pm on 18th and were scrambled with the rest of the squadron at half past two to intercept a reconnaissance Ju 88 escorted by fifteen Me 109Fs. We got split up by some other 109s, and Jerry and I found ourselves alone a fair distance north of the island. We suddenly spotted the 88 right above the sea a few thousand feet below us, heading north back to Sicily. It had lost its escort somehow and thus presented a rare chance for victory. We dived down to it. It must have just come out of a dive itself because our overtaking speed was quite moderate.

Jerry fired at it first and then broke away to the left. He quickly turned back to a parallel course and remained there, just out of range. I cannot remember what damage showed but in his diary he noted: "Very bad shooting on my part".

I then opened fire from 250 yards. Glycol gushed from around the starboard engine – I had at last hit an enemy aircraft. Though I am positive my very first shells hit, the fraction of a second it took them to get there seemed surprisingly long, something I had noticed when firing at the ground. The 88 slowed down noticeably in seconds, suggesting damage to the engine itself and not just to its cooling system. One of my cannons stopped after a second or two, slewing my aircraft badly and spoiling my aim, but I kept on firing with the other one anyway. The 88's pilot must then have begun to pump his control column back and forth because his aircraft began to pitch up and down as if on a low roller coaster. A good tactic of desperation I thought. I closed to about a hundred yards, without seeing any more hits, and then my other cannon quit. I had seen no return fire at any time, so Jerry may have silenced the upper rear gunner.

I almost made a fatal mistake at that point. We had been taught that after attacking a bomber we should break off downwards and to one side, and in practice attacks on friendly bombers back in England I had always done that. Breaking upwards would give the upper rear gunner a wonderful chance to hit you because your upward motion relative to him would be virtually cancelled by his aircraft's forward motion. You would appear almost stationary to him for a few moments, your underbelly exposed and your private parts vulnerable.

Without thinking, I had it in my mind to break downwards and to one side this time. It struck me in the last split second that that would be fatal when the bomber was only a few feet above the sea, and I pulled off to the left as Jerry had done. We headed back to the island feeling highly vulnerable to 109s, being so low and far from home.

Our last glimpse of the 88 was of it flying slowly, tail down. Both its engines were running although the starboard one, still streaming glycol, could not last. We claimed it as a probable but I think damaged would have been more like it. An 88 could fly very well on one engine. Luftwaffe records (obtained postwar and regarded as more than 90% complete by most historians) make no mention of an 88 having been lost in that region on that day.

Jerry's diary:
July 19th Saw one of our fellows in the water coming back; had been shot up and badly burned; 'water-baby' picked him up; in Hospital now.
[The unfortunate pilot was Plt Off C.B.'Chuck' McLean, a Canadian in 249 Squadron, who was actually shot down on 18th; he was picked up by High Speed Launch 107. CS].
July 20th Scrambled too late on both Bomber raids – maddening. Nearly made it second time but they pulled slowly away from us before we could open fire. We were shadowed by six 109's – two of which attacked. Rod and me about ten miles west of Grand Harbour; did head-on attack at one; played about but they had advantage of height, so we finally broke off.
July 22nd One fellow got DFM today and in the afternoon while protecting a chap in a dinghy he was killed by a 109. Bing got his DFC.
[The pilot mentioned who was lost on this date was Flt Sgt Don 'Shorty' Reid, a Canadian of 185 Squadron, who had claimed six victories. The DFC award went to another Canadian, Plt Off L.P.S.Bing, who was the radar operator of a Beaufighter night fighter operating from the island. CS].

During the morning of 24 July the squadron's two sections of four were scrambled to intercept what turned out to be five Ju 88s, with fighter escort, coming south towards St. Paul's Bay at 18,000 ft. My Spitfire was a VB and therefore good for six seconds firing.

The 88s were in their usual vic formation but their fighter escort was lagging badly behind them. We met the 88s virtually over the centre of the island coming towards us but several hundred yards off to our left. I was on the left end of our forward section and therefore closest to the 88s. A couple of seconds before our leader acted I began a 180 degree turn to the left to get in behind them, so I wound up in a position to attack first. I chose the 88 on the extreme left of their formation, which was the nearest one of course. I curved in behind it keeping slightly below the line of its tailplane to prevent its upper gunner, the best placed one, from getting a bead on me. I aimed at its port engine (itself a bigger target from behind than an Me 109 in fact) and opened fire at 250 yards, the range where the streams of shells from my two cannon, which are 13 feet apart, converge.

Within a second I could see strikes on that engine, which began to stream white and black smoke (glycol the white and fuel the black) and it became enveloped in flame. I then shifted my aim to the port wing root where the fuel tanks were, and then to the fuselage, both of which also became enveloped in flame. The whiteness of fuel-fed flame from an aircraft in full flight surprised me, as did the number of fair-sized pieces coming off this one. I continued firing for the six seconds it took my ammunition to run out, by which time I had closed to 150 yards, and I then broke violently downward into an aileron turn to the left, and kept in it until my ailerons hardened up, my speed being well over 400 mph by then.

When I came out of the dive I was all alone and I saw the 88 streaming fire and smoke and curving down in a great arc to the south-west. I then noticed a parachute high up over the centre of the island, and I could actually see the man in it. I hadn't noticed him baling out but it was hard to distinguish a man from the pieces coming off the aircraft while I was concentrating on firing. It only took me two or three minutes to get back on the ground, my entire sortie being logged as twenty minutes.

126 Squadron's dispersal was along the west-south-west edge of Luqa, and we could see almost the whole island from there. The 88 crashed about three miles to the south-west of

Luqa, and the arc of black smoke it had trailed remained in the air for quite some time. The wreckage burned for a long time, giving off a pillar of black smoke. Our groundcrew brought me a burnt piece of aluminium sheeting they said had fluttered down to the aerodrome from the 88. The parachute seemed to take ages to come down, and it drifted slowly to the north. As it got close to the ground it disappeared behind a low ridge to the north-west. We were not allowed to visit enemy prisoners, so I never met the man in it.

Jerry recorded: "Got off late on a scramble. Joined the others just as they attacked the Bombers. Started to aim at Port Ju 88, when Rod opened fire; it went down in flames. Moved over to next one and opened fire, putting port engine aflame. Was hit in glycol and force landed on Luqa (third time this month). A sergeant saw my Ju 88 go into the sea."

[Three more Ju 88s were claimed shot down by 185 Squadron pilots during this engagement, the total number of claims substantially exceeding actual Luftwaffe losses on this occasion. However, there seems little doubt that Rod had shot down M7+KH of KGr 806, manned by Lt Sepp Hoermann and his crew – CS.]

Shortly after this engagement, I was visiting Headquarters in Valetta where I was given a copy of a signal dated 26 July which was being sent to the commanding officers of all the fighter squadrons on the island, and to the wing commanders (flying) at each of the aerodromes. This read as follows:

<u>Enemy escort tactics</u>
The following is a preliminary interrogation report on a Prisoner of War from a Ju 88 shot down on 24th
July, the contents of which should be brought to the notice of all pilots of Spitfire squadrons:-
<u>Action.</u> Between 1039 and 1113 hrs five Ju 88s with a close escort of Italian fighters and a kind of high cover of Me 109s attacked Luqa. The P of W's Ju 88 was at 15,000′ in formation when it was attacked from the port side and below by a Spitfire with the result that an engine was hit, the machine caught fire and only the P of W (the W/T operator), was able to bale out.
<u>Unit.</u> The P of W refused to give this, but his acquaintance with Wilbertz, shot down 6th July, suggests K.G. 54, part of which at the end of June is thought to have returned from Crete.
<u>Fighter escorts.</u> This P of W is the first German to say that close escort to Ju 88s was provided by Italian fighters. The Me 109s he said, merely had orders to carry out an

independent offensive fighter sweep over the island. No pilots report seeing Italian fighters in this raid and it appears that the pilots mistook the close escort for Me 109s.

My surprise can be imagined when in mid 1990 I found myself talking on the telephone to the man I had watched parachuting down! He was the former Leutnant Heinz Hauser, the 88's wireless operator (right). An English friend of his had had the British Public Records Office searched by an agent, who came up with my name. Heinz's first words to me were, "You saved my life!" I'm sure he was right, but I didn't tell him that was not my intention, though I'm very glad it happened that way; I was always keen to destroy enemy aircraft but not to kill their crews.

Heinz told me he had been slightly wounded in his left elbow, and had broken a leg on one of the low stone fences that parachuting aircrew could hardly keep from hitting anywhere on Malta. He was taken to the UK and then shipped to a prison camp in Canada. He had liked Canada, saying, "the food was so good and they were so nice to us," describing his treatment there as "gentlemanly". When the war ended he was allowed to work as a lumberjack with a logging company for many months, and to buy drinks in the local pub, before being sent home to Germany.

Heinz asked me if I ever came to Europe, and if so would I visit him and his wife. I told him my sister Wendy and I would be in London in May of 1992 after we had spent a week in Malta, and that I would be delighted to visit them. Heinz told me my sister would be welcome too so I asked him where they lived. He said in Frenkenberg, a little town 70 miles north of Frankfurt. I told him I had gone for ten years with a girl who had been born there in 1940 and I mentioned her name. He said she had started school there with his wife in 1946! Sadly, a few months later Heinz died suddenly of a heart attack. His wife asked me to come anyway and bring Wendy, as Heinz had so looked forward to our visit and she and their children would like to meet us. Wendy and I had a wonderful three-day visit with them. I am so sorry I never actually met Heinz; I could tell from what his family and friends in Frankenberg said of him that he was a very fine and likeable man.

The Luftwaffe's daylight raids on Malta's three aerodromes continued throughout July. Valetta's Grand Harbour had not been bombed for months, but because its famous ack-ack barrage was still in place the track over the island taken by the Ju 88s bombing aerodromes was a wide U-turn around it.

Our squadron was scrambled at four o'clock in the afternoon of 26 July to intercept a raid by seven 88s escorted by Me 109Fs. We were led by Phil Winfield, our CO, and as had become usual, Jerry and I were paired, my being his number two.

On the climb up we were bounced by a few 109s which had appeared unexpectedly after the 88s and 109 escort of a raid on Halfar two hours earlier had gone back to Sicily. They didn't hit any of us, but they broke us up and then withdrew to Sicily themselves. Jerry and I found ourselves alone, common after being bounced, but we just carried on climbing, hoping to intercept the incoming raid we had been scrambled for by listening to the controller's reports on it.

We usually just had time to get up to the 88s' normal approach height – 18,000 feet – before they reached the island. We would then be going north towards them as they came south, though a little off to one side or the other. We would barely have enough time to level off and get some speed before making a 180 degree turn to get in behind them.

The leader of these seven 88s made a bad mistake, however. He got them up to 18,000 feet much too soon. This gave us much earlier warning because the higher an aircraft is the further away a land-based radar station can pick it up. We therefore had time to get well above these seven before we met them, and do it well out to sea.

The controller usually waited until a raid was within twenty-five miles of the island before giving his first report on it. On this occasion he would have said something like: "OK boys, the party's started. There are six or seven big jobs twenty-five miles north of St. Paul's Bay at angels 18 coming south. With them there are about thirty little jobs, angels 18 to 24. Above those are about twenty more little jobs, angels 28 to 32."

(Radar could distinguish between bombers and fighters by the size of the blip, but could not distinguish between German and Italian aircraft. Until they were positively identified, the controller referred to them as "big jobs" and "little jobs", even though Italian bombers had not appeared for several months.)

By this time Jerry and I were in a position for interception undreamed of in the past. We were at 25,000 feet about fifteen miles north of St.Paul's Bay, the favourite landfall for raids approaching on the west side of Valetta.

We soon spotted the raid a few miles in front of us a little to our right, closing rapidly. It was the first and only time we had the thrill of seeing below our own level all the 109s of an approaching close escort. They were mounted up behind the 88s all the way to 24,000 feet, stationed progressively further back the higher they were.

Jerry and I were always dead set on going after 88s instead of 109s when we had a choice, and each one shot down would cost the enemy so much more than a 109. We sensed, though, that in our present position we should not come in behind the 88s in a diving 180 degree turn. 109s could accelerate in a dive much faster than our cluttered up tropical Spitfires, so any that chose to follow us down could have overtaken us easily.

Jerry therefore decided, correctly I felt, that we should be making our 180 degree turn at our present height and thus bring us in behind the topmost 109s of the close escort as a place to start. From there we could dive right through all the close escort 109s on our way down to the 88s. This would make them break to one side or the other to avoid us, thus delaying their starting down after us for some seconds at least.

Fortunately, only one of the top cover 109s seemed to notice us, though we were between them and the close escort 109s. That particular 109 descended a little and made almost half a circle above us. When I diverted a few degrees towards it, it pulled back up again and I turned back towards Jerry. (I have never been able to understand its pilot's inaction, as I can't believe he could have mistaken Spitfires for 109s from right above them.)

Just before the last and highest of the close escort 109s drew abeam of us we made our 180 degree turn to the right, which brought us in behind and a little above them. We were now heading south towards St. Paul's Bay, as if we were part of the whole procession, an amazing position. We then began our dives, I on Jerry's right and a little behind him. We saw at a glance, and were surprised we hadn't realized it during previous raids, that the 109s were arranged in sections of four line abreast, rising up from and behind the 88s like a great staircase.

As we came down behind the highest section, the topmost stair of the staircase as it were, the left hand pair of 109s in it broke to the left and the right hand pair to the right. I did not look back to see whether any of them had recovered and were following us down because we were quickly closing on the second section down.

The 109s of that section broke the same way as those of the first. In the third section down, though, the pilot of the 109 second from the right was obviously unaware of us. He was almost directly in my path and stayed there. Though I was already too close for proper aim I decided to chance a shot at him anyway, notwithstanding my October 1941 resolution never to shoot unless I could hit for certain. I knew if I simply carried on our positions would be reversed in seconds. I aimed as best I could and fired. It was all too hasty and I saw no hits.

A second or two later I passed about ten feet over the 109's right wing and looked down into its cockpit, getting my first glimpse of an enemy. He swung his head up to the right in a flash and looked at me. I saw his helmet, oxygen mask and dark brown leather jacket. I felt slightly in rapport for a moment! Our positions were then reversed. To spoil his aim for a few seconds I raised my left wing, skidded up left, skidded back down and carried on with my dive, finding myself a little further behind Jerry than before.

The 109s of the sections remaining between us and the 88s turned our way like the ones in the first two. The 88s were looming up a little below and ahead, and our speed was now well over 400 mph. I could not tell, thanks to the poor rearward vision customary among fighters then, whether any 109s were following us down. By then I did not care, though. I was beginning to find the presence of large numbers of enemy aircraft inspiring, high speed dives in pursuit of them intoxicating, and the immediate prospect of a good shot intensely euphoric. Though normally a rather gentle soul, I found myself saying out loud: "I don't give a shit who gets killed as long as *somebody* gets killed!"

There's many a slip 'twixt cup and lip in air fighting however. We now realized that we were overtaking the 88s so quickly we would only be able to fire very short bursts, and then our ailerons were becoming so stiff with the high speed we would be unable to make corrections in time for proper aim.

As we closed on the 88s their gunners began firing streams of tracer at us, which we always ignored while attacking. Jerry fired a hasty burst at an 88 on the left side of the formation, seeing a single strike on it. Seconds later I fired a hasty burst at one on the right and saw no result at all. We now had to pass over them because our speed and stiff ailerons prevented our breaking down and to one side in the proper manner. To make things as hard for their gunners as possible we made the steepest turns we could manage, Jerry to the left and I to the right.

When I was well off to the right I looked across at Jerry and saw a stream of glycol coming from the nose of his aircraft, showing he had been hit in or around the engine. The whole enemy procession, by now almost over St.Paul's Bay, carried on, leaving us alone at 18,000 feet.

Jerry switched off his engine to prevent its catching fire or seizing, and started to glide down to a forced landing, his third that month. From that height he could glide for six or seven minutes and reach any of the island's three aerodromes with thousands of feet to spare. Judging a gliding approach to one would not be so easy, however. I began to weave about a thousand feet above him, to provide some cover against any curious 109s.

He called up the controller, told him he had a dead engine, and asked which aerodrome he should land on. The controller said Halfar, a small aerodrome on the south-east coast, with no runways. This told us he thought Luqa was the 88s' target, though I never knew how he could judge because the three aerodromes were so close together. About two minutes later the 88s indeed dropped their bombs on Luqa, destroying a Spitfire and damaging four twin-engine aircraft there, though not hitting a runway.

A deep anxiety now took over. Most of rural Malta was divided into very small plots of land surrounded by low stone walls. The only place an aircraft could force-land safely was squarely within the boundaries of one of the three aerodromes. Death or a broken back threatened any fighter pilot who misjudged a gliding approach to one of them on a dead engine. If he were too high he would crash into the first wall beyond the far boundary. If too low he would crash into one of the walls between himself and the near boundary at about 75 mph.

All the time Jerry was gliding down he kept weaving back and forth near Halfar to get rid of his excess height. At about a thousand feet he lowered his wheels, straightened out on a southerly course towards the aerodrome, and put down his flaps, thus committing himself.

The late afternoon sun caused his shadow to appear on the ground to his left, racing over the walls between him and Halfar's northern boundary and closing in on him as he sank lower and lower. It was not far off his wingtip as he neared the last wall. From above I could not tell whether he was going to clear the wall or crash into it. He cleared it, to my indescribable relief. As he levelled off for landing his propeller stopped wind-milling and his shadow slid under him. He came to a stop well within the aerodrome, got out of his aircraft and waved to me.

When I landed at Luqa four or five minutes later I learned that Phil Winfield had been badly wounded and taken away in an ambulance. He and Rip Jones had got back together after the squadron had been broken up on the climb, and had intercepted the 88s, then homeward bound, north-east of the island. Rip Jones claimed one of them, but a bullet fired by a gunner in one or another of them passed through the right side of Phil's cockpit and into his stomach. I looked over Phil's aircraft and wished I hadn't. It was a hot day and I still remember the sight and smell of blood and bits of yellow fat left in the cockpit after he landed it and was lifted out. He recovered and returned to England, a much paler and thinner man. Sadly and most unluckily, when he was recuperating at Bournemouth he was killed by a bomb dropped by an FW 190 during a low level hit-and-run raid.

When Jerry got back to Luqa he told me that only his glycol tank had been hit, and not his engine. It occurred to me that if he had found he was going to hit a wall on his final approach he could probably have saved himself by switching the ignition back on for a few seconds. His propeller was windmilling enough to restart the engine, which could have run without glycol for a few seconds at least.

That evening we discussed our failure to down any enemy aircraft. We concluded we should not have begun an attack on escorted 88s from so many thousands of feet above them. We should have settled for the uppermost 109s of the close escort instead, having been in a matchless position to attack them. The unexpected gift of great initial height had blinded us to the drawbacks of high overtaking speed.

A sadder and wiser pair we rose the morrow morn.

Two days later in the late afternoon of 28 July, the two sections of our squadron were vectored onto three Ju 88s heading west over Kalafrana Bay at 18,000 ft – escorted as usual by Me 109Fs.

We turned left into them. I was the furthest away and therefore the last to attack. One of the 109 escort came right down among us firing away but we ignored him. As was all too common, most of our pilots attacked the nearest 88, a couple attacking the one in the centre. Both those 88s caught fire and started down in seconds. I flew across behind the others and attacked the third 88 all by myself, aiming at its port engine and opening fire from about 250 yards.

I was flying a Mark VC Spitfire, of which each cannon was belt-fed with 120 rounds, good for twelve seconds of fire. The port engine of my 88 caught fire immediately, and I carried my aim into the port wing root and then the fuselage, and then the starboard engine, all of which caught fire too. The 88 headed downwards but I kept firing for the full twelve seconds, until the engines came out, the wings came off, and all the burning pieces fell like a shower of golden rain into Kalafrana Bay about a quarter to half a mile from the shore.

I think that firing all my ammunition in one twelve-second burst was an emotional reaction from having been fired upon so often on sweeps over France with rarely a chance to fire back. A twelve-second burst was unnecessary and very dangerous because every second spent looking through a gunsight when there were enemy fighters around was a second you were not watching your tail. I resolved never again to fire longer than necessary and I kept that resolution.

Jerry had less luck on this occasion. He recorded: "Squadron intercepted raid of three 88's between Takali and Halfar. All were in flames within 15 seconds and a fourth 88 was shot down. My cannons had no ammunition and one machine gun jammed after twenty rounds so I was out of the running. Rod got one of the 88's, a flamer over the island." Despite his cannons not having been loaded, Jerry had joined four other members of the unit in attacking the bombers initially, and his combat report had stated:

Turned port into bombers. Fired from 200 yards closing at port 88 – a two- or three-second burst and aircraft immediately burst into flames around port engine and front of fuselage. It turned to port and down. I turned into the middle Ju 88 and fired a short burst and saw a trail of white smoke… observed the starboard 88 going down almost vertically in flames. [This was probably the bomber which Rod had just attacked. CS]. Also saw four Spits chasing an 88 at deck level five miles south-east of Kalafrana, which trailed white smoke, turned to port and crashed into the sea. [The three Ju 88s shot down were all from II./KG 77, and were 3Z+EM, 3Z+BP and 3Z+HP, the latter, flown by Uffz Albert Fuehrer, being that shot down by Rod. CS]

The 'July Blitz' ended on 28th, so the fighter squadrons only had enemy fighter sweeps to contend with for the next couple of months, except for one small day raid by escorted Ju 88s in the morning of 10 August, and the famous convoy 'Pedestal' (13 merchant ships and a tanker) which we were told was due to arrive from the west on 13th.

Jerry's diary:
July 30th Watched a Spit attack a 109 while on beach bathing. It went down in flames and crashed about half a mile out to sea. Pilot bailed out but apparently his 'chute burned because he splashed in shortly after from several thousand feet.
July 31st Intercepted two Squadrons of 109's 20 miles west but couldn't get near them. While flying with Rip one intrepid beggar came up behind us firing at Rip. I turned into him but he dived quickly and fired from well out of range. When 15 miles off Sicily a Squadron of 109's passed us going back; turned to chase them, but they stooged home.
August 1st Usual sun-bathing and Pictures in evening. No Bomber raids and very little Fighter activity. Saw a Spit go down in Flames. Pilot safe.
August 5th Rod and I went on deck level sweep along Sicilian Coast at dusk looking for E.Boats to shoot up. Saw none but shot at what I thought to be one; which I saw after was a rock. Got back in dark OK. 'Jerry' blood wagon picked up one of the hated Huns 15 miles out. We didn't reach it in time and they got off scot free.

On the morning of 10 August, before the one small raid of that day, Jerry and I were on immediate readiness together but we were not scrambled and were put back to thirty minutes. As we had begun to notice that some holes in the silk liners for our leather gauntlets were getting larger, and an army despatch rider happened to be nearby with his motorcycle, Jerry suggested that I ask him if he would take me to station stores to get some new liners. The man took me on the seat behind him and I arrived back in about twenty minutes with the gloves. In my absence the small raid had begun to materialize, and Ops had put a pair from our squadron on standby to protect some minesweepers outside the Grand Harbour. Jerry had been chosen to lead the pair but in my absence my number two position with him had been switched to another pilot from a four, and I was put in the other pilot's place. For the first time I was therefore not Jerry's wingman, but I sat down beside him waiting for developments.

He was in a reflective mood. At home he had always been full of energy and in the thick of things, pursuing various interests and rarely wasting a minute; he would do school essays and other assignments during lunch, usually stood first or second in his class. While we were down waiting he said to me, "What we are doing here is very important of course, but we waste an awful lot of time just sitting around!" I have never forgotten that because all the time I was on Luqa aerodrome I never had a thought for anything but the prospects of scrambling and intercepting, and surviving till the evening 'Stand Down' order. He also said, "I just know I'm going to come in with that convoy [on another destroyer] on the 13th."

In a few minutes his newly constituted pair was scrambled and I watched it take off and disappear over the harbour in a wide climbing turn. A while later the section I had been put into was scrambled but when we got to height all enemy aircraft had headed for Sicily. We were then told to drop down and search for one of our pilots thought to have bailed out about ten miles north of the island. I searched very carefully, you may be sure, but nothing was found.

When we landed my flight commander, Rip Jones, told me that it was Jerry we had been searching for. In accordance with my practice on memorial occasions I immediately put into neutral that part of my brain which ponders such matters and carried on quietly. After a while our new CO, Brian Wicks, told me Jerry had been picked up by Air Sea Rescue. A few minutes later he told me it was not Jerry who had been picked up but another of our pilots, David Ritchie, who had gone missing the day before and who, we subsequently learned, had been floating in his dinghy for about twenty-four hours, unable to see because his face and eyelids had been bruised when he bailed out – a dreadful ordeal.

The pilot who had substituted for me as Jerry's wingman said that when the controller announced that the 88s were withdrawing Jerry left the minesweepers without orders and climbed north with lots of power on, but that he himself could not keep up with him. A pilot from Takali said he had seen a parachute appear to the north but the account was rather vague.

There were no more raids that day, but a number of succeeding pairs from other squadrons took off through the afternoon and carried on the search for Jerry. We were conserving fuel desperately at that time, sending out only two or three pairs in succession to search for missing pilots, but I am sure more pairs were sent out searching for Jerry than was usual simply because I was there. I did bring myself nonetheless to ask the CO if I might take off at late dusk by myself to have a look for a light on the sea because Jerry had a floating flashlight on his Mae West on which he had put much faith. He said I could and I did, the first and only time I flew in the dark there. I found no light, however, and landed back on a flarepath. The delayed ride back in the bus was subdued. I found I could not suppress the usual inner feeling of relief at having survived another day myself, and somehow felt guilty about it.

Decades later, when the records of the Luftwaffe's losses kept by its quartermaster general were made public (having been obtained by RAF Intelligence at the war's end), they showed that a Ju 88 (3Z+ET of 9 Staffel, Kampfgeschwader 77, flown by Fw Helmut Streubel) which had been on the raid of 10 August failed to reach Sicily. No Malta fighter pilot claimed to have attacked an 88 that day, so it has been said to be likely that Jerry shot it down and was then himself shot down, probably by one of the escorting 109s because they did claim several Spitfires destroyed on the raid though Jerry's was actually the only one lost.

It may have been noted that Jerry seemed to have been a magnet for return fire. During my time on the island I destroyed four bombers but my aircraft only once received just one harmless bullet from return fire. It was a matter of luck, of course, but Jerry wasn't a good shot and so could not hit as early in the burst as I could and may therefore have given rear gunners too long a shot.

Jerry was eventually presumed killed in action. I often wonder what he might have done in peacetime. A poem had been written by Flt Lt John Pudney of 242 Squadron during 1940 entitled 'Missing', which could almost be called 'tailor-made' for Jerry, with only one word needing to be changed. It was included in a volume of war poetry called *Dispersal Point* (published by Bodley Head), and reads as follows:

Less said the better.
The bill unpaid, the dead letter.
No roses at the end
Of Smith, my friend.

Last words don't matter,
And there are none to flatter.
Words will not fill the post
Of Smith, the ghost.

For Smith, our brother,
Only son of loving mother,
The ocean lifted, stirred,
Leaving no word.

Of course, Jerry had not been an only son, but the rest is deeply relevant.

I next flew three days later, on 13 August, as the 'Pedestal' convoy came within range of the island. My first sortie was a dawn patrol over the ships, which we found near Pantelleria, and this proved uneventful. The second sortie was a different story as four of us returned mid morning to help continue the cover. We were led by wingo flying of Luqa, Prosser Hanks, who led our CO, Brian Wicks, Flt Sgt Arthur Varey and myself to the area. We arrived at 1125 just in time to see five Italian Savoia S.79 torpedo-bombers launching an attack. I understand from subsequent research that the bombers were escorted by a flock of Macchi C 202 fighters. Apparently, the ships' crews reported that we became involved with this escort, and they thought that ack-ack fire from two destroyers may have shot down two of the Savoias, one of which was seen to crash into the sea on fire when it released its torpedo at long range.

I don't recall being interfered with by the fighters, but while we were at 5,000 feet we saw an S.79 flying away from the convoy to the west at about 800 feet. We dived down onto it whereupon it jinked from side to side, obviously as an evasive tactic, and Prosser Hanks attacked, then broke away left. I (flying as his number 2) attacked from astern and slightly to the starboard, firing a four-second burst. The starboard engine caught fire, following which the aircraft blew up and crashed into the sea in a mass of flames. (I later learned that it was an S.79sil – which indicates the torpedo-carrying version – from the 132 Gruppo Austonomo Aerosiluranti of the Regia Aeronautica, flown by Tenente Guido Barani).

Redge Round, a New Zealander, was in my Malta draft. We met in June 1942 in West Kirby near Liverpool, a depot for those going overseas. He was fairly short and stocky, and, at twenty-eight, considerably older than most of us. He was rather sad to have been posted from his squadron, as I was from mine, and said, "You get to know a bunch of cobbers, and then you have to start all over again." He was very likeable, and he and I went to pubs a few times together; when we had had enough to drink he wound say, "Let's grease the old bum and quietly slip away!"

After we flew off *Eagle* to Malta I never saw him again because he went to 249 Squadron at Takali and I to 126 at Luqa. We officer fighter pilots at Luqa's detached mess at St. Julian's Bay used to swim in the bay on our days off. In the morning of 25 August, a day I had off, I was sitting on our beach in the bay with some other pilots. At about noon some thirty Me 109s came over on a fighter sweep, and 249 and 185 Squadrons were scrambled to intercept them. We heard engines overhead and guns firing, as usual.

After a while the 109s withdrew and things became quiet again. But we soon became aware of a lone Spitfire just north of the bay some thousands of feet up, its engine apparently idling. It was quietly and lazily rising and falling in a gradually descending spiral. It seemed intact and no parachute was in sight. It continued on down until it became lost to our view behind Fort Spinola, across the bay north from us. It crashed into the sea some hundreds of yards north of Dragonara Point. We heard shortly afterwards that poor Redge was the pilot. He would probably say he had "greased the old bum and quietly slipped away".

At this time much of the Luftwaffe had been withdrawn from Sicily for the summer campaigning in Russia. After the end of July, apart from the excitement of the Pedestal convoy, hostile activity over the island was much reduced, particularly by day. The odd small formation of Italian bombers came over from time to time, usually at great height, but mostly the opposition was reduced to fighter sweeps to try and bring the Spitfires up to fight. In these circumstances further deliveries of Spitfires from aircraft carriers allowed the island's defences to be brought up to an almost unheard of strength, and we even began some offensive sweeps over the Sicilian coastal airfields.

This situation continued throughout September, but I flew only seven sorties during that month as I suffered attacks of both sinusitus and sandfly fever, which laid me low for the whole of the latter half of the month.

The final major attack on the island came during October – and was therefore known to us as the 'October Blitz'. It was occasioned by the terrible losses Malta's striking force was having on the Axis supply lines across the Mediterranean at this time, as the Eighth Army (now commanded by Montgomery) was preparing for the great Alamein offensive. Rommel and his Afrika Korps were suffering from extended lines of communication, and were failing therefore to build up strength at anything like the same rate as the British Commonwealth forces.

In consequence, our quieter period during September was rapidly ended as new Luftwaffe units arrived in Sicily from the Eastern Front to try and batter our defences into submission once more.

11 October was the first day of the October Blitz and therefore the first time we were to see a full daylight bombing raid since 28 July, the last day the 88s appeared in the July Blitz.

Early in the morning the squadron was scrambled to meet the first raid of that day. As we climbed above the haze over Malta the upper sky became more beautiful than any I had ever seen in the Mediterranean; it was bright blue and crystal clear, with a magnificent bank of cumulus cloud far off to the north-east. As we continued our climb the cone-shaped upper part of Mount Etna, 150 miles away, came into view as always, seeming to float on the perpetual haze which hid its lower slopes and all the rest of Sicily. It was the only part of the outside world we could see from high over Malta, so it made a superb north point.

Rip Jones was leading the squadron and I was leading Blue Section, keeping just behind and below Red. We were vectored first to Zonqor Point and then out to sea to the north-east, towards the great bank of cumulus. Two or three minutes later he told us that about ten enemy bombers escorted by about seventy fighters were coming towards us from thirty miles away, and that we were to level out when we got to 18,000 ft.

When we were almost up to 18,000 ft we suddenly caught sight of the oncoming raid, ahead of us and slightly to our right. It was the most awesome sight of our lives, in large part because the background cumulus presented the whole array to a single glance. It comprised nine Ju 88s in three vics abreast, slightly above us and still quite a way off, with a close escort of about forty Me 109s rising above them in tiers of six abreast like a staircase, to 24,000 ft, all surmounted by a top cover of about twenty 109s stepped up from 28,000 to 32,000 ft and making vapour trails. Ranging ahead and to each side at about 22,000 ft were a few pairs of 109s seeking to find, pounce on and scatter formations of intercepting Spitfires, though none of them showed any signs of having spotted us.

Just as we reached the height of the 88s the cannon panel on Rip's starboard wing blew off. He turned away and down, and in confusion told Red Three to take over the squadron instead of telling me, the deputy leader. This should not have made any real difference because the 88s were fast drawing abreast of us to our right and it was obvious that all each one of us had to do was make a 180 degree turn to the right to get in behind them, choose one and fire at it. It caused some hesitation though, no doubt because Red Three was considering whether to bring the remainder of Red Section in behind Blue. As our closing speed with the 88s was about 500 mph it was vital that we start turning in towards them a few seconds before they actually drew abreast, or else our attack would develop into a drawn-out chase right under the close escort – a hopeless predicament. I only saw one of Red Section's pilots begin to turn in time, and even he did not turn sharply enough. I began about the same time he did, but so as not to lose one more second I turned so sharply that the other three pilots in my section got left behind. Another circumstance flowing from an armourer's failure to secure Rip's gun panel.

I decided to attack the 88 on the far side of the formation, the one on its extreme left, to avoid being embroiled in any ganging up on the nearest one or two as had happened before, so I headed right across and behind the whole formation. I need not have worried about ganging up though, because no other pilot of the squadron completed the inward turn except the Red Section pilot who had turned in sufficient time, and though he opened fire at the nearest 88 he was well out of range, an error more the rule than the exception in the first half of the air war.

As I began my passage across, the rear gunners in the 88s began firing their machine guns at me continuously, the tracers from them looking like coils of thrown white rope. Though I kept slightly below the level of the tailplane of each 88 as I passed behind it, in order to keep out of the line of sight of its upper gunner, cross-fired tracer from the 88s on each side never left us.

Part way across I noticed that the 109s making up the first tier of the close escort, though quite close behind the 88s, were about 400 ft above them and me, and it suddenly struck me this would be a good chance to observe the black crosses I knew were on them but which had never actually caught my attention in the past. I therefore looked upwards to the undersides of their wings and spotted them instantly, outlined in white and as startlingly clear as recognition posters showed them to be.

For some reason the 109s seemed to take no notice of me during my passage across, probably because I was more or less hidden under their noses, and I finally arrived unscathed at a point about 250 yards behind the 88 on the far left side of the formation. I opened fire at its port engine, which almost instantly began to pour out white and black smoke quickly followed by flames which grew longer by the second. Cross-fired tracer was coming continuously from the two 88s to the right of the one I was firing at, though that did not worry me much because it was only rifle-calibre.

After about three seconds however one or two streams of tracer began to pass over me from behind, telling me that the 109s were finally on to me and that from the cannon in each one of them about a dozen non-tracing 20mm shells a second would be coming along with the tracer bullets from their two machine guns. The pilots must have been either poor shots or getting in each other's way. I was sure I wouldn't last long if I stayed there though, but I hated to leave because the cannons in my Spitfire were good for twelve seconds firing and although the flames coming from the 88's port engine were now very long it didn't seem to be slowing down much, let alone starting down, which rather surprised me.

After about three more seconds, and with mixed feelings, I stopped firing and started violently down into an aileron turn to the right, a diving spiral a 109 could not keep up with for more than a few seconds because its ailerons hardened up much more quickly than a Spitfire's in a dive. I had scarcely begun this, though, when I changed my mind and started back up. I desperately wanted to see the 88 finished off and it had struck me that coming back up behind it very suddenly might fox the 109 for a few seconds. I got behind it again but this time I fired at its starboard engine, which quickly streamed smoke and caught fire just like the port one. After about three seconds tracer started coming at me from behind again, so after three further seconds, by which time both engines of the 88 were streaming very long flames and it had started to veer away to the left and down, I stopped firing and went down in another violent spiral to the right. I had only one round left to fire but I didn't know it at the time.

I kept in the spiral for about three or four turns, heading almost vertically downwards and feeling immune from the 109s while doing so. When my ailerons got very hard I stopped spiralling, shallowed my dive, and aimed for Zonqor Point. I looked around for the 88 and caught sight of it going down almost vertically, streaming fire and smoke. With only two or three thousand feet to go it suddenly exploded into two main pieces which made great splashes in the sea.

At this point I should have been weaving thoroughly to see if any of the 109s had followed me down, but somehow I felt they would not leave the 88s and I hardly weaved at all, but just looked rearwards on each side. A yellow-nosed 109 suddenly appeared about 150 yards off to my right and behind me, in a dive parallel to mine but faster. Foolishly I carried on in my dive. I was puzzled that the 109 was not directly behind me where he could have been shooting at me instead of passing me and becoming a target for me. It carried right on however and I swung over to get in behind it, though I knew I had little if any ammunition left. Fortunately I glanced over my right shoulder at the same time and instantly found the answer to the puzzle; another yellow-nosed 109 was right behind me, blazing away, obviously the section leader. I broke violently up to the right, whereupon both 109s pulled gracefully out of their dives and soared away. It only then struck me that I had forgotten the adage that if you see one 109 there will always be another one not far away. The leader had wisely refrained from using tracer; but he was a poor shot, and his number two had given the game away by overshooting him, a mistake that would be brought up later no doubt.

Feeling safe once more, I went into another dive, shallower still, and pointed at Luqa, but I weaved and looked behind me so thoroughly this time that I failed to notice the aerodrome looming ahead until I was only seconds away from crashing into it.

I was the first of our pilots to land, and I found that Prosser Hanks was at our dispersal. The armourers told me I had only one round left, so I knew I had fired for a full twelve seconds.

I was thrilled by what had happened, a feeling that lasted quite a while, and I marvelled that Lady Luck had thrown her arms around me so many times in a row. The rest of the pilots landed in ones and twos until all were safely down. We were unanimous in exclaiming that our first sight of the raid had been awesome. We found that almost all of us had fired our guns and, in addition to my claim for my 88, various claims were submitted by the others, which I believe were for one Macchi 202 destroyed and one damaged, one 109 probable and two damaged, and one 88 damaged. Someone told Prosser about my crossing under the escort to the farthest 88 and attacking it twice. He rounded on me and said, "None of this death or glory stuff; I don't give a shit about you, but I don't want to lose the bloody aeroplane." I knew he meant, "Be careful, old boy, we'd hate to lose you," and I was touched.

I subsequently got hold of the intelligence brief from HQ, which stated:

"Sgt Grams was the W.T. Operator of a Ju 88 which took part in an attack on Malta consisting of nine Ju 88's escorted by some 40 enemy fighters including Me 109's. The bombing target was our airfield at Hal Far but when at 15,000 feet North East of the Grand Harbour the raiders were intercepted by Spitfires. At this time the nine Ju 88's were flying in a vic formation of three separate sections and the P.W.'s aircraft was on the extreme left of the left hand section, also in vic formation. While their fighter cover of Me 109's above were being engaged by numbers of Spitfires, one lone but obviously experienced Spitfire climbed up behind the bombers and picked off the P.W.'s aircraft delivering first an attack from level with and astern of the Ju 88's port engine putting it out of action and then making a second and similar attack on the starboard engine after which the Ju 88 broke formation and the Spitfire, its task accomplished, broke down and away. The Ju 88 had only a few seconds to make some ineffective return fire. Only the P.W. was able to bale out and he was subsequently rescued by launch.

Pilot. Oberfeldwebel Hermann Mueller	Age 29	Missing
Obs Feldwebel Fritz Winkelmann	Age 29	Missing
W.T. Uffz. Guenther Grams	Age 20	Slightly wounded
Gunner Obergrefreiter Alfonz Newmann	Age 23	Missing"

I have subsequently learned that the aircraft I had shot down was B3+YL of I./KG 54.

My next action of note occurred three days later during my

second sortie of the day in Spitfire EP310 (which I had flown twice on the preceding day also). In the early afternoon of 13 October six Ju 88s escorted by twenty-five Macchi 202s and forty Me 109s approached Malta in a wide curve from the south-east to bomb Luqa aerodrome. Wing Commander Prosser Hanks was leading the two sections of my squadron and we found ourselves about 2,000 ft above the 88s over Luqa heading the opposite way. Prosser tried to half-roll down to come in behind them but he wasn't high enough above them for that. He came down through them and wound up under them, too low to shoot. His aircraft was badly riddled by return fire.

I was sure we hadn't been high enough above the 88s to half-roll down to them without coming out below them, so I did a half-spiral down to the left and though I found myself behind and level with them I was then well out of range. I was faced with the prospect of trying to overhaul them from a position directly underneath their escort, not a safe tactic, when I saw what I thought was an Me 109 not far below me on my right, heading east for some reason. I decided to attack it.

I made a half-spiral down to the right and attacked it from behind and a little to its right, firing a three-second burst with slight deflection from about 250 yards. Strikes appeared on its engine and fuselage, a big flash of flame came from around its engine, and it began to stream smoke. I fired another three-second burst and got more strikes on it. It went into a very tight and almost vertical spiral dive towards the mouth of Sliema Bay, streaming even more smoke. As it neared the water I could tell that one or more of its guns were firing because, before it made its own great splash, a pattern of little splashes had appeared on the surface of the water which exactly matched its tight spiralling. It was the fifth enemy aircraft I had destroyed, and I realized, with secret satisfaction, that I had become an 'ace'.

I was not entirely certain it was an Me 109, as it and the Macchi 202 were quite hard to tell apart in the air, one often being claimed as the other, but I had noticed that this aircraft had a white band about two feet wide around its fuselage between its cockpit and its tail, which I knew was a key Italian marking (and one we had in Britain but not in the Mediterranean region, presumably because the Italians had it first).

I therefore claimed this one as a Macchi 202. (It seems strange to me, but all through the war I rarely noticed the markings on enemy aircraft, just their colour schemes.)

When I got back to our mess in St. Julian's Bay, Wally McLeod and another pilot, both of whom happened to be walking by Sliema Bay when the Macchi went in, told me that they thought it was a 109 and explained that German aircraft in the Med had the white band (presumably to match the Italians). I therefore changed my claim to a 109 next day. It was only when I read Chris Shores' book, *Malta; The Spitfire Year*, nearly fifty years later, that I became satisfied it had been a Macchi and learned who the poor pilot was (Marciello Maurizio Iannucci of 352 Squadriglia, 20 Gruppo, 51 Stormo Caccia Terrestre, of the Regia Aeronautica).

Next day, 14 October, I led 126 against the fourth raid of the day, this time flying BR471. When we were moved up to immediate readiness towards the end of that day our CO, Brian Wicks, told me to lead the squadron on the next scramble because he and Prosser would be flying together as an entirely separate pair. Because I believed that Brian felt he had not been notably successful at shooting down Huns (considering that he had been in the Battle of Britain and had come to Malta from the desert) I immediately inferred, as I am sure everyone else did, that Prosser had suggested this free-ranging scheme to Brian because it would naturally provide each of them with better opportunities to knock down a Hun or two than the pilots of a vectored squadron would have. Brian looked a bit sheepish about such a departure; he was a clergyman's son, which may well have made him more inhibited than Prosser, who had more of the buccaneer in him. So when the scramble came Prosser and Brian received no direction from the controller (by prior arrangement I assume) and simply climbed away on their own to gain a vantage point above the incoming raid from which to practise some natural selection.

In any event 126 was vectored to make the first attack on the 88s. We approached them almost head-on, their being slightly to our left and coming south towards St. Paul's Bay. As they were drawing abreast of us and we were beginning our 180 degree turn to the left to get in behind them, I noticed that the first tier of the close escort 109s behind and just above them was much closer than usual. I ordered Blue Section to go up into the fighters, but I think it was actually too late for such a change and that most of Blue Section simply followed Red Section into the 88s.

I came in behind an 88 that was in about the centre of the

formation and opened fire at its port engine from about 250 yards, closing the range quite quickly. A very large flash of flame came from that engine and it streamed glycol. The 88 banked into a left turn and decelerated so suddenly that I found myself almost upon it and had to stop firing after about three seconds and turn steeply to the right to avoid hitting its raised starboard wing. It headed downwards and I lost sight of it for the few seconds it took me to turn back to the left, but when I caught sight of it again it was still going down and still streaming glycol from its port engine.

Just as my 88 was starting down the others jettisoned their bombs and began to make 180 degree turns to the left to head back to Sicily. While they were turning I saw two of them being attacked and hit, and they both headed down streaming smoke from their engines. I can't remember whether any flames were actually coming from either or both of them, but I saw them and the one I had hit crash close to St.Paul's Bay within fifteen or twenty seconds of each other. I called the controller and told him that the 88s had jettisoned their bombs into the sea and turned back; he replied: "Good show". I had never noticed that I had picked up a bullet hole in my port aileron (my first but not my last), confirming to me a growing suspicion that I was not immortal. I felt some surprise that my 88 had gone down so smartly from such a short burst, with apparent damage only to the one engine (though I could have hit the pilot or the controls), and I could not be certain that another 126 pilot had not hit it while I was turning away to the right and back.

Our squadron's whole attack had occurred within sight of a good part of the island so there could have been no doubt in anyone's mind that most of the 88s had survived to head for home. In fact I think we were all in agreement that only three of them had gone down. When we landed and were making out our combat reports we discovered that about seven of us claimed to have fired at 88s that had gone into the sea, so each of us just claimed a destroyed and left it to Intelligence to sort them out into fractions as appropriate.

That is what had been done on 28 July, when, it will be recalled, the last daylight bombing raid of the July Blitz had occurred. On that day 126 had made a left turn of about 130 degrees in behind a vic of three 88s heading westwards over Kalafrana Bay at 18,000 ft, and within about fifteen seconds all three of them had been sent on their way down in masses of flames and pieces; all our pilots except me had ganged up on the two nearest 88s (on the left side of their formation), very obligingly leaving the farthest one over exclusively to me. Crediting them among our pilots was done simply by our intelligence officer's asking each pilot which one he had fired at and then dividing by the number of pilots who said they fired at that one.

That may not have been fair because most pilots were poor shots in the early years of the war, but as we had no camera guns in our tropicalized Spitfires (because the large ugly air filters blocked much of the field of view we were told) it was probably the only way. (Interestingly, the practise by the majority of a squadron's pilots of ganging up on the 88s on the near side of their formation after the squadron had turned in behind them seemed to be common, and was a bad mistake of course because it gave the ones on the far side a chance to get off scot-free. After 28 July I made a point of passing behind the nearest ones and going for one farther over.)

Reverting to 14 October, Prosser and Brian landed having had no luck whatever. Brian looked more embarrassed than before and even Prosser looked a little sheepish. I do not want to give the impression however that I hold anything against Brian because he went off with Prosser in a free-ranging twosome; he trusted me to lead the squadron, as he should have been able to do. I was amused more than anything else, and even more amused at the way it turned out. Brian was a kindly gentle soul with high personal standards, and Prosser could be very persuasive or even coercive. If I ever get up to what Laddie Lucas called the 'Celestial Bar', Brian and Prosser will be among the first inmates I will look for. Brian will certainly be there, if only as compensation for having had to grow up as a clergyman's son, but I cannot be sure about Prosser or myself.

When we arrived at the aerodrome the next morning, our intelligence officer, a mild man who always gave me the impression that he wished he were in some gentle place far away where air fighting had never been heard of, told us that each of the seven or so of us who had claimed an 88 the day before had been credited with a destroyed. I asked him how that could be when only three had been seen to go down from our attack, as he himself had been able to see from Luqa. He said that Air Headquarters had stated that if a pilot claimed a destroyed and said he had seen it go in he would be credited with it. I was disgusted, all the more because I had long suspected that the policy inherent in that statement had been tacitly accepted as the basis for allowing claims many times before, but I still did not want to believe that we had quite come down to that. [This view would certainly explain why so many of the claims made over Malta by defending pilots have proved very difficult to justify against recorded Axis loss details. *CS*].

Because I had fired only a three-second burst at my 88 and had only hit it in one engine as far as I could tell, and had lost sight of it for a few seconds and therefore could not be sure that no one else had hit it, I felt I would always have a lingering doubt about being credited with a whole destroyed unless the entire matter were sorted out as it had been on 28 July. I thought it was a cop-out by Intelligence, although I realized it would have been harder for them with a formation of eight bombers than three. In any event I told our intelligence officer I wanted to reduce my claim to a damaged. This was a rather odd result because I knew my 88 had gone in, but at least I could be certain that I had hit it first and started it on its way down.

Twenty-four hours later my growing doubts regarding my immortality received considerable reinforcement. The events of the day were also to confirm the inferiority of the aircraft that we were flying to those of our opponents. The Spitfire V was the only Spitfire which was outclassed by the enemy. The 109F, however, was the best of the 109s. It was faster and better at height than the Spitfire V and much faster than the tropical Spitfire V. The air filter fitted under the nose of the latter made it ugly and slowed it down badly, proving again that for aeroplanes handsome is as handsome does. The 109 had a small wing and because of this it could not turn as tightly as the Spitfire. The Spitfire's tighter turn usually enabled it to evade the lunging attacks of the 109, almost always made from above and behind, as long as the pilot of the Spitfire could see the 109 coming. This was not easy because the fuselage of the Spitfire, like the 109 and nearly all other fighters in the early years of the Second World War, was constructed in such a way that it occupied the space behind the pilot's head. For the pilot it was like driving a car with no rear window.

During the second raid of the day Prosser had led four Spitfires (one of them my BR471) to the north of Zonqor Point to intercept some 88s approaching at 18,000 ft, escorted by 109s. By the time we got up to that height we were too late. The 88s had gone but some of the 109s lingered and made a few passes at us from above and behind, firing as they went through us, and climbing right up again, in their usual manner. They were hoping we wouldn't see them coming, and be like sitting ducks. We managed to see them each time however, and turned sharply to pass in front of them at right angles to their line of flight, in our usual manner. This made us hard to hit, because they could only hold the proper lead with their gun sights for an instant, and we would usually pass safely between the rounds they fired at us. This always seemed remarkable to me. The 109F had a twenty millimetre cannon firing a dozen explosive and armour-piercing shells each second through the hollow propeller shaft and two synchronised machine guns just above it firing three dozen rifle claibre-sized rounds a second. These machine-gun bullets were not very formidable but the cannon shells, like our own, could smash through anything.

After a while the 109s which had been attacking us headed north to Sicily, leaving us high up with nothing to do, about two or three miles north of Malta's Grand Harbour.

Suddenly I spotted two yellow-nosed 109s far below us, near the surface of the sea, heading north to Sicily. I reported them to Prosser on the R/T and he quickly told me to lead on down to them. (His distance vision was not what it had once been.) We rarely had the pleasure of seeing 109s below us. They dreaded being there. By diving on them from well above we could build up enough speed to catch them yet still be able to turn inside them if they should try to turn out of our way.

I began the dive down to the two 109s and Prosser followed me keeping to my right and slightly behind, but for some reason the other two pilots of our section did not come with us. As Prosser and I got lower I began to notice that in spite of all the speed we had built up in the dive, the 109s were a bit further ahead of us than I had expected. They had obviously dived down just before I spotted them and still had great momentum. When we got down to their level, a few yards above the sea, they were still 500-600 yards ahead of us, side by side, the left hand one directly in front of me and the right hand one in front of Prosser. They were slowly pulling away, although we were going at full power. Our 20mm cannons were lethal at that range but to aim them accurately we needed to be within about 300 yards.

An idea struck me: if I fired a few rounds over the top of the left hand 109 he would see my shells splashing in the water in front of him and might turn to avoid my line of fire and I could then cut the corner and get closer to him. I began to fire a few rounds accordingly and saw them splash in the sea in front of the left hand 109. The right hand 109 then peeled off to the right. I thought how lucky Prosser was that he would be able to get in a good shot at that one by cutting the corner to the right. I fired a few more rounds over the 109 in front of me and then happened to notice, with some surprise, that Prosser was still on my right. He had not noticed the right hand 109 turning away. For some reason I glanced down at my left wing and happened to see a small bullet hole in it just a few feet from me. I assumed I had picked it up earlier, when we were sparring with the 109s high up, but had failed to notice it. I then fired a few more rounds over the top of the 109 in front of me but he still would not turn.

Quite fortuitously, I looked again at the bullet hole in my left wing and saw a second one about a foot from it. It took a long second for me to realize that there must be a 109 behind me, that a fearful stream of bullets and shells must be passing over my left wing a few feet from me, and that a slight and almost inevitable change of pressure on a rudder pedal by the 109 pilot or myself would bring that stream right into my back if I kept straight on. I turned violently to the left and upwards, following blindly the rule of turning always towards the attack, which was just as well because I would probably have collided with Prosser if I had turned to the right.

In an instant things began to happen. Exploding balls of fire making sharp cracking bangs appeared on the left side of my engine. The aircraft shook as if poked from behind by long metal rods. The cockpit filled with the smell of cordite. The engine oil pressure dropped to nothing. The oil temperature shot upwards. But the engine kept going without missing a beat. Over my left shoulder I saw the yellow nose of a 109 about 100 yards behind me and closing in. Puffs of smoke were billowing from its guns and being blown back over it. It came so close it almost touched me as it passed behind.

To survive ditching a Spitfire in the sea was almost a hopeless prospect; to bale out safely it was necessary to get up to about 600 feet. As soon as I was pointing back to Malta I straightened out and climbed at full power setting. We had been told that if a Rolls-Royce Merlin engine ever lost its oil pressure you should flog it, not nurse it. To my great relief I reached 600 feet and then 1,000. The engine kept delivering full power. I marvelled how it could do this with no oil pressure. I switched the R/T over to emergency and called,

"Mayday! Mayday! Mayday!", the oral SOS. In a fraction of a second the operator in Malta replied: "Keep transmitting, we've got you!" Soon I was at 2,000 feet and Malta looked closer.

To my wonderment and admiration the engine kept going till I reached 3,800 ft and was almost at the coast of Malta. By then acrid smoke was pouring through the cockpit and the power was failing. I baled out into Sliema Bay, opposite the Sliema Point Battery. From here I was swiftly picked up by one of the resident rescue launches and returned to the squadron not too much the worse for wear.

It seems that I was saved from being shot down by Prosser, who reported shooting down my attacker from my tail, and who I understand may have been Feldwebel Gerhard Stockmann of 2./JG 53, who was wounded and came down in the sea to the south of Sicily. Anyway, I could never ask for greater luck than I had on that October morning when two bullets, times and spaced by chance, gently warned me not to linger.

Prosser provided me with a nice little confirmatory note regarding my bale out, which enabled me to claim my caterpillar badge. This was provided to all users of their products by the manufacturers of the parachutes with which we were supplied. Prosser cannot have thought my escapade had done any great harm, for three days later on the 18th I was promoted to command 126 Squadron's A Flight.

By this time the daily appearances of formations of Ju 88s on four or five occasions was coming to an end. We believed that we had made it too hot for the Luftwaffe to continue to this intensity, and while raids still came in on occasion at dusk, the main Axis effort over the island now resolved itself into fighter sweeps and low level attacks by small formations of bomb-carrying Me 109s. We now know that Feldmarschal Albert Kesselring, the Luftwaffe commander in the Mediterranean, had indeed called a stop to daylight bombing attacks at the end of the day on 17 October.

Scrambles continued throughout the rest of the month, but with much less chance of engaging incoming raiders. From the 24th we began hearing news of the Eighth Army's new offensive on the Alamein Line. Next day sections from both 126 and 229 Squadrons were scrambled after one of the new fighter-bomber attacks on Takali aerodrome. Flying BR311, I was able to record in my logbook: "Bounced four 109s from 24,000 ft; four-second burst – flash from cockpit and pieces off – dived into sea – confirmed by rest of section and 'Y' Service." It seems that I had intercepted Messerschmitts from a newly-arrived unit, Schlachtgeschwader 2, and had shot down 'White 16' from that unit's I Gruppe, Unteroffizier Willi Diepenseifen being lost with this aircraft.

This was to be my final success over Malta, although not my last sortie there. I undertook half a dozen more scrambles and patrols, the last of these on 6 November when I and my number two were engaged in a twenty-five minute dogfight with twelve to fifteen 109s at 22,000 ft over Grand Harbour – albeit without any results on either side.

Two days later I went down to Luqa at dawn as usual, but feeling really ill. After our arrival the intelligence officer came round to tell us about the Anglo-American landings in French North-West Africa – Operation 'Torch' – which were just taking place. The medical officer then arrived, took one look at me and despatched me to hospital at St.Paul's Bay, where I was kept for a month with a fairly severe case of jaundice. When I came out I weighed just 134 pounds. I have always been considered to be somewhat slender, but my normal weight is 194 pounds – which I think, speaks for itself.

On my release by the medics, I was posted back to the UK tour-expired. I left Luqa on 12 December aboard a Hudson, passing over Tunis during the hours of darkness to land at North Front aerodrome, Gibraltar. It was the 17th before I was able to depart on the next leg, leaving in a Catalina flyingboat (again at night), destination Mount Batten, Plymouth. It was not to be, however, for due to bad weather over the Bay of Biscay, we were forced to turn back. Over the R/T we learned that it was equally bad at Gib, so landed instead in North Africa, at Arzeu, near Oran.

From here I was to gain a new experience when I accompanied the crew on an air-sea rescue sortie to pick up the six members of the crew of a Wellington which was still floating in the sea about fifty miles north of Oran. Next day we flew back to Gibraltar, where on 21st I got aboard an Albemarle glider-towing aircraft, arriving at Lyneham with the dawn.

Just before I reached England the *London Gazette* of 4 December 1942 carried the citation for the award to me of the Distinguished Flying Cross, which read:

Flight Lieutenant Smith has been responsible for the destruction of six enemy aircraft since his arrival in Malta. One day in October 1942 he led his flight in a determined attack on nine hostile bombers with a large fighter escort, and in spite of intense opposition by the fighters, Flight Lieutenant Smith personally destroyed a Junkers 88, while one Macchi 202 was destroyed by other pilots of his flight. This officer has always displayed the greatest determination and courage and during recent hard fighting has been an inspiration to all.

CHAPTER TEN

SECOND TACTICAL AIR FORCE

So it was that Rod returned to the United Kingdom to commence a very different phase of his wartime activities. Despite his momentous tour on Malta, his recent illness and receipt of his DFC, there was to be no rest – at least not initially. No sooner was he back than a non-operational, but nonetheless testing, appointment was forthcoming as an instructor at 53 Operational Training Unit at Llandow in South Wales.

53 OTU was a fighter training establishment, equipped with Spitfires and Hurricanes. Its task was to 'hone' newly-trained fighter pilots to operational readiness before they were posted to their first squadrons. It could be a daunting task. Rod's stay was fairly brief, however, and having joined the unit in early January 1943, a week later he was detached to 3 Flying Instructor's School at Hullavington, Wiltshire, where most of his flying was undertaken in Miles Master advanced training aircraft. His mentors do not seem to have thought too highly of their aggressive fighter pilot pupil in the role of instructor, for the end of his course here found him classified (rather oddly) as "Below average as instructor, but above average at night flying"!

On completion of the course at 3 FIS he did not return to Llandow, but was posted instead at the end of February to 55 OTU at Annan. The airfield here was located on the north shore of the Solway Firth, just within the southernmost part of Scotland, and but a few miles to the west of the famous Gretna Green, where runaway couples could marry without parental consent at the age of sixteen.

His stay at Annan was to be somewhat more protracted, for he remained until the end of August 1943. Much more to his personal taste was his despatch on 31 August to the Fighter Leader School at 52 OTU, Aston Down, in Gloucestershire to attend the Fighter Leader Course. He graduated from here on 26 September with an "Above average as a pilot" grading, and then at last he was granted a much-deserved home leave.

Transport was not immediately available, and it was 18 October before the vessel upon which he had been allocated a berth, set sail for Canada. He disembarked here six days later. Rested, restored and ready for further action, he re-embarked on 14 December, landing back in the UK on 21st.

In the intervening period since he had departed Malta, the whole course of the war had changed. The start of this improvement in the fortunes of the Allies had begun just as he completed his time on the island, with the Eighth Army's victory at El Alamein, the Anglo-US landings in French north-west Africa, and – unknown to him at the time – the opening of the great battle for Stalingrad on the Eastern Front which was to end so disastrously for the Wehrmacht.

1943 had then seen the invasion of Sicily in July, just at the same time as the greatest armoured battle of the war was being fought out at Kursk. Following this cataclysmic struggle there would be no further major German offensives in the Soviet Union, while events in the Mediterranean were causing Adolf Hitler to withdraw units from the hard-pressed east, and direct them southwards in an effort to save the situation in Italy. In September a foothold on mainland Europe had been gained here with invasions of Calabria on the 'toe' of Italy, and at Salerno. These events coincided with the deposition of the Italian dictator, Benito Mussolini, and an armistice which took Italy out of the Axis 'camp' before the month was out.

Throughout this period too, the Allied cause had been subject to constant reinforcement as the great democracy of the United States moved fully onto a war footing. Having played an increasingly active and important role in the Mediterranean area from late in 1942 onwards, the Americans had also been building a mighty strategic air force in England, which had approached maturity during 1943. Now a combined RAF/USAAF bomber offensive around the clock was causing sufficient damage both industrially and in terms of civilian morale to cause the withdrawal for home defence purposes of Luftwaffe fighter units and anti-aircraft batteries from the Eastern Front, just as their comrades on the ground were heading for Italy.

It was against this far more optimistic background that, after a short period of re-acclimatisation, Rod rejoined the units of the RCAF with a posting on 6 January 1944 to 401 Squadron. He now stepped into an arena where he was to serve 'cheek by jowl' with most of the great names of Canadian fighter aviation during World War II.

401 Squadron had served longer in the UK than any other Canadian fighter unit. It had arrived in 1940 as 1 Squadron, RCAF, in time to play an active and successful part in the Battle of Britain. Renumbered 401 Squadron in March 1941, it had a long and illustrious history during the difficult days of the cross-Channel sweeps throughout 1941-43. Recently re-equipped with the splendid Spitfire IXB, it was based at Biggin Hill, one of the RAF's most famous fighter airfields, and was led by Sqn Ldr Lorne Cameron, an experienced fighter pilot at this stage of the war.

The squadron now formed a part of the 2nd Tactical Air Force which had been set up during the previous year and was now being readied to support the planned invasion of occupied France. As such, it was administered by 126 Airfield – a mobile organisation which could move rapidly from base to base as required; at this stage it also controlled 411 and 412 Squadrons. 126 Airfield, which coincidentally carried the same number as Rod's old squadron on Malta, was one of two such RCAF Spitfire bases in 2nd TAF, the other being 127 Airfield, containing 403, 416 and 421 Squadrons. These six squadrons from the two airfields, all operated at this stage under the control of 17 Wing, which was commanded by Grp Capt W.R.MacBrian, and was led operationally by Wg Cdr R.W.'Buck' McNair, DSO, DFC & two Bars, one of Canada's 'greats', who like Rod had served with great distinction on Malta during 1942.

Notable characters in 401 at the time of Rod's arrival included Flt Lts Jackson Sheppard, W.S.'John' Johnson, Bill Tew and Alex Halcrow, Flg Off Bob Hayward and a young Flg Off, Bill 'Grissle' Klersy, who would distinguish himself greatly during the forthcoming year. At this stage many experienced pilots who had been retained in Canada as instructors, had finally been released for operations in Europe. Apart from bringing with them a wealth of flying skill, this meant that during the rest of the war RCAF squadrons tended to have a considerable number of flight lieutenants on strength – far more than there were flight commander posts for them to fill. At this stage Rod was one of these.

A settling-in period followed his arrival, there being no great pressure to push recently-arrived pilots into action before they were fully ready. As a result it was 25 February before Rod flew his first operational sortie with 401 – withdrawal cover to USAAF B-17 Flying Fortress bombers from Lâon in France back to Friston in England.

At this time the Luftwaffe was seen over the French and Belgian coastal areas on only rare occasions, most of the Jagdgeschwaders making their attacks on the bomber formations further east, after they had passed beyond the range of many of the fighters then seeking to escort them.

However, by the early spring of 1944 the USAAF had also brought into action several units of Martin B-26 Marauder twin-engined medium bombers, which in due course were destined to operate in a more tactical role as part of the new US Ninth Air Force, which was being formed on parallel lines to 2nd TAF. These bombers were now available to attack targets along the coastal belt, or just inland therefrom, and these could often be relied upon to bring up at least a few German interceptors.

Such was indeed the case on 7 March when the Canadian wing took part in a 'Ramrod' escort to B-26s bombing in the Creil area. "Actually saw eight or ten 109s!" exulted Rod's logbook on this occasion. Eight days later B-26s were accompanied to Aulnoy. This time results were much more positive – though not for Rod: "Bounced eight 190s over Cambrai. Squadron got four. I did poor shooting."

Early April brought a number of changes. On 8th Rod received orders to move to 412 Squadron (the unit with which he had first flown operationally during 1941, it may be recalled); here he took up the role of flight commander once more. 401 Squadron was just departing for 11 Armament Practice Camp at Fairwood Common to be initiated into the fighter-bomber role, for which Rod had already received training when at the Fighter Leader School. 412 Squadron had already attended 11 APC, and its Spitfire IXBs were already fitted with bomb shackles, ready to carry a 250 lb or 500 lb bomb beneath the fuselage.

Just at this time Buck McNair was stood down as wing leader of 17 Wing as his eyesight was becoming adversely affected as a result of burns he had suffered when shot down during the previous year. To take his place the commanding officer of 412 Squadron, Sqn Ldr George Keefer, DFC & Bar, an ex-Western Desert fighter pilot, was promoted and departed a couple of days after Rod's arrival on the unit. The unit was then joined by Jackson Sheppard from 401, who took over command. Rod also discovered on arrival that he was replacing Malta's greatest fighter pilot, Flt Lt George Beurling, DSO, DFC, DFM & Bar (known also as 'Buzz' or 'Screwball'), who left on the day of Rod's arrival to return to Canada.

As with 401, 412 Squadron had its share of experienced pilots, one of whom had been with the unit for some months already, but who was destined to become the RCAF's top-scorer of 1944; this was Flg Off Don Laubman.

Rod's arrival was followed by a steady increase in the tempo of operations as preparations for the still-secret Operation 'Overlord' got fully into their stride. On his first full day with the squadron, 10 April, Rod was again involved in escorting B-26s on a Ramrod, similar sorties being flown during the next two days.

On 15 April 126 Airfield moved from Biggin Hill in Kent to Tangmere on the south coast in western Hampshire, and from here three days later 412 Squadron undertook its first dive-bombing operation against a target listed by the codename 'Noball' at Mogenville. The Noballs were construction sites where launching equipment was being set up for the V-1 'Flying Bombs', which had not yet started being launched against south-east England. While pilots were not initially sure of the nature of these new targets, the authorities were very acutely aware of their purpose, and they quickly became priorities for attack. Two more such raids were made next day, and thereafter operations became increasingly sustained during the rest of April, May and into early June. Rodeos, Ramrods and various bombing attacks were launched on most days.

On 23 April, however, the unit was stood down for five days in order that all its Spitfires might be fitted with the new gyro gunsight (GGS). Throughout this period Rod's targets were entirely on the ground, the Luftwaffe failing to make any appearances when 412 Squadron was in the air. One of the highlights for him occurred on 30 May when during a Ramrod to Eindhoven in Holland, he was able to shoot up a train.

Changes had occurred in the administrative structure of 2nd TAF in the meantime. The airfields had become wings in their own right with their commanding officers joined by their own wing leaders. For the time being 126 Wing's commander continued to be Wg Cdr K.L.B.Hodson, DFC & Bar, who had commanded 401 Squadron earlier in the war, while George

Keefer moved from 17 Wing to lead 126 in the air. At the same time 17 Wing, and other such 'big wings' had been re-christened 'sectors', but would be disbanded in July. A third RCAF Spitfire wing had also been formed, 144 Wing comprising 441, 442 and 443 Squadrons.

At last 6 June 1944 brought the long-awaited D-Day, as British, Canadian and US troops stormed ashore on five beaches on the Normandy coast. For the time being the RCAF Spitfire wings reverted to the fighter role, joining many other RAF and USAAF fighter units in providing standing patrols over the beachhead areas and the huge fleets standing offshore. 412 Squadron undertook three such patrols on this first day, Rod being involved in all of them. During the second he and his flight gave chase to four FW 190s, but these escaped into cloud. Little else would be seen during the rest of the month, and before June was out the squadron, which had moved across to a landing ground at Bény-sur-Mer in Normandy, known as B-4, on 18 June, was once again involved in dive-bombing and strafing. The targets now were mainly of a transport nature, road traffic, trains and even marching columns of men, etc, being attacked in the area immediately behind the battlefield.

At last, after seven months back on operations, the moment Rod had been waiting for occurred on 7 July:

"While on an armed reconnaissance south-east of Falaise in the Argentan area during the early afternoon, eight or more enemy aircraft were sighted by Red One at three o'clock to the squadron at the same level when we were flying at 4,000 ft. I turned to meet them head-on and chased one short-nosed FW 190 for a couple of minutes. I gave him a couple of bursts of three-four seconds approximately, and saw strikes on the fuselage. He pulled up smoking and jettisoned his hood. He caught fire in the cockpit and the pilot came half out and burned for a few seconds. He then fell clear of the aircraft and it crashed to the ground. I saw a white puff but I do not know if it was a parachute as there was lots of Flak."

July also saw another round of changes within 126 Wing. At the command level Keith Hodson handed over to Grp Capt Gordon McGregor, OBE, DFC. This was occasioned by the disbandment of 144, the third RCAF Spitfire wing, its three squadrons being shared out between 126, 127 and an RAF wing. When 442 Squadron joined 126 Wing therefore, command of this enlarged organisation became a group captain appointment.

Gordon McGregor was no stranger to the squadrons, however. He had commanded 1 Squadron, RCAF, in 1940, when he had claimed five victories. After a long spell back in Canada, he had served with 2nd TAF's 83 Group (of which 126 and 127 Wings were a part) since February 1944. At the same time George Keefer completed his tour, his place as wing leader being taken over by Wg Cdr B.Dal Russel, DFC & Bar. Dal Russel had flown in 1 Squadron with McGregor during 1940, for which he had received his DFC. In July 1943 he led 17 Wing, and following the April 1944 reorganisation had gone to 127 Wing as wing leader. With a Bar to his DFC, he had dropped rank to stay at the front, commanding 442 Squadron in 144 Wing. Now, with the move of that unit to 126 Wing, he again became a wing leader – a role which he would continue to fulfil until January 1945. He was indeed a most worthy new member of the 126 Wing team.

On 2 August 412 Squadron's commanding officer, Jackson Sheppard, who had by then claimed five victories, was shot down during a rare engagement with German fighters, and crash-landed. Sqn Ldr Dean Dover was immediately posted in from the newly-joined 442 Squadron, to take his place. Sheppard had managed to evade capture, and was back on 13 August, but was then rested, being awarded a DFC. Also during July Sqn Ldr Hugh Trainor had been posted from 411 Squadron to command 401 Squadron. After a long fallow period prior to the invasion, Trainor had claimed eight victories and a share in a ninth during little more than a month after D-Day, for which he also had received a DFC.

Apart from the events of 7 July, Rod's activities with 412 had remained of a ground attack nature as the Allied armies at last pushed the Wehrmacht back and began the great encirclement around Falais. Now, as the fighting on the ground spread out, came a succession of moves. On 8 August it was to B-18 at Cristot, and then on 29 August to B-28 at the old Luftwaffe fighter base at Evreux, to the east of Paris. By now the pursuit was on as the Wehrmacht pulled out of France with all possible speed. B-29 at St Andre-de-l'Eure on 1 September was followed next day by B-26 at Illiers-l'Eveque, and then B-44 at Poix on 3rd. Three days later the squadron reached B-56 at Evere on Belgian soil, but here the wing's odyssey slowed as re-equipment with the latest Spitfire IXE took place. Whereas the Mark IXB had retained the armament of the Mark V – basically a pair of 20mm Hispano cannon with four .303in Browning machine guns, mounted two in each wing outboard of the cannon, the Mark IXE carried a pair of 0.50in Browings inboard of the 20mm cannon, plus the standard pair of the latter. This was a considerably more effective armament, the 0.50 packing a considerably greater punch than the 0.303.

It was at this time that Operation 'Market Garden', the great airborne assault took place on 17 September. This was designed to capture bridges across the Dutch canals at Vegel, the Maas and Waal river bridges at Grave and Nijmegen respectively, and critically, the Rhine bridge at Arnhem. This venture was a gamble aimed at securing a quick crossing of the main water barriers before north-west Germany, which it was hoped British 2nd Army, part of Montgomery's 21st Army Group, could exploit to bring the war to an early close.

As is now well-known, the US 82nd and 101st Airborne Divisions secured their objectives at the first three locations, although one of the canal bridges was demolished by the Germans before it could be secured. However, the British 1st Airborne Division, reinforced by the Polish 1st Independent Parachute Brigade, found Arnhem unexpectedly strongly defended, and having been dropped largely too far from their objectives, failed in their attempt to secure the Rhine bridge after a heroic and costly battle. With the single road to the area under observation and constant artillery and anti-tank fire, 2nd Army's XXX Corps was unable to get through in time to link with the paratroops.

However, the vitally important bridge over the Waal at Nijmegen was in Allied hands, and became a prime target for increasingly desperate attempts by the Germans – particularly by the Luftwaffe – to destroy it. On 21 September therefore, 126 Wing moved up to airfield B-68 at Le Culot to which 127 Wing had also flown in three days earlier. The two Canadian wings were to play a major part in providing the air defence of the bridge, and it was here that Rod was about to achieve his greatest period of success in aerial combat.

Both wings commenced patrols over Nijmegen on 25 September, much of the action on this first day devolving on 127 Wing, and upon Mustangs of the RAF's 122 Wing. 127's squadrons were able to make claims for nine German fighters, while 126 Wing's claims amounted to five, two of them by 412 Squadron pilots. Rod led a low level patrol, recording in his logbook only "Saw an Me 109!" – the first sighting for him in two and a half months.

How different the next day was to prove! Soon after midday on 26th he led a high level patrol in Spitfire MJ461 VZ-H during which:

"... when at 2,000 ft I sighted about 12 Me 109s on the deck just east of Nijmegen Bridge going east. I chased one for a couple of minutes and fired a burst of cannon of about four seconds from 400 yards astern. I saw strikes in the wing roots and fuselage and he streamed glycol. He flew on for a few seconds and then crashed.

I then chased another one of another gaggle of about 12 plus flying parallel to the left of the first gaggle. I fired several bursts from 300-400 yards, dead astern but my starboard cannon then stopped. I closed the range to 100 yards and fired a short burst. Pieces came off and clouds of smoke and he crashed a few seconds later. I used camera in both cases but GGS only in the first combat."

Apart from Rod's two claims, two FW 190s were claimed by Don Laubman, now a Flt Lt, and two by Flt Lt Wilf Banks (his 7th and 8th since D-Day), while Flg Off Phil Charron, who had flown with Rod in 126 Squadron on Malta, claiming two victories during the October Blitz there, got his fourth of the war. One more was claimed by a fifth member of the squadron and one by a pilot of 416 Squadron from 127 Wing. It is now known that during this engagement JG 11 suffered the loss of at least four Messerschmitts and two Focke-Wulfs. The squadron again engaged Messerschmitts later in the afternoon, claiming two of these – one each for Laubman and Charron.

Next day, 27 September, proved even more successful. Rod was to fly three times in MJ461. On the first sortie, commenced soon after 0800 in the morning, he:

"... was leading 412 Squadron just north-east of Nijmegen. We sighted ten plus Me 109s below cloud heading for Nijmegen. I attacked one from 250 yards astern (GGS fitted, not used) and gave a four-second burst. I saw strikes on fuselage and wing of e/a and he crashed into the Rhine. The pilot baled out but his chute streamed and he hit the Rhine.

Twenty minutes later I saw a single Me 109 just east of Nijmegen Bridge diving towards the bridge. He was below cloud at 5,000 ft. He saw me and pulled back towards the cloud. I attacked from 300 yards astern and fired two three-second bursts just as he entered cloud. I saw strikes and pieces fly off and he fell immediately out of cloud and crashed on the edge of the Rhine. The pilot fell out, I saw no parachute."

Don Laubman added claims for two more, and Flg Off Lloyd Berryman a further pair. 421 and 441 Squadrons had been active in the same area at this time, adding six more claims to the Canadian total; II./JG 77 lost nine Messerschmitts, with two more damaged.

It was but the start, however. By the end of the day 2nd TAF fighters had listed 45 claims – very close to actual Luftwaffe losses – but of these, 126 and 127 Wings had been credited with 41! 412 Squadron had engaged twice more, both Laubman and Berryman each claiming a third success for the day during these later sorties.

28 September proved to be a somewhat quieter day, but 29th brought a further slaughter of the German fighters. Rod flew one early sortie in VZ-K, but then received the news that he was posted to command 401 Squadron with immediate effect. This order had actually been issued on 20 September, but had only just reached the wing. On 19 September 401's existing commander, still Hugh Trainor, had been obliged to bale out near Helmond when the engine of his Spitfire failed after being hit by Flak; he had become a prisoner for the duration.

Taking over his new command, which, conveniently was located at the same airfield, Rod was back in the air later that same morning, now flying MJ448 YO-W. At approximately 1030 the 13 pilots he was at the head of spotted an estimated 30 plus Messerschmitts and Focke-Wulfs. With 421 and 443 Squadrons from 127 Wing and some Canadian-flown Typhoons of 438 Squadron in the area, Rod reported:

> "I was leading 401 Squadron on low patrol in the Nijmegen area at 4,000 ft. We sighted about thirty plus Me 109s in a fight with some Typhoons at the same height. I attacked one from about 200-400 yards astern and fired two or three short two-second bursts (GGS fitted not used). I saw many strikes on fuselage and wing roots of e/a, pieces came off and his starboard wheel came down. He dived straight into the ground from the base of the cloud. I saw no-one bale out.
>
> I then attacked another Me 109 from astern at about 100 yards range and fired a three or four-second burst (GGS not used). I saw many strikes on fuselage and wing and pieces came off. He gushed glycol and crashed into the ground just west of the first 109. I saw no-one get out. Cine camera gun used."

The results had again been greatly in the Canadians' favour, 401 Squadron alone claiming nine Bf 109s. Double claims were also made by Flt Lt H.J.Everard and by Flg Offs John

Hughes and Doug Husband, although on this occasion one Spitfire failed to return, Flg Off C.G.Hutchings being shot down and killed. During this same series of engagements the pilots of 421 Squadron had claimed seven victories and 443 Squadron two. A little later Rod's old 412 Squadron colleagues submitted five claims, while 416 Squadron rounded out the morning with another seven to bring effectively to a conclusion what had undoubtedly been the greatest period of success for the RCAF fighter units of the war.

Thereafter, a reduction in Luftwaffe activity led to a resumption of bombing duties, the wing moving first to B-84 at Rips on 3 October, and then back to B-80, Volkel, on 14th. Both these airfields were on Dutch soil, the former to the north-east of Eindhoven, the latter a few miles to the south.

The move to Rips led to Rod's final, and perhaps most famous combat. During the early afternoon of 5 October he took off in MK577 YO-F to patrol over Nijmegen, which was now under occasional attack by the new, very fast Messerschmitt Me 262 jet fighter-bombers of Kampfgeschwader 51. Rod's logbook entry was perhaps a little more detailed and 'personal' than his official combat report. Because of the importance of this particular engagement and the controversy which, sadly, later surrounded it, it is probably worth including both, as well as his later commentary upon the event.

a) Rod's logbook entry

"While leading squadron on routine patrol over Nijmegen Bridge at 14,000 ft an Me 262 was sighted 500 ft below in front coming head on. We attacked and Hun turned and dived down towards bridge half rolling at very high speed. F/O MacKay and F/L Everard damaged him first with a few strikes. I then attacked him with three others. He zoomed and F/L Davenport and I cut him off and fired simultaneously. I fired approx 8 sec burst 350 yds astern, small deflection, and his starboard jet unit caught fire. I turned down to starboard and he turned down behind me. Uncertain as to whether he attacked. He fell in flames just SW of Nijmegen. Pilot came clear before a/c hit ground. Killed. Claims: F/L Everard, F/O Mackay, F/L Davenport, F/O Sinclair, self."

b) Composite combat report

"1353-1508
5 miles NE Nijmegen
Enemy height 12,000 feet

Own height 14,000 feet

I was leading 401 Squadron at 13,500 feet in the Nijmegen area about 5 miles north-east of the bridge. We were flying on a north-easterly course when I sighted an Me 262 coming head-on 500 feet below. He went into a port climbing turn and I turned starboard after him with several other Spitfires chasing him. He then dived down towards the bridge, twisting and turning and half-rolling at very high speeds. He then flew across Nijmegen, turning from side to side. I saw a Spitfire get some strikes on him and he streamed white smoke from the starboard wing root. He flew on at very high speed still and I managed to get behind him and fire two three-second bursts at 200-300 yards approximately. He zoomed very high and I saw strikes on him in the port and starboard nacelles. A small fire started in the starboard nacelle and then a big one in the port nacelle while I was firing. I broke down to starboard under him and he turned down to starboard behind me. I thought at the time he was trying to attack me, even though in flames. He passed me and crashed in a field about two miles south-west of Nijmegen. He was painted green with yellow decoration on his long nose. He looked like the silhouette. The fuselage seemed to be fat in plan view and it seemed to be triangular in cross-section with apex up. He rolled at high speed (480) much better than a Spitfire and the turns were very tight at high speed. The pilot seemed to handle his aircraft very well but the aircraft did not seem to be tremendously fast in the combat low down.

GGS fitted not used. Cine gun used.

I claim 1/5 Me 262 destroyed.

R.I.A.Smith Squadron Leader

I was flying Red 4 to Flight Lieutenant Everard when we sighted the Me 262. I followed Red 3 (Flight Lieutenant Everard) into his attack. After a couple of spiral turns, Flight Lieutenant Everard was slightly out of position and told me to go in to attack. I got on the tail of the aircraft, saw strikes on the after part of the fuselage and the port or starboard wing root. The aircraft was extremely manoeuvrable. The pilot was hot and put the aircraft through everything in the book. We were about 2,000 to 3,000 feet when Squadron Leader Smith came in to attack. The starboard nacelle burst into flames, the aircraft pulled up to the right then dove down (burning) on a Spit' (Squadron Leader Smith) seeming to want to ram the Spit'. The Me 262 then crashed into the deck. GGS II used.

For this I claim 1/5 Me 262 destroyed.

J.MacKay Flying Officer

I was flying Red 3 in a north-easterly direction at 14,000 feet when Red 1 spotted the E/A diving at 13,000 feet towards 6 o'clock. I half-rolled after it and it started a slow spiral going

straight down. I opened fire from 900 yards and followed it, closing in all the time. At 5,000 feet he began to level out, heading south. Throttling back, not to overshoot, I opened fire with machine-guns only from 150 yards. A streamer of white smoke came from it and it accelerated rapidly, drawing away. I then informed Red 4 to have a shot then break off. Two minutes later I saw the E/A come flaming down and hit the deck. Circling the wreckage from 300 feet, there was little left to describe it except that the bits of wreckage covered an area of 150 yards. In the centre of the debris was a large oil fire and the biggest piece of wreckage was not more than eight feet long.

I claim 1/5 Me 262 destroyed.

H.J.Everard Flight Lieutenant (above)

I was flying as Blue 1 in 401 Blackout Squadron, when the Squadron spotted a Me 262 at about 12,000 feet north-east of Nijmegen. Red Section fired first, bringing the Me 262 across in front of Blue Section. I turned in behind firing 4 or 5 second burst, saw strikes, but was crowded out by two other aircraft coming in from above. This aircraft was destroyed immediately after. Strikes were observed along the wings and fuselage. Before making my attack I observed strikes, or pieces flying off from the attacks made by Red Section. This aircraft dived and turned down to the deck. The turns were very tight.

I used cine gun and cannon and machine-guns and new gyro sight.

A.L.Sinclair Flying Officer

I was flying as Yellow 1 Blackout Squadron when we sighted a Me 262 at 12,000 feet 5 miles north-east of Nijmegen. There was a great mix-up as all twelve Spits dove for the Jet Job. I waited until he made his first break then came in 20 degrees line astern at approximately 400 yards and observed strikes in fuselage. I then continued the chase which was composed of rolls, dives and turns at approximately 375 miles per hour. I finally closed into 300 yards line astern and emptied the remainder of my guns, approximately 10 or 12 seconds, into the kite, observing strikes all in engines and fuselage. The aircraft was burning all this time. The pilot seemed to be unhurt and put up a good fight all during this. At the last realising the fight was up he attempted to ram Red 1 on the way to the ground when he crashed and burned.

I used camera and got 8 feet film. Cannon, machine-guns and gyro sight functioned properly, no ammo left.

I claim 1/5 Me 262 destroyed.

R.M.Davenport Flight Lieutenant

In his typical meticulous fashion, Rod subsequently wrote up the course of this fight in some detail:

"In the afternoon 401 Squadron, which had moved to a small grass field near the village of Rips in south-east Holland two days before, was sent to do a patrol above the Nijmegen road bridge. Two things were unusual about this patrol. One was that it was set unusually high for the Tactical Air Force, 13,000 feet, and the other was that the sky had become almost clear after two or three weeks of quite low cloud ceilings. All was quiet until 'Kenway' called me up and said there was an aircraft to the north-east coming towards us at 13,000 feet. The Squadron was in open battle formation over Nijmegen at that moment, so I turned it north-north-eastwards, took it up another 500 feet and levelled it off three or four miles north-east of the town. Almost immediately I spotted an aircraft dead ahead of us about 500 feet below. It was travelling south-west towards Nijmegen, head-on to us, very fast. I quickly reported it to the squadron then swung out some distance to the right to give myself enough room to swing sharply back to the left. I planned to turn all the way round to the south-west, so that I would be able to pull in close behind the aircraft at a small enough angle to its path to be able to aim ahead of it, if it should be obliging enough to keep on coming. Two or three other pilots did the same thing.

I quickly recognised it as an Me 262. It kept on coming and had obviously failed to spot us, probably because we were more or less between it and the sun, and it would, therefore, have to pass right through us. I felt a peculiar thrill. At long last here was a jet plane that had made a mistake and was going to leave itself open to a burst of fire, if only a short one because of the speed with which it would be able to draw away.

I then began my final swing back to the left and around to the south-west. Just before it began to pass through us it climbed to the left slightly and my feeling of thrill intensified. I was fast pulling into position behind the '262 for a perfect shot, and I was already aiming along its path ahead of it.

But that perfect shot was not to be. Another Spitfire in a tight left turn like mine, suddenly appeared quite close in front of me and almost in line between the '262 and me. If I fired I would risk hitting the other Spitfire, but for an instant I was tempted to fire a short burst anyway. I resisted the temptation however. Having to pass up that shot was hard to swallow and on top of that I was afraid that the '262 would simply keep on going and get clean away without a shot being fired at it.

However, a second or two after he passed through us the '262 pilot rolled into a fairly steep dive, then half-rolled the other way to get himself upright and began banking and swerving from side to side. All the while he kept in the dive and crossed Nijmegen in a generally south-west direction. All of us dived down after him. I am as certain as I can be that he must have closed his throttles quite a bit as he entered his dive, natural enough in ordinary circumstances, but in his position another mistake. The Spitfire that had come between it and me (which I later found to have been that flown by John MacKay) managed to get within range fairly early in the dive. For several seconds, though, that Spitfire seemed to be withholding fire for some reason. In a burst of impatience, not knowing who was flying it, I called out "For God's sake shoot – that Spitfire!" I'm sure my call was unnecessary, of course, and that its pilot was doing his very best contending with the diving and swerving of the '262.

I then saw MacKay open fire, and immediately two or three cannon strikes appeared on the trailing edge of the wing next to one of the jet nacelles. Strange-looking smoke began to trail from the place struck by MacKay's shells and for a moment I thought that the engine might catch fire, but this did not happen.

'Tex' Davenport and I had to pull out at about 7,000 feet because we were about to collide with each other, so I lost sight of the action for quite a few seconds. When I was able to look again I saw it had pulled out of its dive and was about 3.000 feet over the south-west edge of Nijmegen, still heading south-west. It was no longer trailing smoke and was increasing its lead over several Spitfires which were still chasing it but were then out of range.

I thought the action was over and that the '262 had got away but, quite suddenly, it zoomed up into the most sustained vertical climb I had ever seen, leaving far behind it the Spitfires which had followed it all the way down. To my great surprise and elation its climb brought it up to where 'Tex' and I were. As it soared up to us, still climbing almost vertically, the sweep-back of its wings became very noticeable. Its speed, though still very considerable, was beginning to fall off and with full power on I was able to pull up in an almost vertical position to within about 350 yards behind it, the maximum range. I aimed at one of its engine nacelles and within two or three seconds a plume of fire began to stream from alongside one of them. The '262 was then slowing down more than I was and I was able to close the range to about

200 yards. I did not know that 'Tex' Davenport was behind me and was also firing!

By now both the '262 and my Spitfire had reached the limit of our zoom-climbs, and slowly we both stall-turned to the right in formation. Halfway through our stall turns, when our noses had come down level with the horizon but our wings were almost vertical, I felt as if I were in slow motion line abreast on the '262, to its right, directly below it. As the '262 was only about 100 yards above me I had a remarkable and unhurried look at it, side on. To my surprise I couldn't see the pilot's head, although the canopy was still fully closed. He must have had his head down for some reason.

It began to dawn on me that when we had completed our stall turns we would be facing almost vertically downwards with our positions reversed. The '262 would be close on my tail and I would be helpless. My nose went down and to the right. I had no control for quite a few seconds.

Because of the Spitfire's lack of rear vision the '262 was out of sight behind me, which was probably just as well in the circumstances. 'Tex' said later that it fired at me but no-one else reported that. In any event, after what seemed an age during which I wondered if cannon shells would come smashing into me from behind, the '262 appeared a few yards away on my right. It was diving almost vertically downwards, as I was, but it was picking up speed more quickly and the plume of fire it was streaming had grown much bigger. It plunged on down and crashed within our lines just south-west of Nijmegen, sending up a billowing column of smoke."

401 Squadron's pilots had shot down Hauptmann Hans-Christoff Buttmann of 3 Staffel, KG 51. He had managed to bale out at an altitude of about 100 feet, but his parachute had no time to deploy and he was killed on impact. This success, the first time a jet had been shot down by aircraft of the British Commonwealth forces, was the subject of a great celebration that evening. However, the leading RAF 'ace' of the war, Grp Capt J.E. Johnnie Johnson, who had been flying as a wing leader with the RCAF, recorded in his autobiography, *Wing Leader*, "Later that evening Dal Russel phoned to say that some of his boys had shot down a 262. This was the first time that this type of enemy aircraft had been destroyed, and Dal and his wing were celebrating the event. It was a good thing; but it was an ominous sign that the destruction of a single aircraft should receive such acclaim."

He was right, of course, although his statement was not wholly correct. While 401's victory was the first jet shot down by the British Commonwealth forces, two had already been claimed by the USAAF – one by an Eighth Air Force pilot as early as 28 August 1944, and one by a Ninth Air Force fighter on 2 October, three days before this success. But this would be of little concern to Rod Smith; he had just fired his guns at another aircraft for the last time.

The above reports seem fairly straightforward and conclusive, so where did the controversy spring from? When the then Flt Lt Hedley 'Snooks' Everard wrote his autobiography *A Mouse in my Pocket*, which was published in 1988, he presented a somewhat different view of the engagement:

"Conditioned by years of searching empty skies, I became aware of a moving speck ahead and below my flight path. It was approaching rapidly and as I radioed this information to my comrades, the wary bandit half rolled into a vertical dive. A similar manoeuvre and my Spit was screaming for the deck about 800 yards behind the unrecognizable aircraft. A glance at the airspeed indicator confirmed that I had exceeded the maximum safe flying speeds for Spitfires. Although the flight controls stiffened up alarmingly, I pursued my prey whose German markings were now visible. When it appeared that the target and I would become two smoking craters in the blurred countryside, the invader commenced his pull-out. It became evident that I must pull-out of the dive more sharply to get within firing range. I 'blacked-out' as the excessive gravity forces buffeted my aircraft. As vision returned my aircraft gave a sudden lurch. Ahead the strange twin-engined fighter filled my gunsight. Soon cannon strikes were seen in the right engine which immediately streaked dense white smoke. A barely controllable skid in my aircraft eased as I decelerated rapidly. A horizontal distance of some 100 yards separated our two aircraft when I glimpsed another Spitfire 200 yards astern pouring cannon fire into the crippled Hun.

In rapid succession three other Spits made high speed passes, all registering strikes on the now flame streaked fighter. As the last Spitfire began its attack the German pilot tumbled out of his cockpit. Although we were about 700 feet above the ground, which is marginal altitude for safe fighter bail-outs, the victim's parachute failed to open. Over my shoulder I saw both he and his burning aircraft hit the ground. The Nijmegen Bridge loomed ahead of me and in minutes I limped into our airfield narrowly avoiding a crash landing. Both wings of my Spit were wrinkled and I knew it would never fly again.

At a long hectic debriefing it was recorded that we had shot down the first jet-propelled aircraft by British Forces. To remember this unique occasion we attack pilots agreed to share the kill and each claimed a one fifth victory. We learned that evening that an American Mustang escort fighter had destroyed a similar ME 262 a few days earlier."

Readers will no doubt compare this description with the combat reports submitted at the time – particularly Everard's own. How this all came to cause considerable distress to Rod will be recounted later.

Following the destruction of the Me 262 the squadron returned to bombing activities, moving as already noted to Volkel on 14 October where the metalled runway would be more suitable for autumnal flying than the grass surface at Rips. Ten days later the squadron was despatched to England to attend APC at Warmwell to update on latest bombing and strafing techniques, and here it remained until 4 November, when the return flight to Volkel was undertaken. At once operations commenced again, but time was nearly up for Rod, and on 21 November his second tour ended. By now he had flown for 1,150 hours, 15 minutes, and of these 470 hours, 25 minutes, had been while on operations. With thirteen and one shared victories to his credit in aerial combat he was placed sixteenth on the list of Canadian top-scorers. Three days after handing over the squadron, the award of a Bar to his DFC was published in the *London Gazette*. It read:

Since being awarded the Distinguished Flying Cross, Squadron Leader Smith has completed numerous sorties against the enemy. In four days he achieved the remarkable feat of destroying seven enemy aircraft. As squadron commander this officer led 412 Squadron on six missions in three days during which period it destroyed 27 enemy aircraft and damaged nine others. This was accomplished during the enemy's persistent efforts to destroy bridges in the Arnhem and Nijmegen area which were vital to our ground forces.

CHAPTER ELEVEN

HOME

Posted home to Canada, Rod arrived at the Report Depot at Lachine on 22 December where he stayed over the Christmas period, before progressing to 2 AC at Winnipeg. Here he was to serve until the start of June 1945 with one small break when he spent three weeks at 4 Service Flying Training School, Saskatoon. However whilst here he experienced the beginnings of postwar financially-motivated bureaucracy, when an attempt was made to have his acting rank as a squadron leader removed since he was no longer commanding a squadron. The same was happening at this time to Sqn Ldr W.G.Dodd, another notable RCAF fighter pilot. Winnipeg opposed the intention vigorously, reporting that the jobs these two were now doing required a Squadron Leader rank to provide the necessary authority. The commanding officer of 126 Wing had also recommended strongly that Rod should retain his acting rank in recognition of his outstanding service. Winnipeg reported that this matter had coloured the thinking of both pilots who had been considering remaining in regular service with the peacetime RCAF, but now wished to be released as soon as possible.

Although the result was that his acting rank was permitted to be retained, the matter had obviously upset Rod deeply, for whilst still planning a future in aviation, it was no longer his intention to remain in the RCAF, and he sought early release. Although the war with Germany had ended on 8 May, that with Japan was still continuing without an obvious early conclusion. Nevertheless, plenty of aircrew were available, and many of those veterans of the European fighting who wished to return to civilian life could be accommodated. Hence on 4 June he was posted to 6 Release Centre at Regina, from where he was discharged two days later.

His intention now was to become involved in aeronautical engineering, and to that purpose he entered McGill University, Montreal, almost at once, from where he would graduate with a Batchelor of Engineering degree during 1949. His connection with the air force had soon been renewed, however, for in November 1946 he joined the RCAF Auxiliary, where he rejoined 401 Squadron – now known as 401(P) Squadron (Aux) 'City of Westmont'; the original 401 had been disbanded in Germany in 1945. With this new unit he did, however, still retain his acting rank as squadron leader.

With the coming of peace the rundown of Canada's once-mighty air force had been rapid in the extreme. By the end of 1945 thirty-five of the forty-four operational squadrons had been stood down, the remaining nine all having been disbanded by June 1946. Meanwhile a peacetime establishment had been set of 16,000 regular servicemen, backed by 4,500 auxiliaries and 10,000 reserves. Provision was made for the formation of eight regular squadrons and fifteen auxiliary units, the latter initially providing all the air defence and attack capability. This was not as bizarre as it may first appear, for the latter were almost entirely formed of experienced wartime aircrew during the initial period. Even before the last of the wartime units had disappeared, the first seven auxiliary units had begun forming, six of them to be equipped with fighter aircraft.

The problem which immediately arose was that such aircraft were no longer available in Canada, requiring orders to be placed for new aircraft. Initially North American P-51D Mustangs were ordered from the USA, followed by De Havilland Vampire F.3 jet aircraft from the UK. In the first instance however, the new units had to make do with the large supplies of Harvard trainers left over from the Commonwealth Air Training Scheme. Postwar austerity was already beginning to be felt, however, for at the end of 1946 the newly-agreed establishment of the regular RCAF was reduced to 12,735.

By the time that Rod had completed his studies at McGill, he had decided that the world of aviation no longer appeared to offer good opportunities, and immediately upon his graduation he commenced new studies when he entered Osgoode Hall Law School in Toronto. The move to Ontario required by this change in focus made it virtually impossible for him to stay with 401 Squadron, and in January 1950 he transferred to the locally-based 400 'City of Toronto' Squadron, which like 401 was flying Vampires but at Downsview airfield. Initially it was the official view that he could not be carried on the strength of his new unit as a supernumerary squadron leader – or even as a flight lieutenant – and at the end of 1949 he was informed that if he wished to transfer it would have to be in the much more junior rank of flying officer. To this he acceded, but once again officialdom was confounded by those who appreciated his qualities, and the transfer was actually made to become a supernumerary flight lieutenant.

It was good fortune therefore that when in November 1950 a new 411 Squadron was to be formed at the same base, and which again was to be Vampire-equipped, it was Rod who was selected as commanding officer with a strongly-recommended promotion from flight lieutenant direct to acting wing commander coupled with a promotion in his substantive rank to squadron leader. In September 1952 a further promotion to substantive wing commander followed; he had been more than vindicated, at last.

All these units also retained Harvards for practice flying and general 'hack' use, and on 19 May 1951 he undertook a special very long trip in Harvard 3324. Initially he flew to Vancouver and back, then to North Bay, Kapuskasing, Armstrong, Winnipeg, Rivers, Regina. Lethbridge, Penticton, Vancouver, Pont Bay, Vancouver, Penticton, Lethbridge, Regina, Winnipeg, Armstrong, Kapuskasing, North Bay and home to Toronto. In total during this trip he had spent thirty-two hours and ten minutes in the air.

Sadly, however, this was all about to end, for during 1953 Rod and a fellow pilot were on foot on the airfield when a Vampire opened to full throttle just as they were passing the tail, Rod taking the full force of the jet efflux to the right side of his head with disastrous impact on his hearing. Clearly, this made it impossible for him to continue flying, and in the first instance he was transferred to 14 OP Wing, which was also Toronto-based. He applied for transfer from the auxiliary to the supplementary reserve, but the medical board which he was then obliged to attend received the report: "Wg Cdr Smith has developed perceptive deafness of the right ear, to a degree where hearing has been almost completely lost. The ENT Specialist believes the condition to be permanent and progressive." The result of this damning report was that he was recommended not for the transfer he was seeking, but for release from the service on medical grounds. He therefore departed the RCAF for the last time at the start of 1954.

The following year saw him complete his legal studies with a Barrister-at-Law degree and a call to the Ontario Bar. In

1954 he joined the firm of Lawrence, Shaw & McFarlane in Vancouver, being called to the British Columbia Bar.

Rod's career as a barrister was to be a notably successful one. In 1964 he moved to join Campney & Murphy, becoming a partner in this firm two years later. He was to remain in this role until his retirement in 1989, having held the office of chairman of the Civil Justice Section of the British Columbia Branch of the Canadian Bar Association for two years, and having been member of various other sections of the association. Unknown to many of his colleagues he also devoted considerable amounts of his spare time to the legal aid system, assisting those who could not afford normal legal representation and advice.

His connection with flying had been maintained during this time, and he had become an active and committed member of both the Royal United Services Institute of Vancouver, and of the Canadian Fighter Pilots Association. Indeed, from 1961-1962 he was president of the former, whilst from 1983-1987 he held a similar post at the head of the Pacific chapter of the latter.

Dale Kermode, an old colleague of Rod's, provides a personal view of him at this stage of his life:

"I clearly recall the first time I ever met Rod, at Campney & Murphy, soon after I arrived on 1 October 1975. Urbane. Distinguished. Courteous. And beneath the affable surface, there was scrutiny…

If you passed the character test, he was a very loyal friend. Fools were not suffered gladly; those with questionable moral standards, even less.

If you were on the wrong side of Rod Smith, it would be your fault, not his. If you were his friend, you knew you were honoured.

From Rod I learned, and remembered, the following:

– Do not try and bullshit Rod, or a brief withering remark or circumspect stare would quickly follow. Honesty is always the better course. Be sure that the mind has moved, before the mouth does.

– When writing letters, or briefs, or anything that must occupy the mind and time of others, eliminate all redundancies.

– Martinis must be served very cold, and very dry, preferably commencing at an hour nearer noon than midnight, and while on a seagoing vessel.

Now, just a couple of stories.

As a young bearded new associate of his, Rod invited me to join him for lunch at the club. I did not fit the visual mould. I respected Rod for not being concerned with that. First, to the anteroom for the world's best bread, slathered in butter. Numerous gentlemen (as the members all then were) stopped to say hello, and Rod introduced them all to me. Then to the main dining area. Rod asked if I wished to go to the washroom first. I said no. Throughout lunch, there were many introductions. At the end, I did go to the washroom. In the mirror, I saw a grotesquely large dollop of butter was hanging from my beard, near to where it should have, but did not enter my mouth. Neither Rod nor I spoke of the discomfort he must have felt, presenting me to his peers over the previous 90 minutes or so, looking like I had just eaten from a trough.

And then there was his 'vessel'. Meticulous. Rod gave me the ultimate honour of commanding it as it moved the last few feet into its mooring at RVYC, after my wife and I had spent a weekend with him on it. I took my task seriously. My job was to provide gentle reverse as required to eliminate forward motion as it berthed. We had entered his covered moorage. Rod was on the dock, getting ready to secure the lines. I was gently reversing as required. Rod gave me a brief affirmative glance that assured me I was performing the job well. Suddenly, he looked at me aghast as the diesel engine started to roar, and the vessel moved to full reverse. My God, what was happening? I was about to fail in the one assignment given to me by the vessel's astute commander. Rod leapt back on to the boat and seized the controls. I felt awful. I had let him down.

Thankfully, we soon found out that the netting he had put up to stop the birds from hanging around and doing their thing on the vessel, had caught the throttle control on the flying bridge. As the boat moved forward, the throttle moved back….

I do not mourn Rod's Passing, or the manner of it. To the end, I know he would have remained rational, logical and considerate of others, after reflecting on a full and rewarding life, fully satisfied that there is no hereafter, and that this is it."

PART TWO

RETROSPECTIVE

Increasingly, Rod became deeply interested in the history of World War II and of aviation generally. He was to read deeply and to attend many seminars of fighter pilots, usually in the United States. An avid reader and a profuse letter writer, he was to become involved in a number of extremely enlightening correspondences, sometimes over a considerable period of time, and on occasion with people notable within the world of aviation. Some of these exchanges were of much import, and a selection of the most interesting follow. They all demonstrate Rod's great knowledge of the subject, and above all the analytical, well-argued cases he was able to present – aided beyond doubt by his legal training and experience. On occasion his erudition seems to have caused some obvious discomfort to his 'opponents'.

The Battle with Bee

In *Aeroplane Monthly* for September 1993, the well-known fighter and test pilot, Wg Cdr R.P.'Bee' Beamont (right), presented an article in the second of a series entitled *Tangmere Summer*. Rod wrote a long letter to Bee which was to be the start of an extended – and at times slightly acrimonious – correspondence. It was not, however, the first time they had 'met' by letter.

During 1987 Rod had sought to assuage his passion for knowledge regarding matters aerodynamic by

seeking information from Bee, via a third party, regarding the performance advantages which might have been offered by the inclusion of an annular radiator in the construction of the Hawker Typhoon and Tempest fighters. On 3 July 1987 Bee wrote to the third party – one Frank MacLeod – in the following terms:

Chris Thomas has passed me your question and Rod Smith's profile – he certainly had a busy war! He was right about the Spit IX, but he would have liked the Tempest V in 1944 – there was nothing to touch it below 20,000 feet, except the Me 262!

On the Typhoon Napier annular radiator, I knew Mike Rodneys (who was in charge of Napier flight test) and he said it was worth "about 25 mph". The high figure could have been a 'one off' piece of optimism by Napier's PRO – they were trying to sell it to the air force!

On the Tempest it probably produced about 460 mph at rated altitude – compares with 470 on the leading edge wing radiator Tempest I and 438 on the Tempest V.

The latter was chosen for production since the radiator was already in production for the Typhoon, and since the performance was considered adequate – it certainly proved to be against 109Gs, 190s and the V-1 flying bombs.

Rod responded directly on 8 March 1988:

Dear Mr Beamont,

Thank you ever so much for writing, at the request of Chris Thomas to Frank MacLeod of North Vancouver on July 3rd last year concerning my questions about the increase of speed given to the Tempest and the Typhoon when fitted with the experimental annular radiator. I apologise for this very late reply.

A few months after joining a Spitfire (Vb) squadron in June 1941 I began to think, particularly when flying close line astern, that our aircraft were being held back too much by such things as the protruding tailwheel, the half-open wheel wells, the myriad little holes and bumps for the four .303 Brownings (themselves quite unnecessary in my view) and the protruding rivet heads on the after part of the fuselage. We never seemed to be able to catch a 109F or, later on, a 190, but they seemed able to catch us all too easily. I realized when I took the Pilots' Engine Handling Course at Rolls-Royce in March, 1942, that much of our trouble sprang from our single speed supercharger (Merlin 45) but that is another story. I began to be disappointed and amazed by any item on any fighter I flew which created drag and which I thought could have been avoided by a little more determination in detail design.

One day in the fall of 1941 my squadron (412 RCAF at

Wellingore, a satellite of Digby) received word that it was to convert to Typhoons. A few days later we received photographs and some specs. I was appalled when I saw the radiator. The brute size of the aircraft and its thick blunt wing would have been disturbing enough in themselves. I have always thought that for aeroplanes handsome does as handsome is. The Typhoon radiator looked to me like a giant bullfrog's throat with a hole in it.

It seemed the reverse of good aerodynamic form and to throw away all the speed advantage of a liquid-cooled engine over a radial in exchange for the drag of both. I was enormously relieved when our conversion was cancelled.

In February 1941, on a visit to Duxford, I saw a Mustang I. Although its wing and tail seemed angular, I was much taken by its general and detailed cleanliness, and I thought its radiator was in the only proper place – below and behind the pilot, and well ducted. Because it had an Allison, though, I mentally wrote it off!

In the spring of 1942 I saw some tropical Spitfire VBs and Cs at Renfrew waiting to be loaded on the USS *Wasp*. I was astounded by the ugly Vokes filter cowling under the nose. It seemed to me that the man who designed it didn't love aeroplanes very much. The VC was downright appalling. It had four cannons and a big bulge on the top of the wing to cover the belt feeds, and myriad little holes and bumps for its alternate four Brownings and fish-tail exhausts. With its grim 90 gallon 'slipper' tank (a dreadful thing) it looked as if it could hardly get airborne. Ten weeks later I found myself flying them in Malta. The extra pair of cannons were of course instantly removed on arrival at Malta (a single Merlin can't throw four cannons around the sky with any panache) and the four Brownings were removed from the VBs and literally dropped in the dust. There was no time for foolish theories of the Air Minister in Malta. Anyone who couldn't destroy any German aeroplane with two Hispanos didn't belong in the air force. The Tropical VBs and Cs were about 20 mph slower than the temperate VB, which was about 20 mph slower (and lower) than the 109F. However, they were good enough to intercept Ju 88s, and 109Fs that were foolish or trapped in close escort. Extra drag and single-speed blowers were more infuriating in Malta for me than anywhere else because they spoiled so many opportunities.

In the summer of 1943 I got a chance to fly a Typhoon IA, with 12 Brownings and partial rear vision. I was serving the usual six months-plus sentence as an OTU instructor at 55 OTU at Annan in Scotland, on Hurricanes. Paddy Woodhouse was our station commander and he got the Typhoon for two or three weeks, somehow, for his own amusement. I was intrigued by the Sabre, with its 24 cylinders, sleeve valves, its H shape and other intricacies, although it had a bad reputation at the time. I wasn't interested in the aeroplane but I must say it was beautifully finished, with all butt-joints, flush rivets and a paint-job worthy of one of his late Majesty's aircraft. I didn't let it swing on take-off but it seemed to move crabwise to the right for a short time as soon as it was airborne. It was simple to fly and child's play to land I thought. The engine was super-smooth, a great delight. Fortunately it behaved itself. Open fields in that area were not plentiful. I was disappointed that the airspeed, at about plus one boost and cruising r.p.m. (3,150?), was only about 270 low down. The Spitfire I at zero boost and 2,400 indicated 245 mph low down, at plus one boost, and the Spitfire IXB at plus two and 2,400 about 235 mph.

I have concluded that the low down cruising speed of an aircraft is a good indication of its drag, comparatively speaking, particularly if the type of supercharger is the same as in the aircraft being compared. I always look on my single flight in a Typhoon as an occasion where I took a beautifully designed engine for a ride in an aeroplane.

I did not know about the experimental annular radiator until many years after the war, although I was aware of the Tempest I with wing radiators in September 1943 when Philip Lucas brought it to the Fighter Leader School at Aston Down. He gave us a talk on the development of the Typhoon. After he finished I told him, facetiously, that the Tempest I was the first good looking monoplane Hawkers had ever made. He wasn't particularly amused. Actually, I rather liked the look of the Hurricane when it was just far enough away that its large size and wing thickness were not so noticeable. It looked like a Hart with its top wing blended down into the bottom one, and the Hart was very beautiful. I think that Sydney Camm lost his nerve when it came to cantilever monoplanes for a few years at least. But I am digressing.

The wing radiators of the Tempest I should be ruled out because they took up the space where the forward fuel tanks should be. I was amused (digressing again) by your comments on page 29 of your *Testing Years* concerning the deletion of the leading edge fuel tanks from the early Tempest Vs. What could those idiots in Air Ministry have been thinking about when the Mustang had showed up every other fighter aeroplane in its world badly on that score (and on almost all others!). I suppose some guy in Air Ministry must have been languishing in the old Air Exercises days and pre-Battle of Britain dogma. Even the final Tempest V didn't have nearly enough fuel for a 2,200 h.p. engine, in my view.

I realized from *Typhoon and Tempest at War* and William Green's books that the wing radiators gave about 30 mph over the Tempest V and I thought the annular radiator would give about the same. The 25 mph mentioned in your letter confirms this. This is an enormous deficiency; a commanding lead in the fighter war. Using the formula that speed varies as the cube root of the power, I have calculated that it would take about 400 more horsepower to get a Tempest V up to 460 from 435. This really means that at 435 the Tempest V was throwing away 400 h.p. just to bring its radiator along with it. I believe the Sabre was fully capable of pulling a fighter designed on Mustang principles to 500 mph. Incidentally, one snag with the annular radiator, which might well have been conclusive against it, was the need for an extension shaft. Michael J.E.Bowyer (not Chaz) says on page 100 of his *Interceptor Fighters* (1984) that *"Napier's annular radiator involved a 1ft long untried propeller shaft."* (Some German engines had optional extension shafts for annular radiators.)

I enjoyed your two books mentioned above enormously. I enjoyed very much your comments on rear-vision on pages 33 and 34 of *Total War*. Geoffrey Quill had the same difficulty as mentioned in his first book. At least you got (from your personal efforts I am sure) a beautiful rear-vision canopy. The poor old Spitfire got a handful about two months before the war ended, when it would have been almost a pleasure to have been shot at from behind – almost, but not quite! How could the Air Ministry ever think there would be no dog-fighting when they knew the stalling speeds of the Spitfire and Hurricane would not exceed about 80 mph? An SE 5 stalled at about 50 and a good 1930s sports car went faster than 80.

Your comments on pages 18 and 30-32 of *Testing Years* concerning national reluctance to call a spade a spade and reflecting the gunsight, respectively, were priceless. It was never necessary to tug one's forelock too vigorously in the presence of 'experts'.

I enjoyed your comments about *"one rather lurid and often-quoted biography"*. It was the translation you referred to, I suppose. If we both have the same autobiography in mind, I must say I wondered which war the author was fighting, particularly from the fall of 1944 onwards. It read like one of those war books that should have been subtitled: *"What Dangers I Braved and What Agonies I Suffered"*. The Hun pilots were so poorly trained at that time, for the most part, that with a Spitfire IXB (max 408 mph) and a baseball bat you could have clobbered almost all the Huns you were lucky enough to find. Their fighters were of course, hopelessly obsolescent, particularly the 109G, which was about as helpless as a stranded Beluga whale.

In your letter you said I would have liked the Tempest V in 1944. You were dead right. It could catch and kill any Hun below 20,000 feet easily (except the 262 as you pointed out) and its extra speed and four Hispanos must have made it deadly for strafing.

On October 14, 1944, two days after your engine dropped you in the bag, I brought my squadron (401) to Volkel and was pleased to see Johnny Heap there, CO of 274 Squadron. The

Tempest Wing was having engine failures and two or three glided into the aerodrome wheels up and fan almost stopped. One came right into our dispersal as we were just starting up for a show. It smashed two or three of our Spitfires and killed one of our groundcrew men. Once when I was acting wing leader, looking out the caravan window, I saw a Tempest, wheels up and fan turning slowly, approach the caravan. It touched down, dropped out of sight into a huge bomb hole, and burst into flames and a pillar of black smoke. It was the last moment of Johnny Heap. The year before I had succeeded him as a flight commander at OTU.

I was delighted recently to be given a 26-year-old copy of your *Phoenix Into Ashes*. I had not known of it, probably because your other books don't list your previous books. I particularly enjoyed your all too short accounts of the Battles of France and Britain. An almost over-weening modesty is about the only fault I find with your books, and a recent reviewer holds similar views. You sometimes use *"one"* when only the sentient pronoun will really do the job!

Because I was fundamentally a Spitfire man I am tempted to comment extensively on your views on the Hurricane set out on pages 46 to 48 of *Phoenix*. However, because this letter is already far too long, and because Britons have a national reluctance to hear a spade called a spade I understand, I will only point out my foregoing comments on drag and say that I have noticed that those who extol the virtues of the Hurricane and the Thunderbolt always stress their ability to take punishment. I'd rather dish it out than take it, although that may sound sadistic! I always liked the Hurricane in bad visibility though, because you had a lot more time to map-read.

If, after reading the immediate preceding paragraph, you ever feel like speaking to me you may get a chance in Washington in the last week of April. I noticed you had been invited to events there. I have been invited to a couple of them.

I had hoped to type this letter, as I am learning to type and word-process, and have the gear, but I have not reached that state yet. I want to write my air force memoirs.

Thank you again for sending your letter. Best regards. Yours sincerely, Rod Smith.

Bee was quite quick to respond to this epistle, and at this stage in friendly terms. On 28 March 1988 he wrote:

Dear Rod,
Thanks for your letter – it was nice to hear from an inmate of Volkel!

I know from experience that it is no use trying to talk to a Spitfire man about any other aeroplane – but I will attempt to dispel some of the mythology in your letter!

The radiator of the Typhoon was moved forward from its original 'Hurricane style' position to reduce drag, which it did.

In 1942/43 we used plus 2½ lbs boost for low level penetration which gave about 295 A.S.I. – a lot faster than Spit Vs, XIIs and 190s – and especially at full throttle which gave about 380 at sea level.

Spitfires looked pretty, but if you didn't want to get caught you needed a Typhoon!

"Sidney Camm lost his nerve on cantilever monoplanes"! Oh well, Hurricanes destroyed more e/a in B of B than Spitfires, guns, balloons, Home Guard and anything else handy. I liked them – easy to fly and land – excellent gun platform, and out-turn anything in the sky up to 20,000 ft.

I once had a set-to with Sqn Ldr Mike Lister Robinson flying a Spit 2 of 609, in my Rotol Mk I Hurricane – there was absolutely nothing he could do to get me off his tail, except dive away as I 'shot him down'.

"Tempest Vs didn't have nearly enough fuel" – none of ours had enough, but with our drop tanks I led several three-squadron wing sweeps from Newchurch to Emden and the Ruhr, which wasn't bad.

The Tempest V was really a superb fighter in 1944 – but as you say it could have been better with the Tempest I's leading edge radiator – I did my best!

Glad you liked my books – a new one at publishers Patrick Stephens – title *My Part of the Sky*. My 1939-45 diaries, out later this year.

Afraid I'm going to miss the Washington visit at end April. Going to the 'Gathering of Eagles' at Montgomery in June instead – should be fun. Sorry I'll miss meeting you – we'd have had a lot to talk about. Very best wishes to you, Bee Beamont

P.S. A major advantage was dive placard – 500 for the Typhoon and 545 on the Tempest, both with good roll rate left.

A 190 tried to get away over Cleve one day in October 1944, by a rolling vertical dive – I caught him with one burst, at 510 according to my No 2. Try that in a Spitfire! (any Spitfire).

A gap of nearly five years followed, but during September 1993 Bee produced his article for *Aeroplane Monthly*, and this time Rod could not resist letting fly with something of a broadside dated 1 October 1993 – and this time fully word-processed:

Dear Bee,

In your article which appeared in the September issue of *Aeroplane Monthly*, the second of your *Tangmere Summer* series, you said three things about the Mustang that seemed quite wrong to me and I would like to point them out to you.

Before I begin I should perhaps remind you that in 1987 you very kindly answered, through a friend, some queries I had about the effect of Napier's experimental annular radiator on the speed of the Typhoon and Tempest V. In March of 1988 I thanked you in a long letter in which I digressed to tell you how relieved I was when, in 1941, I learned that my Spitfire squadron's slated re-equipment with Typhoons had been cancelled. You responded with a very interesting letter which you began by saying that you knew from experience it was no use trying to talk to a Spitfire pilot about any other aeroplane! In actual fact, my love for the Spitfire, though ever enduring as regards the Mark I, began to wane with the Mark V and reached its nadir with the Tropical V. It was rekindled with the Mark IX but nearly all the credit was due to Rolls-Royce.

Turning to your *Tangmere Summer* article, my first point and one I could never let pass, concerns the following paragraph:

"It [the Mustang] could get as far as Berlin – although, as a fighter pilot was quoted as saying at the time, "Who the hell would want to do that?"

I would have thought you would be one of the last persons to sanction or appear to sanction a statement like that. The motto of the Royal Artillery, oddly enough, is the perfect response to it. If the paragraph was meant as hyperbole or facetiousness it didn't come across to me that way. No one could ever have doubted that when the Fortresses headed for Berlin (or anywhere else in the German hinterland for that matter) the Luftwaffe's day fighters would have had to come up in maximum strength, and a Battle of Britain in reverse would therefore be looming A chance to take part in it, flying a long range fighter which 'Bomber' Harris said *"fought like hell all the way"*, should surely have seemed like a fighter pilot's dream come true.

U.S. 8th Air Force Merlin Mustangs began to escort Forts to northwest Germany in mid December 1943 and by early March of 1944 to Berlin. We fighter pilots of the Royal Air Forces in Britain had been kept for years on such a pathetically short leash that Lille (and much later, with a miserable drop tank, Brussels) seemed like Ultima Thule to us. Wouldn't any one of our pilots worth the powder to blow him to hell jump through hoops for a chance to range far and wide over Germany proper? Wouldn't it simply have come down to whether he wanted to get in a real fight of not? In the months following December of 1943 quite a few 8th Air Force Mustang pilots were able to shoot down a dozen or two Huns apiece, which illustrates an intensity of combat hopelessly beyond our reach by that time.

I escorted Forts once, in February of 1944, when I was with 126 Wing at Biggin Hill on Spitfires, but it was only for the last part of their home stretch, by which time, no doubt, the 8th Air Force Mustang pilots were heading for their officers clubs and the surviving German fighter pilots were half drunk. I felt like a page whose knight, after a heavy day of battle, has gone off to a marquee for libations with his peers. Our own stamping ground, which had become a backwater sometime in 1943 thanks to the 8th Air Force, virtually dried up when the Merlin Mustangs got into full swing. Although we didn't know it at the time, we were victims of Portal's wholly unfounded and therefore senseless declaration that any long range fighter would be inherently and irremediably inferior to a short range one, a declaration which Churchill said *"closed many doors"* (and which I have taken to calling 'Portal's Curse'). I have noticed that in your books you have been consistently critical of the RAF's tolerance of low fuel capacity for its fighters.

My second point concerns your extreme criticism of the pilot's vision from the Allison Mustang. You said that though you had previously flown Hurricanes, Spitfires and Typhoons in combat, and also a number of other fighters, you had seldom flown one with *"such appallingly restrictive vision"*. You went on to say that *"the canopy seemed to consist of more metal than transparency"* adding up to *"totally inadequate combat vision"*, and that you were *"sure that it would never be accepted by the RAF for the combat role"*.

In fact, until mid 1943 the pilot's vision was very poor from all British, American and European fighters except the FW 190. This is commonly attributed to some early nineteen thirties theory that because the speed of the forthcoming monoplane fighters would be so high, fighter versus fighter combat would become a thing of the past. What puzzles me is that anyone who was in a position to conform with such a theory must have known that the stalling speeds of those monoplanes would only be about half as fast again as that of the SE 5 of 1917, and that the speed of any aircraft soon falls off to just above its stalling speed in a continued tight turn. The Japanese army and navy air forces were the only ones that rejected the theory. In 1940 they came up with all round vision for their 'Oscar' and 'Zero' respectively, and although their canopies were not one-piece their vision was infinitely better than that of any other contemporary fighter.

In any event the vision from the Allison Mustang can hardly have been as bad as you said it was. At least it had transparent panels on each side behind the head-armour (as had the Spitfire, the P-40, the early P-47 and the Me 109) so it (like them) was like a car with no rear window. Your beloved Hurricane, though, had no transparent panels behind its head-armour. So it was like a truck, having dreadfully limited vision to the rear.

As to your saying that you were sure the Allison Mustang would never be accepted by the RAF for the combat role because of its vision, I say it was a good thing the Americans weren't as inhibited as that. The first Merlin Mustang was the P-51B, and its vision was virtually identical to the Allison Mustang's. (I include the P-51C with the B because they were identical). The first Mustang with all around vision, the P-51D, didn't arrive on the scene until March or April of 1944. Because the P-51B began to escort Forts in mid December of 1943 it therefore carried the whole load for three or four months with the vision that you have criticized. Those months, which included 'Big Week' and the first escorts to Berlin, encompassed the Mustang's most glorious days, the Hun falling *"like Lucifer, never to hope again"*. As for the RAF, it received about a quarter of the P-51Bs produced and it did use them in the combat role, though it fitted them with Malcolm hoods which gave considerably improved but far from all around vision.

My third and final point concerns your saying that the maximum diving speed ('Vne') of the P-51D was 485 mph IAS, which you contrasted with the 454 mph IAS of the Tempest V. I had always understood that the Mustang's Vne was 505 mph IAS, so I checked a wartime USAAF pilot training manual for the P-51D and found that it gave that figure as the Vne up to 5,000 ft. I also checked a USAF postwar flight handbook and found the same figure but the 5,000 ft limit had been raised to 9,000 ft. I then telephoned to my friend Edward Horkey (who at age 24 was the aerodynamicist for the Mustang and now lives in Phoenix) and he confirmed the 505 figure. I don't have the pilot's notes for the Tempest so I don't know what altitude it was permitted to hold 545, but I have calculated that the Mach number for this figure would be .86 at 10,000 ft and an impossible 1.06 at 20,000 ft. I therefore assume that the permitted altitude wouldn't be great because a Mach number of .86 seems very high for an aircraft with a large radiator under its chin, but I and my calculations could be wrong of course. In any event the Mustang seems to have been remarkable with regard to Vne, because it was the first production aircraft to reach and exceed the 500 figure and it appeared more than two years before the Tempest.

Although I only flew a Mustang twice (a P-51D, in 1951, when I was in the Auxiliary in Toronto), I can say that ranging in it far and wide over southern Ontario with no fuel worries, cruising 25 mph faster than a Spitfire having the same engine, and dogfighting with a Vampire and another Mustang, confirmed all that I had heard and read about it.

As for your beloved Tempest, I admit that for medium and low altitude fighting and ground strafing it was superb, but it didn't get to squadrons until the late spring of 1944. I also admit I would rather have had it than the Spitfire from Normandy on, but it didn't get to the continent until the end of September. As to both of those aircraft however, I find it hard not to conclude that the

RAF's putting up, after mid 1941, with an internal fuel capacity of only 85 gallons for the Spitfire's 1,200+ horsepower, and three years later accepting one of only 132 gallons for the Tempest's 2,200 horsepower, demonstrated not just an acceptance of false doctrine but a slackening of the will to go first class.

With best regards, Rod Smith

Following this epistle, a degree of icyness entered Bee's reply, which was dated 8 October 1993:

Dear Rod,

I was surprised at the tone of your letter of 1 Oct.

In your RAF service you obviously did not acquire their sense of humour. You are in a minority of one among the many responses to my *Aeroplane Monthly* articles in interpreting my 'Berlin' quote as serious!

And I don't need a lecture on the great achievements of the 8th AF P-51s in their courageous and vital long range bomber escorts which turned the tide of the air battle for Germany – I have often mentioned this in my writings.

Nor do I need to be told about the British short range fighter design philosophy which was of course based on the vital need to defend the UK. We had no spare resources to consider any future possibility of extending the war across Europe.

It was a good thing that USA came in when they did – late – and were able to develop the British requirement and specification Mustang (it was not a US original spec) to do what the 51s later did so well.

You are wrong about the early series Berlin aircraft. The B model did have the original (A model) cockpit vision, but the C model (in RAF service) had the British designed Cobelle bubble canopy which was a great improvement.

And I don't need a lecture about Hurricane vision either after a combat tour on them in France and the B of B!

You certainly could not see adequately through the canopy but you could slide it back and look all around behind. We did in the B of B even at 20,000, and doing so saved me from 109s often – and lost me my goggles on one occasion.

The briefed 485 IAS for 'my' P-51D was probably a Tangmere limitation pending clearance of makers placard speed by A & AEE, Boscombe Down – but that does not affect the argument.

The Tempest V Mach set was shown to be higher than the Vampire!

You are also incorrect about the Tempest operations. 150 Wing began operations over Normandy, Belgium, Holland, and later Germany, from Newchurch, right through from May '44 until we moved out to 2nd TAF (Grimbergen and then Volkel) in Sept. Air superiority and especially ground-attack with excellent results.

The trips to Germany were daylight bomber-escorts with drop tanks and averaged 600 miles and 2 hrs 15 mins – not a bad cruise speed for those days, and not the *"pathetically short reach"* which you ascribe to all British fighters.

Finally you did not check your facts in claiming the Mustang was the first to reach and exceed 500. The Typhoon IB (series production) was cleared to 500 Vne in its introduction to RAF service in September 1941.

Regards, Roland Beamont

Not long after this exchange, Bee produced a two-part eulogy of the Hurricane for *Aeroplane Monthly*, the second part of which appeared in the February 1994 issue entitled *Hurricane Testing*. This time Rod could not resist having his say on the subject which he had refrained from pursuing in his March 1988 article. Now, however, he did not write to Bee direct, but to the editor of the magazine, Richard Riding, enclosing a seven-page critique; copies of both were passed to Bee at the same time.

The result of this was that Rod was invited to turn his letter into an article for the magazine entitled *In Defence of the Spitfire*, which subsequently appeared in the August 1995 issue. Bee would respond immediately, in a letter which the magazine printed in the October 1995 issue. The controversy was steadily hotting up, for in September, meanwhile, another article defending the Spitfire appeared, entitled *Spitfires: A Test Pilot's Defence*. This had been prepared by Rod's great friend Alex Henshaw, in consultation with another friend, Jeffrey Quill; both were, of course, well-known ex-test pilots, with whom Rod had been corresponding for some time.

Under pressure of this assault, Bee was persuaded to produce a final letter which appeared in the issue of December 1995, after which the matter was laid to rest. The articles referred to have not been repeated here as they appeared in the various issues of the magazine, since those interested should be able to access them in back copies without undue difficulty. However, the various letters, including that from which Rod's article was developed, are set out chronologically here:

To Richard Riding, Editor, *Aeroplane Monthly*, 18 March 1994

Dear Sir,

Re: Roland Beamont's Article – *Hurricane Testing*
(Your February 1994 issue)

I enclose a seven page letter to you dated yesterday taking issue with certain comparisons in Roland Beamont's above article which seem to mark the Spitfire down (to say the least) and which I am sure are not sound. I hope you will publish this letter, or (considering it is too long for your Skywriters page and so late in arriving) such parts of it as you may see fit.

I have very much enjoyed reading Bee's books but not all his articles. I also took issue with three points in the section of his *Tangmere Summer* article which dealt with the Mustang and appeared in your September issue. My first impulse was to write a letter to you about those three points for your Skywriters page but I decided to write to Bee instead. His reply showed we were on different wavelengths. The Spitfire and the Mustang are the two wartime fighters I respect and admire the most. Though I only flew a Mustang twice it lived up to its billing. I once flew an early Typhoon, mainly because I was intrigued by the design of its engine. Bee seems very caught up on Hawker aircraft, understandably to some degree of course. But if he can criticize the competition I should be able to criticize Hawkers....

The study of WWII aircraft, engines, guns and air battles has been a pastime of mine for decades. I was a fighter pilot and I am writing my memoirs with a stronger than usual technical flavour. I enclose a profile I wrote in 1984 to a format of Pat Barnard's, for the Douglas Bader Foundation, which shows a qualification to write about fighters; moreover, in 1949 I graduated from McGill University in mechanical engineering with additional advanced math with a view to postgraduate studies in aeronautics. I took law instead however and practised here in Vancouver until I retired four years ago.

Let me assure you I am not blinkered about the Spitfire. I have many criticisms with regard to its development after 1940 though not its handling. I feel that trying to push it through 1941 and half 1942 without cleaning it up, giving it a two-speed supercharger drive and increasing its fuel effectively was simply and predictably exchanging success for failure and throwing boundless opportunities away. I would have switched to a Merlin Mustang in early 1944 like a shot, though if I had known the RAF ones were not going to be kept constantly in the mainstream with the Fortresses I might have had second thoughts....

Yours truly, Rod Smith

Same addressee and heading, dated 17 March 1994:

In his above article comparing the first marks of the Hurricane and Spitfire in the Battle of Britain, Roland Beamont made some surprising errors which gave a highly distorted and unfavourable picture of the Spitfire. I feel they should be corrected, if only because 'Bee' is so well known as a test pilot, Typhoon squadron commander and Tempest wing leader that what he says may be taken to be unchallengeable by persons without a personal experience or knowledge to the contrary.

Bee flew Hurricanes in the Battles of France and Britain. I missed both those battles, having been only seventeen when the war began, but as a consolation I flew in the defence of Malta in 1942, in effect a miniature but intensely concentrated Battle of Britain. I flew Spitfires from the spring of 1941 to almost the end of 1944 and though I never flew a Hurricane operationally I instructed at a Hurricane OTU between tours. Bee flew one operational sortie in a Spitfire which was entirely uneventful.

Everyone acknowledges that the Hurricane was essential in the Battle of Britain, if only because there were not enough Spitfires, but not many realize how slow the Hurricane was and the ramifications of that. It could catch Heinkel 111s and Dornier 17s (though that was no great feat, Bomber Harris having said that even a bad fighter was bound to catch the average bomber). It was accordingly given that job for the most part, and while doing it could frequently attack Me 109s and 110s that were unfortunate enough to be tied down in close escort positions. Everyone also acknowledges that Hurricane pilots deserved much honour. Attacking a heavily escorted bomber was very dangerous, and facing much faster enemy fighters day after day was terribly nerve-wracking.

Turning to Bee's errors, the most surprising was his saying that the Vne (the maximum permissable diving speed) of the Spitfire and the Hurricane *were the same at 400 mph IAS*. In fact the Spitfire's Vne was 470. The Hurricane's was either 380 or 390, but even accepting Bee's 400 figure there would still have been an astonishing difference of 70 mph between the two aircraft. Of more practical significance the Vne of the Me 109E was 469 mph, effectively the same as the Spitfire.

Bee also said that the Spitfire was about 30 mph faster than the Hurricane but in fact it was about 45 mph faster. Both were powered by the Merlin III so their top speeds were reached around 18,000 ft. The Spitfire's top speed in Battle of Britain trim was about 350 mph (not the 367 or 362 that used to be put forth) and the Hurricane's was about 305 (not the 310 to 325 still put forth). In his famous despatch Dowding gave the 305 figure as the average of Fighter Command tests on five Hurricanes. The 45 mph difference between the two types is confirmed by a comparison of their cruising speeds low down at the normal cruise settings for the Merlin III (zero boost and 2,400 rpm). Under those conditions the Spitfire's IAS was 245 mph and the Hurricane's 195. The apparent difference of 50 mph reduces to 44 mph after correcting for their respective pitot head position errors. Though I took lots of maths and physics at university I am only an amateur aerodynamicist, but because both aircraft had the same engine I calculated with some confidence that it was not aerodynamically possible for the Hurricane to narrow the gap at any greater heights or power settings. Of more practical significance, the Me 109E's top speed was about the same as the Spitfire's so the gap between it and the Hurricane was also about 45 mph. This was of enormous significance because a lead of 10 mph was a great advantage, one of 20 was usually commanding, and one of 30 or more indicated obsolescence in the slower aircraft.

The very great differences in top speed and Vne meant that the Hurricane could never be in the same class as the Spitfire and the 109. Those differences were mainly the result, of course, of the Hurricane's very thick wing which had a very blunt leading edge to boot (reminding one of the thick high-lift wings of the Fokker trimotors of the 1920s). Consequently the Hurricane had to rely almost entirely on its turning ability to survive against the 109, endlessly crossing its 'T' when attacked by it. A competent pilot not tied down in close escort had no fear of the Hurricane, being able to attack or evade repeatedly and at will.

Bee went on to say that while the Hurricane could be "corkscrew" dived at full bore, vertically and with full aileron and nothing would break either then or in the subsequent strong pullout, in that manoeuvre there was:

A strong likelihood of pulling the wings off a Spitfire – many did, and this was a clear incentive to the Spitfire pilot not to do it; but if circumstances included a 109 on your tail this presented a dilemma.

(Likelihood means probability!) A corkscrew dive was the best way to end an attack on a bomber escorted by 109s, or to escape from a number of 109s bouncing from different directions at the same time, and it was as natural as breathing for a Spitfire pilot to go into one of those circumstances. He had no thought whatever of his wings coming off and he knew that the 109's ailerons hardened up in a dive so much more quickly than his own that it wouldn't try to corkscrew with him for long. In the corkscrew dives that I did and saw others doing in Spitfires in Malta in 1942 (we called them "downward aileron turns") I never saw a 109 that kept corkscrewing for even one full rotation.

Bee seems to have had his mind on the wing failures that happened to some Mark V Spitfires in early 1942, following the installation and improper loading of heavy items of operational equipment in the rear fuselage throughout 1941. This caused the centre of gravity to creep back and reduce longitudinal stability to the danger point, so that too quick a pullout from a dive could cause the aircraft to do a pitch-up (nose and tail suddenly reversing positions), something no wing could stand if the dive speed was very high. Things like this happened in the best-regulated aircraft firms. Tails began to come off the fine new Me 109Fs in early 1941, and just after wings began to come off Spitfire Vs in early 1942, tails began to come off Typhoons, all with fatal results to their pilots as a rule.

In any event, because pitch-up troubles did not appear in Spitfires until more than a year after the Battle of Britain, Spitfire pilots in that battle had no reason whatever not to do a corkscrew dive or a fast pullout from one. In his autobiography Jeffrey Quill described the pitch-up problem with the Spitfire V, as well as the simple solution to it – fitting a six pound 'bob-weight' in the elevator control system and reducing the Vne to 450 mph IAS (which became standard for all Spitfires from 1942 on). It was not a question of wing strength; the Spitfire's wing though the thinnest of all the wartime fighters, was immensely strong. If a Hurricane pilot had ever tried to dive his aircraft to the speed a Spitfire could survive to he would have exchanged his mount's thick blunt wings for some graceful feathered ones long before he reached it.

Bee went on further to say:

The Hurricane's gun platform stability was much superior to the Spitfire's and the 'pippa' could be held spot-on in... combat manoeuvres far better than with the Spitfire, whose low directional damping tended to result in 'hosing' rather than precision shots.

That sounds like sheer revisionism. An uninformed person would infer from it that the Spitfire, instead of being far and away the top-scoring British fighter of the war, had rarely been able to shoot down enemy aircraft. I did some practice dogfighting in a Hurricane and I never found it was the slightest bit easier to hold the sight on with it than with a Spitfire, in fact I would put it the other way round. As for *hosing* rather than *precision* shots, among fighter pilots the Spitfire was famed and beloved above all other types for its beautiful response to its controls. If you could hit with any fighter you could hit with a Spitfire. If any pilot in the three Spitfire squadrons I was in had said that he had got on the tail of an enemy aircraft but had failed to shoot it down because his aircraft was an imperfect gun platform he would have been sent to tow drogues in Lysanders and laughed off the aerodrome.

Bee also said:

...Hurricanes, used in larger numbers and mainly at the bomber streams and escorts below 20,000 ft, saw much more of the action in the Battle of Britain and achieved a clear majority of the successes.

The *saw much more of the action* proposition is very doubtful because most of the action was fighter-versus-fighter. The numbers of Spitfires and Hurricanes actually shot down, 718 altogether, were fairly proportionate to their original strengths, and more than twice as many German fighters were actually shot down as bombers, 826 to 388 (leaving out the 59 Stukas shot down on the fringes in the beginning). And I wouldn't accept the *clear majority of the successes* proposition either unless I knew massive research had been done in which every RAF combat report had been closely examined and matched against the Luftwaffe Quartermaster General's loss records. The proposition could well be true though, considering that there were about half as many Hurricanes again as Spitfires, that almost 40% of the German fighters shot down were Me 110s, and that even a fine fast twin like the 110, having no business fighting against singles, was almost as easy meat for a Hurricane as for a Spitfire when it was tied down in close escort.

Bee went on further to say that when he got on the tail of Michael Robinson's Spitfire II with a Hurricane in late 1940:

I had no difficulty staying in the slot behind his tailwheel... The demonstration convinced us all... that our Hurricanes (and our knowledge of them) were, in the prevailing circumstances, much safer for us!

I never had any difficulty staying on the tail of a Hurricane with a Spitfire. Once the pilot of either one got on the tail of the other he should have been able to stay there because the difference between their wing loadings was less than a pound and the Spitfire's wing gave nothing away in efficiency. As for being *much safer for us*, Hurricanes only had to turn inside 109s to be safe, not apparently Spitfires; but this was a thing Spitfires as well could do with perfect ease because the wing loadings of both of them were only 80% of the 109Es.

Finally, Bee, after acknowledging that the Hurricane's performance after 1940 was no longer adequate for the major air defence and air superiority roles in the West, went on to say:

But the Hurricane still continued to give good value worldwide in the campaigns where the latest and more powerful fighters were not available to the enemy.

Pilots who served overseas became cynical about the aircraft they were given, so I doubt that many pilots who flew the Hurricane overseas would agree it gave good value. Except as against the Fiat CR.42 and the Macchi 200, the Hurricane when on its own failed in every theatre, the drag of its thick blunt wing proving an insurmountable handicap. When a mere dozen Me 109Es of JG 26 came to Sicily for short periods in the early part of 1941 they devastated Malta's Hurricanes without losing one aircraft. 109Es easily overcame Hurricanes in Greece and Crete, and tiny numbers of them commonly frustrated our air operations over the Libyan desert. As for more powerful fighters being available to the enemy, the Zero and the Oscar both had less power than the Mark I Hurricane and a lot less than the Mark II but they quickly despatched both marks over Singapore, the Dutch East Indies, Malaya and Burma. The Hurricane's air combat swan song was heard over Colombo in Ceylon on April 5 of 1942, when 36 carrier-borne Zeros escorting 91 Vals and Kates shot down 21 of 35 Hurricanes scrambled to meet them, for the loss of one Zero and six Vals. Though most of the 35 Hurricanes had been scrambled too late, some of them with Zeros actually overhead, 30 of them were the powerful Mark IIs. An enemy aircraft which combined superior speed with tighter turning was the fighter pilot's ultimate nightmare.

Turning to the genesis of the Hurricane and of the Spitfire, both Sydney Camm and R.J.Mitchell have been said to have had genius, and rightly so. Camm's Hart and Fury biplanes of the latter twenties and early thirties and Mitchell's trophy-winning monoplanes of the same period were the most beautiful aircraft of their day, the leaders in a field where handsome does as handsome is. Even great designers occasionally fail or fall short of real success however. Mitchell had two failures (his S.4 of 1924 and his Type 224 of 1934) but fortunately they were both irrelevant to the war. Unfortunately Camm fell short of real success with his first two monoplane fighters, the Hurricane and the Typhoon, both of which failed to stay the course in the role they were designed for – air combat. He later admitted to embarking on the design of a monoplane with some fear, which probably accounts for both those aircraft having been too big and no doubt lay at the root of his choice of the thick blunt wings for them which proved so limiting to their careers. Making that choice for the Hurricane is difficult enough to justify because it was more or less a contemporary of the 109 and Spitfire, but making it for the Typhoon a full three years later is impossible to justify. (The Tempest was a Typhoon corrected late in the game, though it was formidable when it finally arrived.)

Anyone who thinks the Hurricane could look forward to any real future after the Battle of Britain should read Sholto Douglas's correspondence, beginning in January of 1941 (two months after he had taken over from Dowding) concerning the fighters to be chosen for that year. His remarks on the new and more powerful Mark II Hurricane (let alone on the Mark I) were devastating *"...not good enough... far below the 109 in speed... inferior in climb... seems clear cannot compete on anything like level terms with the enemy's fighters..."* He said the same remarks applied but with even greater force to the Mark I, adding that it was: *"inferior in all respects to the (Mark) II and would shortly become obsolete."* (He ended by saying that some of them would no doubt be useful overseas!)

By contrast the Spitfire was destined to remain a frontline fighter to the end of the war. The heart and essence of the achievement of Mitchell and his design team, to put it in one sentence, was in coming up with a fighter which, though weighing only a few hundred pounds more than the Me 109E, had 40% more wing area and yet unbelievably had no more drag if as much. Hence the priceless gift of tighter turning with at least equal speed. If the 109 was a cobra, the Spitfire was a cobra convertible to a mongoose, instantly and at will; for a 109 coming upon a Spitfire it was one pass and away, for a Spitfire it was one pass and stay no matter which one made the pass. (It is sad to reflect that in the spring of 1941, four years after Mitchell's death, this priceless gift went into eclipse for a year and a half upon the arrival of the new and cleaned up Me 109F, which turned out to be a lot faster then the new but not cleaned up Spitfire V – but that is another story.)

Yours truly, Rod Smith

Bee's response was not unexpected:

Sir,
In his *Defence of the Spitfire*, your contributor blends half-facts with mythology to support his curious condemnation of the Hurricane, but if he should read my Hurricane piece again (*Hurricane Testing*, February 1994 *Aeroplane*) he would find that it in no way claimed overall superiority of that aircraft in 1940.

Spitfire pilots love Spitfires and rightly so for they are beautiful to look at, and to fly – well, most of them; and they were in their various developments nearly always superior to, or at least on a par with, the best the enemy could produce.

But none of that is justification for denigrating and dismissing the Hurricane in the Battle of Britain, as is so often done by revisionist historians and, of course, some Spitfire pilots. Rod Smith dismisses my qualifications for expressing an opinion by saying that I only flew one *"entirely uneventful"* operation in a Spitfire. Quite so, but I did fly many hundreds of Hurricane operations in a two-year continuous operational tour, many of which were not so uneventful; and, after that, over 400 test flights on Hurricanes at the Hawker factory before going on to take part in handling evaluations on Spitfire Mk Vs, VIIIs, XIIs, XIVs, Seafire XVs, XVIs, 21s and 22s at various times at the Handling Squadron and later CFE. So I became a Spitfire fan myself, but it did not affect my objectivity in assessing Hurricanes in combat.

On other points which seem to have wound him up: many pilots were indeed killed when their Spitfire wings came off. I saw one happen, and he was in an "aileron-turning" dive at the time. No Hurricane ever failed in this way to my knowledge and its structural integrity was probably unique. Smith's reference to Typhoon structural failures is of course irrelevant.

And whatever the Luftwaffe deemed prudent to publish about their losses, it is an established fact that a significantly greater number of enemy aircraft were shot down in 1940 by Hurricanes than by Spitfires.

Never mind. Rod Smith's roseate memories of his superb Spitfire IX (in which he served with distinction later in the war) have probably coloured his judgement. No amount of wittering on about comparative Vnes (and a design Vne of 470 mph is not a practical operating limit if, as in the Spitfire Mk I, the ailerons became 'solid' around 400) and wing-loadings etc can ever alter the basic facts which are that although the Hurricane was slower than the Spitfire in the Battle of Britain it did not matter a damn when charging Heinkels, Dorniers and Ju 88s.

The Spitfire won the high-altitude war in 1940 on its own, and the Hurricanes won it with the help of Spitfires below 20,000 ft – but, and I admit it, it didn't look so pretty.

Roland Beamont

Rod's own response followed within days:

I would have thought Roland Beamont, in his letter responding to my article (*In Defence of the Spitfire*, August 1995 *Aeroplane*), would have condescended upon particulars more than he did.

He began by saying that revisionist historians and Spitfire pilots often denigrate and dismiss the Hurricane in the Battle of Britain. I have never come across anything like that, though I have occasionally heard and said myself that if all the Hurricanes had been Spitfires victory would have come more easily. I was born just too late to take part in that battle, and I was immensely pleased to become a Spitfire pilot fairly early in 1941. I would like to make one thing clear however; If in the summer of 1940 Mephistopheles, though refusing me a Spitfire had offered me a Hurricane instead, I would have accepted terms for the latter which would have made Faust look like one of the prefigured saints.

There is nothing wrong with criticizing one's own weapons fairly, even after victory. The euphoria of the Battle of Britain victory, however, seems to have spawned a tacit agreement not to look the Hurricane too closely in the mouth. As far as I know, my article was the first really close look to be published. It would never have been written, though, if I had not thought that Bee had grossly downgraded the Spitfire in his article (*Hurricane Testing*, February 1994 *Aeroplane*).

Two points in his article triggered me. One was that in a corkscrew dive at full bore there was a *"strong likelihood"* of pulling the wings off a Spitfire. The other was that the Spitfire's *"low directional damping tended to result in 'hosing' rather than precision shots"*. Both were nonsense, and the second sheer revisionism to boot.

Bee alleged that I *"dismissed his qualifications for expressing an opinion"* in three ways. The first was by pointing out that his one operational sortie in a Spitfire had been uneventful, the second by omitting his long and eventful two-year continuous operational tour in Hurricanes, and the third by omitting his Hurricane production testing and his evaluations on many aircraft, including a number of marks of Spitfire.

I don't think a long profile was called for. I did say at the beginning of my article that Bee flew Hurricanes in the Battles of France and Britain; it was appropriate for me, though, to point out that neither of us actually tangled with the Hun while flying the other's favourite aircraft. I also remarked on Bee's being so well known as a test pilot, Typhoon squadron commander and Tempest wing leader (the Typhoon reference showing he had more guts than I had!).

In response to my saying I would not accept Bee's proposition that Hurricanes achieved a clear majority of the successes in the Battle of Britain unless I knew that all combat reports had been closely checked against the Luftwaffe Quartermaster General's loss records, Bee said:

<u>*Whatever the Luftwaffe have deemed prudent to publish about their losses*</u> *it is an established fact that a significantly greater number of enemy aircraft were shot down in 1940 by Hurricanes than by Spitfires.* [underlining mine]

Bee doesn't seem to realise that the QMG worked for Goering (Milch in reality), not Goebbels, and that any publication of his records would have been of great value to the RAF. All Luftwaffe units had to notify him of their losses so that he could produce replacements.

At war's end a small Air Intelligence task force was dispatched to Germany to find records of losses. They were discovered in the QMG's office, although those for 1944 and most of 1945 were never found. Copies of those found were lodged in the Imperial War Museum and no serious historian impugnes them to my knowledge. The revelation in Churchill's memoirs that German aircraft losses for September 15 of 1940 were 56 instead of 183 was based on those records (though the disparity on that particular day was well above average).

Bee went on to say: *"Rod Smith's roseate memories of his superb Spitfire IX in which he served... later in the war have probably coloured his judgement."* Hardly. A Spitfire pilot never confuses his Mark IX days with his days on the early marks. Johnnie Johnson first flew a Mark IX after harrowing years in Mark Vs over France. He told me that when it lifted off the runway and pointed its nose skyward as a higher angle than he had ever experienced before he said to himself: *"I'll live".*

Bee remarked that although the Hurricane was slower then the Spitfire, in the Battle of Britain *"it did not matter a damn when charging Heinkels, Dorniers and Ju 88s"*. The faster aircraft could obviously charge sooner and more often, however. And in the third part of his *Tangmere Summer* article (October 1993 *Aeroplane*) Bee said that Ju 88s in 1940 *"often dived away from our Hurricanes"*.

The Spitfire's ailerons issue seems to have wound Bee up (he said the pulling-off-wings issue seemed to have wound me up). He said that a design Vne [referring to the Spitfire's 470 mph IAS] was not a *"practical operational clearance if it is limited by 'solid' ailerons above 350 as in the Spitfire I, a condition not experienced in the Hurricane all of which were cleared to 400 at the factory."*

Though a Mark I Spitfire's ailerons were firm at 350, a roll at that speed was still quite easy. They only began to get very heavy at 400, and at 450 (a realm beyond the Hurricane incidentally) they were much too heavy but could still give some control. They never became 'solid' but at 470 were very nearly so. More to the point, most pilots who flew a Bf 109 said its ailerons were virtually solid at about 400 mph and immovable beyond that, which squares with my experience when aileron turning downwards away from them.

Bee added that the stiffness condition was *"not experienced in the Hurricane all of which were cleared to 400 at the factory and dived to that and beyond as a matter of course operationally."* I dived a Hurricane to 400 once or twice, and found its ailerons getting a bit mushy at that speed. I did not realise I was going at least 10 mph above the aircraft's Vne. I had not read the Pilot's Notes for it, and I never imagined that the RAF's most numerous fighter in the Battle of Britain would have had a Vne so incredibly low. I actually felt nervous at 400 and was ashamed of myself. I recovered some of my self-esteem thirty years later when I read Bee's autobiographical *Phoenix into Ashes*, in which he said his production testing of Hurricanes included a dive to 400 mph *"with the whole thing seeming ready to burst at the seams"*.

As I got deeper into this letter I began to realize it was directed more at Bee than anyone else. I will send a copy to him.

Bee did not respond directly to this letter, perhaps because the further article by Alex Henshaw was practically upon him. He did respond to the latter – and obliquely to some of Rod's comments – in the concluding correspondence of this 'match' in December 1995:

Sir,
When invited to comment on *Spitfire: a Test Pilot's Defence, Aeroplane* September) I felt that nothing would be gained by adding to the flow of verbosity already given to the subject, but the subsequent mail and calls from the Hurricane lobby giving

strong support to my views has suggested that in fairness to them I should respond.

For over half a century the Spitfire 'club' have missed no opportunity, and indeed made many of their own, to feed the ever-grateful media with highly coloured accounts of the 'superiority' of the Spitfire, and the 'inferiority' of the Hurricane in the Battle of Britain, and the latter claim has never been justified by the facts.

Indeed, in his own article attacking mine the author has written to the effect that in one-on-one combat between a Spitfire and a Hurricane (presumably he meant Mk Is in each case) it was always the best pilot that won and not the best aircraft. In fact the only way a good Spit pilot could get a Hurricane off his tail was to break the circle, roll out and accelerate away – by which time he would of course have been 'shot down' by the Hurricane!

This of course proves the point that in many important aspects the types were very closely matched.

The fighter battle in 1940 was mainly fought by three excellent types, the Messerschmitt Bf 109E, the Spitfire (I and II) and the Hurricane.

Each type had some advantages over the others and some disadvantages. For example, the 109's superior armament and negative-g fuel injection system gave advantages over their opponents.

The ruggedness and manoeuvrability of the Hurricane were superior to those of the others below 20,000 ft, and its gun platform stability at least as good or better than the others; but the Spitfire's sustained manoeuvrability and performance on up to about 30,000 ft showed overall superiority there.

So no-one can claim with veracity that one type was superior in all aspects.

What can be said with certainty is that the Royal Air Force won the Battle, and that it did not do so with inferior equipment.

Perhaps our pilots had a slight edge before losses eliminated so many of the experienced leaders, but Galland's and Molder's men, who were also of formidable calibre, had the distinct disadvantage of having to operate their very short-endurance 109s at the extreme limit of their radius of action from their forward bases on the Channel coast.

It is perhaps too much to hope that the Spitfire 'club' will ever admit for the record that the Hurricane was in fact the very effective mainstay of Fighter Command's attack on the Luftwaffe bomber fleets and escorts in 1940, and in doing so scored a higher proportion of all establishable victories between July and October 1940; but historians today should, if they can overcome the boredom factor, read all the recent hot air and form their own unbiased conclusions.

A Test Pilot's Defence went on to give details of the later Mk

Vs and even 22s, but what this was supposed to show in relation to comparisons between the Spitfire and Hurricane remains obscure.

However, if it was intended to suggest that in all its developments the Spitfire was "the best", the author has apparently mis-remembered the flying-bomb battle in 1944, when $2^1/_2$ squadrons of Tempest Vs destroyed more V-1s than all the Spitfires put together, including the Mk XIVs. (Newchurch Tempests 638 – Spitfire Mk XIVs 322). The Tempest was significantly faster at low level and in the dive (fully manoeuvrable Vne 545 mph) and thus more able to catch the small, fast V-1s effectively, and also the later 190s, Ta 152s and Me 262s in the closing months of the war.

The mythology so persistently promoted by the Supermarine Tendency has now become accepted fact in many books, which relegate the Hurricane to a claimed position of embarrassing inferiority in the Battle of Britain. It was never in such a position – my own squadron pilots actually petitioned our CO to prevent our being hastily re-equipped with Spitfires in September 1940. We were more than satisfied with our 'Rotol' Hurricanes at the critical point in the Battle – and it is more than time that the record be clearly and unequivocally put straight.

Roland Beamont

Having considered the above cut-and-thrust of discussion, the reader is warmly recommended to accept Bee's advice in the final letter to *"Read all the recent hot air and form their own unbiased conclusions"*.

Rod, however, was to return to this topic some five or so years later when it was author Bill Gunston that he took to task for much the same reasons. Once again it was Rod's favourite magazine, *Aeroplane Monthly*, which hosted the article which raised his ire and had his fingers bouncing across the keyboard of his word processor – addressed on this occasion to the new editor, Michael Oakey, and dated 5 March 2001 – some considerable time after the offending item had appeared:

Dear Mr. Oakley,

Re: <u>Bill Gunston's Article RAF Wings</u>
(AM April 98)

I have always enjoyed and had high regard for Bill Gunston's books and articles on aeronautical subjects, particularly those on aero engines, but two passages in his article *RAF Wings* (*Aeroplane Monthly* April 1998) disappointed me. The first passage was demeaning of three of Britain's greatest aircraft and their engines – the Schneider Cup Supermarine S.5, S.6 and S.6A, the S.5's Napier Lion, and the S.6 and S.6A's Rolls-Royce 'R' engines. The second passage was demeaning of the Supermarine Spitfire.

The first passage was on page 7 of Bill's article, where he said that those three seaplanes won the Schneider Trophy outright for Britain by *"brute force and ignorance"*.

Though he was likely being facetious in adopting such a well known phrase for this passage, *"brute force"* misleads the uninformed because the speed of any particular piston-engined aircraft cannot increase more, proportionately, than the cube root of the total horsepower made available to it. And cube roots have a habit, discouraging to designers, of increasing less and less as the numbers they are cube roots of increase more and more. It is therefore wrong, when victories have been won in the world's hardest-fought aviation contest, to dismiss as *"brute"* the *"force"* [thrust] of the propellers driven by the engines of the three victorious seaplanes. So the passage was also demeaning of Napier, Rolls-Royce, Sir Henry Royce himself, A.J.Rowledge (chief designer of the Napier Lion and the Rolls-Royce R engines) and James Ellor (designer of the R's superchargers, superb for their day). All the more demeaning in the case of the R because, though developed from Rolls's large Buzzard engine with a pressing deadline, its frontal area was kept to low. As for *"ignorance"*, a mere glance at the three seaplanes themselves reveals the most advanced aerodynamics of their day. Their performances confirmed this, so the passage was demeaning of Supermarine, and of R.J.Mitchell in particular.

The will to win shown by each of the three firms may seem too American for some tastes but it proved to be no bad thing in the long run.

Bill's second passage that disappointed me was on page 13 of his article where he said *"...the... Hurricane... was... by far the most important aircraft in the Battle of Britain..."*. Nothing facetious about that. It was even more demeaning of Supermarine than the first passage, and particularly of Mitchell again, and also of his new young aerodynamicist, Beverley Shenstone, because it implied that the Spitfire's contribution to the Battle was minor.

It reveals either that Bill does not fully appreciate that fighter performance was the most vital aspect in World War II daylight air battles, or that he has been unduly influenced by what Hurricane booster Roland ('Bee') Beamont calls the 'Hurricane lobby', membership in which seems to require one's reason to have been plucked from one. In either case to promote the false, even unintentionally, is to betray the genuine. Britain and the world should be forever grateful that the low drag of the Battle of Britain Spitfire, which gave it a speed equal to the Battle of Britain Me 109, was superbly combined with generous wing area, which gave it the ability to turn much tighter than the Me 109. Bill did add that, *"In the long term a more important aircraft was the Supermarine Spitfire…"*. But he went on to say, *"Unfortunately it was difficult to make, and it reached the RAF more than six months after the Hurricane and at a much lower rate of delivery."* The uninformed would infer there were hardly any Spitfires in the Battle, instead of almost two for every three Hurricanes.

Bill's technical editorship of *Flight*, his massive knowledge and his huge number of fine published works are impressive qualifications to express aeronautical opinions. I believe, though, that I'm more qualified then he to assess the combat-worthiness of the RAF's World War II fighters.

He was unfortunate enough to be too young to get his RAF wings until the year the war ended. Though I was cursed by being too young to take part in the Battle of Britain, and was far away in my native Canada during it, I became old enough and was lucky enough to begin flying Spitfires on a few sweeps over France in the fall of 1941 and the spring of 1942, and then in the defence of Malta in the latter half of 1942, and eventually in the invasion of Normandy and through to Holland in 1944. I shot down a few of the enemy and got shot down myself. Though I never operated on Hurricanes, I did instruct at a Hurricane OTU between tours and was astonished to discover how much slower the most numerous RAF fighter in the Battle of Britain was than the Spitfire.

Having taken part in air battles does not fully qualify one to assess fighters, however. Much of my claim to be more qualified to assess them than Bill is based on the study, reading and research I have done since the war. In 1949 I graduated in mechanical engineering from McGill, where I took additional advanced math to qualify for postgraduate studies in aeronautics. I changed my mind and became a lawyer instead, but in the decades since I have delved into most aspects of air war history, my emphasis with respect to the technical aspect having been on fighters, engines and guns. I have long been convinced that although fighter pilots can win air fights, only designers can win air battles (though commanders-in-chief can throw victory away).

Everyone concedes that there weren't enough Hurricanes or Spitfires for either of them to have won the Battle without the other, so Britain and the world should be thankful for both of them. But if every Hurricane had been a Spitfire instead, it would have been won sooner and much more easily. If every Spitfire had been a Hurricane, though, it would have been lost, because the Hurricane could never stand up to the Me 109 on its own.

Adolf Galland's opinion of the Hurricane makes a good starting point because his tactical sense was second to none. His statement that the Hurricane was *"a nice aeroplane to shoot down"* is well known. Not known to all, though, as far as I'm aware is what my old friend Johnnie Johnson told me Galland once said to him about the Hurricane: *"We weren't afraid of it; it was like a Sunday afternoon picnic.*" On pages 44-45 of his fine book *The First and the Last* (English version 1955) Galland describes his first combat, which was over Belgium on May 12, 1940, when he and a companion dived on what he identified as eight *"antiquated"* Hurricanes of the Belgian air force 3,000 feet below them. He shot down two of them, saying *"My first kill was child's play"*; the second appears to have been little more. He shot down a third that afternoon. His summation was: "...*even more experienced pilots could have done little against our new Me 109E. We outstripped them in speed, rate of climb, armament, and above all in flying experience and training.*" He added that he felt *"something approaching a twinge of conscience"*. John Foreman, the fine PRO researcher and author, determined later that the three Hurricanes Galland shot down that day were all from 73 RAF Squadron, which had been operating in France since the beginning of the war, albeit when it had been called the 'Phoney War' there up to May 10.

Any fighter pilot who operated in the first three years of the war would understand what Galland meant by being *"not afraid"*, and therefore, conversely, *"afraid"*, of a particular enemy fighter. At the root of it was the fear of dying. Its presence or absence revealed how a pilot rated his own fighter against one he expected to come up against. A competent fighter pilot who felt his own was clearly superior did not feel that fear, but if he felt it was inferior or even just more or less equal he would feel it whenever he was climbing up to meet the enemy. The fear was entirely natural, and had nothing to do with cowardice unless a pilot let it get the better of him. If he were normal he would keep himself and his aircraft under full control at all times, and the fear would banish the instant he knew he was in the presence of the enemy. He could then, cool as ice, watch an enemy fighter firing straight at him and take proper action both to avoid getting hit and to fire back whenever practical. (Royal Air Forces fighter pilots only began to feel free of that fear in mid 1942 when the Mark IX Spitfire came out. The Mark IX was actually just a Mark V modified to take the first Rolls-Royce Merlin 60 series engine produced, which had the matchless two-stage after-cooled supercharger that in both the Spitfire and Packard Merlin Mustang became the nemesis of the Me 109 and the FW 190.)

In my article 'In Defence of the Spitfire' (*Aeroplane Monthly* August 1995) which I wrote in response to Bee Beamont's article 'Hurricane Testing' (*Aeroplane Monthly* February 1994) I set out some details of the respective performances of the Battle of Britain Hurricane and Spitfire (the Mark I of each) and Me 109 (the 109E). Suffice it to say that the Spitfire and 109E, with equal top speeds of 355 mph, were 45 mph faster than the Hurricane's 310 mph as well as 80 mph faster in the dive, mainly because of the Hurricane's thick blunt wing; they were also much better at height, the 109 actually having some advantage over the Spitfire up there. A margin of just 20 mph as between single engine fighters was usually commanding. (That, for example, was the margin of the 1941 Me 109F over the 1941 Mark V Spitfire and of the 1942 Mark IX Spitfire over Me 109s F and G, the faster and higher having bested the slower and lower in each case.) A competent 109 pilot who was not obliged to fly close escort to bombers therefore had nothing to fear from a Hurricane because he would have control of any engagement with it, able to attack and disengage at will.

The Battle of Britain Me 110 (the 110C) was only about 10 mph slower than the Mark I Spitfire and the Me 109E, and therefore about 35 mph faster than the Mark I Hurricane. A twin engine fighter was always a target for a single engine fighter, however, unless it were about 60 mph faster, because it was much heavier, slower to accelerate, more cumbersome, and not as tight-turning. The Me 110 was almost invariably limited to close escort throughout the Battle, so our fighters could more or less treat it as a bomber without bombs. It was therefore a liability to the Luftwaffe in a daylight air battle, not an asset.

A key indicator of the respective contributions of the Hurricane and Spitfire to the Battle of Britain is, of course, a comparison of the numbers of Luftwaffe aircraft shot down by each. By good fortune, John Alcorn's article 'B of B Top Guns' (*Aeroplane Monthly* September 1996) shed much light on that and related issues. I am sure I am far from alone in considering John's article to be the most up to date and accurate source for those numbers, largely because of the method he devised for arriving at them. He collated the times and locations of squadron engagements set out in the several credible sources he cited and he linked enemy losses in them with RAF claims regarding them; he apportioned the excess claims on a statistical basis as appropriate, and he also listed the number of days each Hurricane and Spitfire squadron was engaged in the Battle – a new and important consideration. Commendatory comments by Dr Alfred Price FRHistS were appended to John's article; Dr Price's analysis and conclusions are revealing. By further good fortune John updated and supplemented his article by a second one, 'B of B Top Guns Update' (*Aeroplane Monthly* July 2000), which provides a breakdown, also revealing, of the numbers of Me 109s and Me 110s shot down by Hurricanes and Spitfires respectively (the other Luftwaffe types shot down having been virtually all bombers, of course).

John credits the 30 Hurricane and 19 Spitfire squadrons involved in the Battle with shooting down a total of 1,185 Luftwaffe aircraft – 656 by the Hurricane squadrons and 529 by the Spitfire squadrons. Though a further 34 were shot down he was unable to assign credit for them, but the 656 and 529 figures can of course be taken as a sound basis for comparison.

On that basis the average Hurricane squadron shot down almost 22 aircraft and the average Spitfire squadron almost 28, which indicates that although the 30 Hurricane squadrons shot down almost one quarter more than the 19 Spitfire squadrons, the average Spitfire squadron shot down a little over a quarter more than the average Hurricane squadron.

The question can naturally be asked, though, why the number of enemy aircraft shot down by Hurricanes was almost a quarter more than that by Spitfires in spite of the Hurricane's greatly inferior performance. There are three reasons.

The first and most obvious is that there were almost half as many Hurricanes again as Spitfires.

The second reason is that while both Hurricane and Spitfire squadrons were commonly directed against the enemy's bombers and their close escort, the Hurricane's performance was so far below that of the 109 and the Spitfire that where there was a choice the Spitfire squadrons were directed against the 109s not flying close escort, which were usually higher up and therefore much more difficult prey. The great majority of the bombers were Heinkel 111s and Dornier 17Zs, whose top speeds were not only well below that of the Hurricane, but the speed of the formations they had to keep in both for mutual defence and pattern bombing was only about 180 mph. It can be deduced from John's update that of the 1,185 Luftwaffe aircraft shot down, about 473 – 40% – were bombers, of which John credits Hurricanes shooting down 306 and Spitfires 167; the average Hurricane squadron therefore shot down slightly over 10 bombers and the average Spitfire squadron slightly under 9.

The third reason, and much the more important one in Galland's estimation, was that Goering ordered the bulk of his fighters to keep very close to the bombers when escorting them, which allowed even the slow Hurricanes to tangle with the whole array. Goering did this because the bomber crews complained to him that the fighters were staying too far away. They did not realize, and Goering was too stubborn and mentally lazy to analyse the issue, that having the bulk of the fighters in close to them was actually far more dangerous for them. Fighters in close lost the initiative, including the all-important choice of initial position. To stay with the bombers they had both to weave and reduce their forward speed so much they lost momentum. Galland consistently advised Goering of these key facts during the Battle and later Luftwaffe offensives, but to no avail; Galland's own choice would have been for most of the fighters to be moderately above the bombers, with a good portion spread out ahead of them. Goering could not have given an order more fatal to a Luftwaffe victory.

The escorting Me 109s and Me 110s that stayed in close to the bombers as ordered became vulnerable to Hurricanes because the latter could so easily overtake the preponderant He 111 and Dornier 17Z formations (though not Junkers 88 formations so easily, Bee Beamont himself having said that 88s *"often dived away from our Hurricanes"*). The Me 110 was more vulnerable than the Me 109 in those circumstances because of its slow acceleration. John's update states that 504 Me 109s were shot down in the Battle, about 222 of them by Hurricanes and 282 by Spitfires, which means that the average Hurricane squadron shot down $7^1/2$ of them as opposed to 15 – twice as many – by the average Spitfire squadron. John's update also states that 208 Me 110s were shot down during the Battle, 128 by Hurricanes and 80 by Spitfires, which means that the squadron average for both types was about $4^1/4$.

(On the close escort issue I should know whereof Galland spoke. In the summer of 1942 I found myself in a fighter squadron in Malta on daily readiness to intercept Ju 88 bombers escorted by Me 109Fs. We were equipped with the tropical Mark V Spitfire, the worst mark of Spitfire ever made. [Joe Smith, who succeeded Mitchell on the latter's death in 1937, was responsible for it; it was much faster and better at height, however, than the hapless tropical Mark II Hurricane it had replaced in Malta in the spring of 1942.] In what appeared to be even a refinement of Goering's usual order all the Me 109Fs were kept in a tight rigid staircase ascending for several thousand feet up behind the 88s, except for a smaller group too high above them to give any real protection. If a good portion of the 'staircased' 109s had taken up position advocated by Galland instead – moderately above and ahead of the 88s – we would never have got near the 88s because those 109s would have broken us up well before we did. In fact, sometimes just a pair or two of 109s would assume that position and have that effect.)

Another question concerning the Battle of Britain arises naturally: How did the losses of the average Hurricane squadron compare with those of the average Spitfire squadron? John's update shows that 497 Hurricanes and 317 Spitfires were shot down, a total of 814, which means that the average loss for both Hurricane and Spitfire squadrons was about $16^1/2$. This raises the question: If the Spitfire's performance was so much better than the Hurricane's, why did the average Spitfire squadron lose as many as the average Hurricane squadron? The answer lies in John Alcorn's list of the number of days engaged in the Battle by every squadron, which Dr Price pointed out. It shows that the average Hurricane squadron was engaged $15^1/2$ days and the average Spitfire squadron 20 days (almost 30% more, an advantage which Dr Price attributes to the Spitfire's lower attrition rate). The risk of being shot down in a Hurricane was therefore almost 30% greater than in a Spitfire. If the average

Hurricane squadron had been kept engaged the same number of days as the average Spitfire squadron at the Hurricane's attrition rate, 636 Hurricanes would have been lost instead of 497 – twice as many as Spitfires – though there were almost half as many more Hurricanes in the Battle of course.

Further analysis by Dr Price does show, though, that in spite of the lesser number of days the average Hurricane squadron was engaged, during each day it was engaged it managed to shoot down enemy aircraft at the same rate as the average Spitfire squadron did. No doubt the reason for that was the average Spitfire squadron's much heavier engagement with Me 109s, of which it shot down twice as many as the average Hurricane squadron (as well as having shot down as many Me 110s and 85% as many bombers). Tangling with the smaller formations of 109s not trapped in escort and free to use their height advantage was not conducive to a high rate of victories against them, but it had to be done.

Another natural question is how did the Hurricane's low performance permit it to survive the Battle? The answer is that although the Me 109 was by far the most dangerous enemy of Fighter Command, its pilots properly feared the Hurricane's fighting companion – the Spitfire. A 109 pilot free of escort duty could make any number of passes at the slow though tight-turning Hurricane, but against the Spitfire, a foe with equal speed but tighter-turning, it could only be one pass and away (sometimes requiring luck for the 'away').

And it wasn't always easy for a 109 pilot to tell a Hurricane from a Spitfire at about 1,500 yards and over. They had the same camouflage and both had upswept noses, quite distinct from the 109's downswept nose. 1,500 yards was a very short distance when jockeying for position, so a 109 pilot had often to get quite close to a Hurricane to distinguish it from a Spitfire. The Hurricane was therefore sheltered by the Spitfire's reputation when the latter was in the same theatre, though the two did not always have to be in the same patch of sky.

Though Hurricanes held up against the Italian air force for other than technical reasons, when on their own they failed in every theatre where they were up against German or Japanese fighters. They failed in Greece and Crete. A single squadron of Me 109Es from Galland's group that was detached from the Channel coast to Sicily early in 1941 for a month or two devastated the Hurricanes on Malta without loss to itself. It repeated that feat in the Libyan desert before returning north. In his 1966 *With Prejudice*, Arthur Tedder, who commanded the RAF in the Middle East from December of 1940 on, consistently mentions the frustrations arising from the Hurricane's inferiority to the 109. Hurricanes were devastated by Japanese Navy Zeros over Ceylon in April of 1942. Hurricane pilots were fortunate that they almost never met Zeros, because it was faster than they were and could easily turn inside them. A Zero with a Hurricane was 'like cat down cellar wi' no-hole mouse'.

Though the speed margin of the Japanese Army's Oscar over the Mark II (tropical) Hurricane was quite small, the position was much the same as with the Zero. Paul Richey (author of the 1941 *Fighter Pilot*) became Wing Commander Ops at HQ Bengal Command in May of 1943. In his 1993 *Fighter Pilot's Summer* (written with Norman Franks) he says that one sentence in a report he wrote for his AOC concerning operations by Hurricanes against Oscars in Burma read: *"Of course there is no doubt the Hurricane is not up to the job and we must have Spitfires."* The AOC called him into his office and after congratulating him on his report took out a pair of scissors and said, *"There's just one thing I can't let through."* He cut out the sentence about the Hurricane and Spitfires, saying, *"That's true, and both you and I know it, but we must never let the boys suspect it – it would destroy morale."* Paul commented on this in his book by saying: *"As if they didn't know it!"*

That shows, by the way, that good fighter pilots will do their best with whatever aircraft they are given to fight with; no one could say Hurricane pilots were ever surpassed for guts by Spitfire pilots. Because of the Hurricane's failure to succeed on its own, a final question arises: Why do so many Britons consistently maintain that it was a truly first class fighter, and the backbone of Fighter Command, even, in the Battle of Britain?

I believe there are three reasons.

One is the very human desire, perpetuated by the Hurricane lobby, to prevent the reputation of the Hurricane's designer, Sydney Camm, from being tarnished. His pre-war Hawker Hart and Fury were the most beautiful biplanes in the world and performed as they looked. But Camm, lacking Mitchell's and Shenstone's preference for and experience of monoplanes, admitted he had fear of them. It seems he tried to allay it by making the Hurricane's wing thick and blunt, aiming to get the lift and strength of two wings with one. That proved a fatal mistake (which, though it is hard to believe, he repeated with the Typhoon).

Another reason is chauvinism, an incurable corruption of patriotism. Those afflicted can never acknowledge that another country could excel their own in any sphere. And it can be downright dangerous in wartime if a person so afflicted has a say in the choice of his own country's weapons.

The last and I believe the most important reason is that the myths of the Hurricane's superiority over the Me 109 and its near equality with the Spitfire became so deeply embedded in British propaganda during the Battle of Britain that many Britons would think they were being disloyal if they allowed themselves to question those myths. Willingness to accept one's own country's propaganda varies inversely as one's respect for the truth, however.

German propaganda never bothered me because Goebbels had promoted the big lie, and much of it was just amusing. I began to suspect our own propaganda during the Phoney War, and detested it from the fall of France onward. When the Germans broke through at Sedan in 1940 our propagandists labelled our wholesale retreats as *"strategic withdrawals"*. They even said the Germans were *"advancing over a wall of their own dead"*, though a *Life* photographer reported he had a hard time finding one dead German soldier to take a picture of.

Three prominent Air Ministry propaganda themes during the Battle of Britain should suffice to show how misleading its propaganda could be.

The most prominent one was that RAF fighters were shooting down at least three times as many Luftwaffe aircraft of all types as the Luftwaffe was shooting RAF fighters down. John Alcorn's figures show that Hurricanes and Spitfires shot down a total of 1,219 Luftwaffe aircraft of all types whereas the Luftwaffe shot down a total of 814 Hurricanes and Spitfires. The Luftwaffe was therefore shooting down two of those RAF fighters for every three of its aircraft of all types that were being shot down. (The hopeless participation of the RAF's two-seat Defiant fighters in the battle can be totally ignored.)

A second prominent theme was that Luftwaffe aircrew and aircraft were second-rate, but that our fighter pilots faced heavy odds because they were greatly outnumbered. Our propagandists included the Luftwaffe's bombers and its misused Me 110s in the numbers, however, which was false reckoning. Though the return fire from the bombers and 110s was unpleasant, it was trifling compared with the risk of being shot down by Me 109s. The more the bombers and Me 110s could have been able to darken the sky the more diluted the 109s would have become and the less the odds against our fighters (but in fact the number of bombers began to be reduced to increase the ratio of 109s to bombers). At any one time during the Battle the Luftwaffe had roughly 800 Me 109s available for operations over south-east Britain, and Fighter Command kept roughly the same number of Hurricanes and Spitfires to defend that area (being only about half of the total it had on hand because of the need to maintain guard over the rest of Britain). Both sides required constant replacement, of course, because of the 504 Me 109s shot down by Hurricanes and Spitfires, and the 814 Hurricanes and Spitfires shot down by the Luftwaffe (the great bulk by 109s). Fighters escorting bombers over enemy territory needed a ratio approaching three to one over the defending fighters unless they were much superior to the best one of them (as for example the superiority of the Merlin powered P-51 Mustangs escorting Fortresses over Germany in 1944 against defending FW 190A-8s and Me 109Gs). So the Luftwaffe simply did not have enough Me 109s for a great offensive like the Battle of Britain. I doubt that any of our fighter pilots (except those flying Defiants) would have happily swapped predicaments with 109 pilots.

A third prominent theme was that the Me 110 was hopeless, implying that it was intrinsically faulty, notwithstanding that any unescorted multi engine aircraft caught by a 110 in daylight (except for the later De Havilland Mosquito and the Lockheed P-38 Lightning) was in deep trouble. But more than all that, as a night fighter the Me 110 probably sent more Royal Air Force aircrew to their graves than all other enemy fighters put together.

So much for propaganda. It has obscured to this day the fact that the Spitfire was the key saviour of Britain and the world in the Battle of Britain. And it has kept hidden the fact that the Hurricane was the poorest fighter employed in great numbers by any country during the war (though that is another issue). When the Luftwaffe withdrew the Heinkel III and the Dornier 17Z from daylight operations after the Battle of Britain the Hurricane's days of glory were over, and all too challenging days for its pilots lay ahead.

Yours, R.I.A.Smith

P.S. – On page 17 of his article Bill said, *"...the RAD fought its greatest war with almost all of its guns of two types designed in the First World War"* (by which he could only mean the Browning .303 and the Hispano Suiza 20mm cannon). I can't refrain from commending to him, by way of this postcript, *The Machine Gun*, written by the USMC's Lt Col George M.Chinn for the US Navy in 1951. It will show that John Moses Browning designed his famous .30 machine gun in the last year of the 19th century and his even more famous .50 version of it by 1918. It will also show that Hispano Suiza's Marc Birkigt did not begin to design his firm's 20mm cannon until 1933. As a matter of interest, Browning's .50 became fit for aircraft use in 1932, two years before the RAF's Air Staff chose, against all reason, his .30 calibre instead and even had it senselessly modified to take the obsolescent 1889 British Service (Lee-Enfield) cordite-propelled .303 rimmed cartridge. The resulting gun wasn't nearly as trouble-free as the unmodified .30, but fortunately it was good enough not to lose the Battle of Britain. The unmodified .30 (like the .50, the 20mm Hispano cannon and the German guns) was nitro-cellulose propelled and rimless, and it equipped a number of the early American aircraft supplied to the RAF.

This letter was copied to Bill Gunston, Roland Beamont, John Alcorn and Alfred Price.

N.B. This latter question of the guns is one that I never had the opportunity to discuss with Rod. Had I been able to do so, I would have suggested to him that the Air Staff's decision had much to do with the UK Treasury in a period of economic stringency; there were large supplies of British .303 ammunition left over from World War I, coupled with which armament practice using the considerably larger, and therefore more expensive .5 round would have exacerbated costs. This is one of the prices to be paid for being part of a basically peaceful and democratic system.

Guns remained a matter of abiding interest for Rod, and indeed during 2001 he chose to speak on this subject at a symposium in Los Angeles. Responding to a written question deriving therefrom at the start of 2002, he wrote:

I inadvertently left out a couple of key things in my talk which may have left some wrong impressions. Perhaps I should have chosen to give an outline of my 'wartime career', as the others did, instead of choosing to speak on 'Guns and Shooting'.

But I somehow felt the urge to indulge my incurable technical history streak, though I might have curbed it if I had known how many women would be there. I have long believed that although fighter pilots fought air battles and most did their best to win them with what they had, only the designers of the aircraft, engines and guns actually won them.

I got a great kick out of Bill Allen's moderating, though I failed to adapt quickly enough on the Sunday morning when he told me there would be a fourth speaker and we would therefore be limited to 20 minutes each instead of 30. In fact, probably because I was the last speaker and didn't set my stopwatch, I think I went on considerably longer than 30!

I opened my talk by saying that the RAF's choice in 1934 of the .30 Browning machine gun (which they changed into a .303) was a bad mistake because the Browning .50 had become fit for aircraft use two years earlier, and its bullet had about the same muzzle velocity as the .30 but weighed four and a half times as much [in accordance with the cube rule – getting bigger in all three directions like a boat or a fish]. I then said the American choice of the .50 was a compromise.

Actually, because choosing the .50 in the early 1930s was dead right, I should have said that sticking with it too long was the compromise. Furthermore, I failed to say later on, as I had planned, why I thought that was so, and just as importantly to admit that things turned out wonderfully well nonetheless and why I thought they did.

In my view, though, failing to prepare effectively for the adoption in due course of the obvious next size up, the 20mm

(.80), was very risky because the Hispano 20mm shell had about the same muzzle velocity as the .50 bullet but weighed fairly close to three times as much (the cube rule not being applicable as between shells and bullets because shells are hollow though usually filled with some light but nasty stuff).

By the mid thirties General Walter Wever had become chief of staff of the Luftwaffe, in effect its commander-in-chief. Though originally an army officer he had a passionate belief in carrying air war right into the heart of an enemy country to destroy its industrial capacity, and he quickly ordered prototypes of two four engine long range bombers of B-17 size (the Ju 89 and the Dornier 19). He was killed in a flying accident in mid 1936 however, and his successors concentrated on twin engine bombers suitable for both tactical support for the German army and medium range bombing (as well as concentrating on the single engine short range Stuka dive bomber of course).

The Browning .50 could easily shoot down twin engine aircraft but I'm sure it would have been light in the pot attacking well armed four engine bombers, which would likely have become necessary if:

(i) General Wever had not been killed (or had been succeeded by a C-in-C who shared his beliefs); and
(ii) Hitler had not gambled by attacking Russia before defeating Britain.

None of these events could have been foreseen by American service staffs of course (Hitler's gamble having been less than six months before Pearl Harbor) so their failure to plan to adopt the 20mm cannon is hard not to be excused.

Hitler's failed gamble makes the 20mm vs .50 issue moot of course because it not only left Germany without the resources to build up and maintain a four engine bomber fleet, it left the country highly vulnerable to round the clock bombing. The .50 armed US 8th Air Force fighters tore the guts out of the defending Luftwaffe fighters in daylight, especially after the P-51B Merlin Mustang (with just *four* .50s!) arrived in mid December of 1943.

And because of the general lightness of Japanese aircraft the .50 easily reigned supreme in the Pacific.

As I did say in my talk though, I'm sure the 20mm was better for ground strafing.

I would be pleased if you would show this letter to any of your group you think might be particularly interested in the subject. Stocky Edwards told me that when he was invited to a fighter pilots organization in Alabama some years ago he found that American fighter pilots did not appreciate any suggestion that the 20mm would have been a proper replacement for the .50!

And please apologise to Bill Allen on my behalf for not touching on the single 20mm in the P-38; but even I recognize some limits on time, space and complication. I wouldn't be surprised if he thought the gun was better for ground strafing too.

In Combat with the
Canadian Broadcasting Corporation

During the mid 1990s the Canadian Broadcasting Corporation ran a series of television programmes (the 'Valour and Horror' series) dealing and commenting on aspects of World War II involving Canadian servicemen. Many veterans felt that these programmes carried a distinctly 'revisionist' and left-wing bias. The episode which particularly incensed many ex-airmen was one covering the night bombing offensive, entitled 'Death by Moonlight'. This so-called 'documentary' sought to suggest that the British authorities had used Canadians to keep down British casualties. Rod was among those who were incandescent with anger, and on 30 April 1995 he sent a detailed rebuttal to The Honourable Perrin Beatty, president of CBC:

I was a fighter pilot in the Second World War, not a bomber pilot, but I consider that the CBC film *Death by Moonlight*, the bomber segment of *The Valour and the Horror* series, was covertly intended to denigrate all Canadian airmen.

I have learned, belatedly, that Brian McKenna appeared on CBC's *Front Page Challenge* on 11 November of last year and said: *"The CBC Ombudsman dumped all over the series... he had his own agenda."*

I will restrict this letter to *Death by Moonlight* because I took part in the air war and have studied it, as an interest, for the last thirty years.

Because McKenna was the director of the film and co-author with his brother Terence (a background figure it seems), he gravely impugned the integrity of the Ombudsman, William Morgan. And because the introduction to the film says: *"This is a true story... there is no fiction"* (which is repeated on the cover of the videotape) the integrity of the CBC itself is in issue. The CBC therefore seems to be obligated either to sever relations with McKenna or to initiate proceedings to have the Ombudsman dismissed.

The choice should not be difficult. The Ombudsman's adverse report was clearly justified, though his stating that he found no reason to conclude that those responsible for the series *"deliberately set out to distort facts or to mislead their audience"* appears to be misplaced diplomacy. I have never seen a more gross example of fraudulent journalism than *Death by Moonlight*. It is riddled with so many instances of deceit it aroused the disgust of all informed persons.

Those who perceived this differed only as to which instances they found the more disgusting. I found three to be particularly so. The first two involved Bomber Harris, whom Brian McKenna obviously felt he must destroy in order to prevent his 'thesis' from falling to the ground; he therefore portrayed him as a brutally uncaring and untrustworthy scoundrel.

The first instance occurs in a scene where the villainous-looking actor who plays Harris is alone, facing the camera. (A Union Jack is behind him, to stress a constant theme of McKenna's that British senior commanders were forever sacrificing dominion and colonial fighting men.) The actor quotes, more or less accurately, from a paragraph on page 64 of Harris's 1947 book, *Bomber Offensive*. He stops part way through the key sentence however, leaving out the rest of it and a short dependant one which follows it. The words he says are:

I have been amused to read in almost every history or novel about Empire wars what magnificent horsemen and natural good shots the colonial troops were. I have ridden with colonial troops and shot with colonial troops, and been shot at by colonial troops. And I have no hesitation in saying that colonial, and Dominion troops are on average damn bad horsemen and damned bad shots....

The succeeding words which he leaves out are:

....unless and until they have been put through the standard riding school procedure, in the day when horsemen meant something, and the standard musketry drill of the armed forces. After which they are no better and no worse than the British themselves.

This instance of deceit struck me as the crudest one, and all the more so because of Harris's introductory qualifying words (*"admittedly magnificent fighting men from the colonies and dominions"*) were also left out.

The second instance I found to be particularly disgusting is far more material, however, because it shows the film to be fraudulent to its core. It occurs in a scene involving Douglas Harvey, one of the two former RCAF bomber pilots who appear intermittently in the film, speaking mainly of their own experiences. He is alone, facing the camera, and he begins to tell of a visit Bomber Harris paid to his bomber station in Yorkshire in the late fall of 1943 during which Harris addressed the crews of two squadrons gathered in a hangar. The visit is described in detail on pages 71 and 72 of a book Harvey wrote in 1981, *Boys, Bombs and Brussels Sprouts*. In the film Harvey says that Harris bounded up on the platform, and:

...his first words were, "Most of you people won't be here in a

few months". It got our full attention.

Those two lines follow the book fairly closely but the scene in the film ends at that point, leaving out about 45 lines of the book. The two lines in the film would probably lead most viewers who had never fought in a war to believe that Harris was a man who would sacrifice crews without caring, whereas the 45 lines left out give an entirely different picture of him. Harris was actually alerting the crews to the Battle of Berlin, which was about to begin, but he could not tell them the target of course. Though Harvey's book reveals that he himself had a chip on his shoulder about senior officers, the 45 lines left out of the film constitute, in my view, one of the most down to earth tributes to a twentieth century military leader ever written; they show that Harris conquered Harvey on that visit. Here are some key extracts from those 45 lines left out:

[Harris was] the one man, it seemed, who understood what the war was all about. The same guy we would disparage over our beers as Bomber Harris and Butcher Harris. We would picture him standing in his office, a glass of Scotch in hand, looking out the window at the fog or rain or snow and saying, "It looks fine to me, chaps. Send them off." At the same time we had tremendous respect for him, for it was obvious, even at our level, that he fought very hard to get all the many support services the squadrons required to keep operational. We had heard enough about him to know he was a winner.

[Harris speaking] "We are about to begin a series of raids that will demand the best from all of you. We know there will be tremendous losses, but it has to be done. You've all done a splendid job, but the real test is still before you. We must beat Germany to her knees."

Harvey went on in his book (in some of the 45 lines left out) to say that Harris then asked the crews if there were any questions; a sergeant gunner spoke up and asked him why sergeant gunners got less pay than sergeant pilots and navigators for doing the same job; Harris called out, *"Who said that?"*; the gunner yelled back, *"I did"*, and Harris roared, *"Come up here"*. Harvey went on further:

We all waited, straining forward, as the gunner made his way to the platform. This was going to be good. Old Bomber would probably tear a strip off the poor sergeant. But Harris greeted him warmly and shook hands, before asking him to repeat his question. Then he turned to the crowd and said, "I don't know. It's one of those damn crazy things that get started and after a while no one knows why. I don't agree with it but I can't change it."

The direct honest way that Harris answered brought a roar of approval from the crowd, and he went down in our books as a man you could trust. [underlining mine]

Because destroying Harris was vital to the credibility of McKenna's thesis, putting in the 45 lines left out would have undermined the whole foundation of the film of course, so McKenna simply left them out, as he did in the 'colonial' instance. I am sure Harvey himself had nothing to do with such disgusting tricks, and that he deeply regrets ever having met McKenna. That he should be used to give credibility to a film in which denigrating Harris was a fundamental element, without disclosure being made of his deep respect and admiration for him, was fundamental fraud all by itself.

These first two instances of deceit can be exposed in mere minutes by scanning the pages of Harris's and Harvey's books. Tennyson said: *"a lie which is half truth is ever the blackest of lies"*. It is little wonder that when the film was shown in Britain, the first country to endure sustained bombing, one review was captioned: *"The Venom and the Humbug"*.

The third instance of deceit I found particularly disgusting was more subtle and required much more research to expose, but the technique of leaving out material parts was the same. It involved scientist Freeman Dyson, whom McKenna put forward as his sole source of expert opinion regarding the bomber campaign and Harris's leadership of it. Dyson began to work as a civilian mathemetician at Bomber Command headquarters in 1943, when he was twenty. McKenna calls Dyson, *"a brilliant analyst of the bombing campaign"* and puts forward Dyson's views that the campaign was worthless to the Allies and that Bomber Harris was a brutal commander. McKenna took Dyson's anti-bomber-campaign material for the film from two books Dyson wrote decades after the war, but he failed to tell viewers that those books show Dyson to have been a virtual arch-priest of the radical academic left and of its Siamese twin, pacifism.

Dyson wrote that in 1938, when he was fifteen, he and his school friends distributed propaganda leaflets of the Peace Pledge Union, but, *"The rotten society around us blundered along to its inevitable doom, heedless of our warnings"*, led by *"a government which had no answer to any of its problems except to rearm as rapidly as possible."* And further:

I was morally against all violence... Winston Churchill was our archenemy... the incorrigible warmonger... We loved... Mahatma Ghandi... his gospel of nonviolent resistance gave us hope... We were not sure whether Hitler could be successfully opposed with nonviolence... but at least there was a chance.... With bombs and guns we were convinced there was no chance... if we opposed Hitler nonviolently and he killed us, we should be dying for a good cause...That would be better than dying for Mr Churchill and the empire.

All this could be laughed at as precocious sophomorics, except that Dyson maintained these views (with a few short-lived diversions) during the time he was working at Bomber Command, and afterwards as well, though his thinking did undergo a few sea-changes much later in his life.

For McKenna to have included in his film Dyson's anti-bombing-campaign material without disclosing Dyson's extreme pacifist views was another example of gross journalistic fraud. Setting a pacifist to analyse a bombing campaign is like setting a chicken to watch foxes. If McKenna had put forward the views of Dyson he withheld, the film might well have died a natural death. Although revisionists are not hot after Churchill, more than a few Canadians think we owe him something.

In addition to McKenna's fundamental though false proposition that Harris was a scoundrel, the film advanced five supplementary propositions, each of which can easily be shown to be false too. The first was that Bomber Command always had the ability to conduct its operations by precision bombing at night, and that Harris therefore had a choice between bombing factories and area bombing. The second was that area bombing of cities was militarily useless. The third was that bomber crews were prevented from knowing what their losses were because Harris kept them from them. The fourth was that the crews were dupes of Harris because he failed to tell them that civilians would be killed in the area bombing they were doing. The fifth (inconsistent with the fourth) was that by carrying out area bombing the crews were guilty of immoral conduct.

As to the first supplementary proposition, the backbone of every history of Bomber Command worthy of the name is a running description of the problems of finding targets at night. For nearly the first half of the war the main problem was to find a specific city, let alone bomb any particular part of it. (Even the bombing carried out later by the US 8th Air Force in daylight was only relatively precise; the majority of its bombs usually fell outside the targeted factory because its bombing formations averaged about a mile wide and all the bombers in each one dropped their bombs at the same time.) Only in about the last eight months of the war could key installations be targeted with any confidence.

The second supplementary proposition, that area bombing of cities was militarily useless, ignores the fact that every city, industrial or not, was a giant war machine, akin to a nation as a battleship or an aircraft carrier was to a navy. It was a huge provider of armament or other military equipment or training of some kind, a centre of transportation, distribution, food processing, and storage, as well as housing for the many thousands of workers who lived in it. A successful area attack on a city was a military calamity. Although when Albert Speer, the German Minster for War Production, was interrogated after the war he tended to mark down the effects of area bombing, that contradicted what he said to senior members of the Nazi Party in October of 1943 (when he was under the gun) about the problems of war production. He stressed the absenteeism of the workers after air raids, saying:

We have to be clear about one thing, namely that the method of the English and the Americans of bombing the inner city and its civilian population, a lesson they likely learned from our attacks against their cities, in the long run affects production more than an attack against the factory itself. We have to counter this stubborn English strategy by trying to reduce absenteeism. Often, even eight days after an air raid, only 20% to 30% of the employees are reporting for work. (Film No.175, German Documents, National Library, Washington.)

And the remarkable diaries of Dr. Joseph Goebbels, Minister of Propaganda, leave no doubt that Bomber Command's attacks were devastating to the factories themselves and in every other way.

An area attack on a city was a human calamity too of course, but the average German's chance of surviving the five years of bombing was between one hundred and two hundred to one (depending on whether one takes the American survey figure of 305,000 Germans killed in air raids, Dyson's figure of 400,000, or McKenna's figure of 600,000). During four of those five years the British army could not get on to the main part of the European continent to fight, so the only way Britain could come to grips with Germany itself was by area bombing. That was the crux of the matter. A decision not to bomb for fear of killing German civilians would have had two results. One was that most of the million and a half Germans engaged on defending against bombers, repairing bomb damage and dispersal of factories, would have been freed up for military service or war production. The other was that German civilians would have been allowed to go on living in their homes with every normal convenience, producing in the workplace with peacetime efficiency. The British might as well have resigned themselves and all the subjugated peoples of Europe to permanent enslavement.

The third supplementary proposition, that bomber crews were prevented from knowing what their losses were because Harris kept them from them, is patently ridiculous. The whole of Britain listened to the BBC every morning to see whether Bomber Command had been out, and if it had been, how many bombers had been lost and what tonnage had been dropped. Any bomber crewman, briefed beforehand on the number of bombers taking part in each attack and hearing the BBC loss figures after it, could calculate his chances of surviving a thirty trip tour quite closely if he wished to. The approximate probabilities were general knowledge among the crews anyway, though understandably not dwelt on every hour of the day and night.

The fourth supplementary proposition, that Harris failed to tell the bomber crews that civilians would be killed in the area bombing they were doing, and therefore they were witless dupes in carrying out his immoral purposes, is too stupid to discuss. Harris actually complained to Sir Charles Portal, the RAF's Chief of Air Staff, that the BBC news described each area bombing of a city as an attack on military objectives within it. He said this might give the impression to bomber crews that they were doing something to be ashamed of. This shows, as does his address to the bomber crews in Yorkshire, that portraying him as an untrustworthy man was journalistic fraud at its worst.

McKenna's fifth supplementary proposition, that by area bombing cities the bomber crews were guilty of immoral acts, is implied by several false statements in the film. The principal ones were that fighter pilots were given a special campaign medal after the war, that bomber pilots were refused one and treated as an embarrassment, that Bomber Harris was shunned by everyone after the war, and that German fighter pilots were morally undefeated. All this implies a moral difference between a country's defending itself against enemy bombers and bombing the enemy country. The morality in both instances is obviously the same however. It is the moral issue underlying the war itself. If not, one would have to say that while it was all right for Britain to defend herself in the Battle of Britain, she and her allies should not then have gone on to defeat Germany merely to remove the threat of slavery and to liberate Europe from the Gestapo and the SS. Anyone who would say that (and McKenna must) has an ulterior motive.

Though I was a fighter pilot in the war, during the final year of it I made forty-five dive-bombing attacks in fighters in daylight. On a few of them I found myself in the same position as the bomber crews who were the subject of *Death by Moonlight*, so I consider I was among those denigrated by the film. On those few attacks on railway tracks in German towns where the chance of hitting houses alongside them was almost as great as hitting the tracks themselves, I saw a few houses actually get hit by my bombs. Though I naturally felt sorry for any people who might have been in them (and they had little or no warning), I have never felt that my attacks, tiny efforts towards victory that they were, should not have been made.

My fighter pilot friends and I have nothing but deep admiration and respect for Bomber Command and its crews, who were our comrades in arms. In spite of journalistic romancing about the selection of pilots for fighters or bombers being governed by differences in personality and attitude, that was not so. Chance was virtually the sole factor in selection. It all depended on whether, after a class of students at an elementary flying school had graduated, a single engine service flying school (leading to fighters) or a twin engine one (leading to bombers) was ready to take on a fresh class. This often depended on whether the weather had shortened or extended the time for graduation at one school or another. The air force was the biggest lottery in the world, of necessity, and initial selection was just the beginning. If I had become a bomber pilot and had failed to carry out each trip as conscientiously as I believe I carried out each of my fighter sorties I would feel everlasting shame.

McKenna's view of morality is one-sided. Compared with the hundred to two hundred to one chance the average German had of surviving all air raids, every Jew sent to a death camp had only the remotest chance. Sympathy for adult Germans killed in air raids has been mentally buried, understandably, under a landslide of the putrefying remains of the millions of men, women and children who died in the death camps on the orders of the elected leaders of the German people. It is interesting that as the Russian army got nearer to Auschwitz Himmler tried to remove all traces of it, that Ernst Zundel has denied the history of the death camps, and that McKenna made no mention of them. To Himmler, Zundel and McKenna, Holocausts Hardly Ever Happened.

As for moral ground, though it is difficult emotionally to fault German day and night fighter pilots for trying to shoot down bombers which were devastating their country, it should be kept in mind that during every day the war was extended as a result of their successes, a few thousand more inmates of the death camps went to the gas chambers. Those pilots bear their share of their nation's shame. And it is doubtful that many adult Germans could truthfully say they did not know of the death camps. A highly successful German day fighter pilot, Colonel Johannes Steinhoff (who eventually became a commanding general of the postwar Luftwaffe) wrote a book, *The Final Hours*, in which he tells of being terribly burned in a crash at war's end and of reading the first peacetime German newspaper in hospital. He said they called his and his fellow patients' attention:

…repeatedly and in detail to the disgrace of our nation: Auschwitz, Treblinka, Buchenwald… (As if we had not known – but it was unthinkable and we had simply shut our ears to it, there being 'no alternative in the pursuit to ultimate victory'.) [underlining mine]

Only a few days ago the president of Germany, in a memorial speech at Belsen, rejected contentions by much of the older generation that the average German was unaware that six million Jews were being slaughtered in their country's name.

Although neither the civilians nor the servicemen of the Allied countries knew of the death camps until the war ended, they did know of the never ending torture and killing carried out by the Gestapo and the SS in German concentration camps and in the occupied countries.

McKenna stressed the women and child victims in the German cities. The women were old enough to vote and raise their right arms, though, and newsreels suggest the vast majority did. If any of them protested against the area bombing of Warsaw, Rotterdam, London or Coventry, it has not come to light. Every child killed in the war, however, whether by bombing or gassing, was a helpless innocent victim whose fate is difficult to think about. There was one fate worse, though, and that was the life of slavery which would have faced all British and European children had Germany not been defeated. And McKenna failed to bring forward the fact that German children killed would have been saved if they had been evacuated to the countryside at the beginning of the war, as British children were. I don't remember ever seeing a child in London until nearly Christmas of 1944, when the danger there had passed, nor can I recall hearing of British children being killed in air raids, though some were by chance of course. Allied airmen, when they learned after the war that German children had not been similarly evacuated until far into it, were much surprised.

I have no complaints about the CBC's making films about controversial subjects. I agree with what Gerard Veilleux, a former president of the corporation, said on its behalf when the controversy over McKenna's series arose:

...we must not be afraid of controversy or of treating subjects of this kind... we must... however... ensure that any program we broadcast is fully defensible in terms of its adherence to the Corporation's journalistic policies and standards." [underlining mine]

The Ombudsman set out those policies in his report. I find them admirable, and can see they are essential for a Crown corporation which is generally considered to be the 'official' mouthpiece of the nation and is supported by taxpayers of varying stripe. Relevant parts of them (with particularly pertinent parts underlined by me) are:

...the information is truthful, not distorted to justify a conclusion. Broadcasters do not take advantage of their position of control in any way to present a personal bias.

Programs dealing with an issue of substantial controversy on a one-time basis should give adequate recognition to the range of

opinion on the subject. _Fairness_ must be the guiding principle...
...*selection and editing*... must... reflect the essential truth _without distortion_.

McKenna's flagrant disregard of these policies and the sheer falsity of _Death by Moonlight_ demand a searching look at him.

There was a revealing follow-up to that part of McKenna's thesis which held that Canadians were forever being sacrificed by British senior commanders. He was interviewed by journalist Anne Collins about the rising furore over _The Valour and the Horror_ series, and she wrote it up for _Saturday Night_ of May, 1993. She quoted him as saying:

You know in the First World War we lost more men per capita than all the other Western allies, then twenty years later we go and do it again. This time we lose forty-two thousand outright killed and hundreds of thousands wounded in mind or body.

All informed persons know that Canada's per capita losses in the first war were only a fraction of France's, and in both wars were less than half of Britain's. Population and loss figures in the _Canadian Encyclopedia_ show that Canada lost 6.9 men per thousand in the first war. The figures in _Encyclopedia Britannica_ (an American publication since 1910) show that France lost 34.3 men per thousand and Great Britain 17.4, five times and two and a half times the Canadian rate respectively. The same encyclopedias show that in the second war Canada lost 3.7 men per thousand while Britain lost 8.4, two and a quarter times the Canadian rate. New Zealand's loss rates were about twice Canada's in both wars. In the second war Britain lost 38,000 men in Bomber Command alone, not far off the 42,000 which was Canada's total loss for all three of its services during the whole war. There were several reasons for Canada's relatively low per capita loss rate in both wars, but the low figures do suggest that Canadian fighting men were not continually being squandered by their senior commanders, British or Canadian, in either war. McKenna's statement to the contrary, fitting his thesis, was typical of him and of the integrity of his series.

McKenna stated that _Death by Moonlight_ was a tribute to the 50,000 Canadian airmen who flew with Bomber Command. That is deceitful and therefore insulting. Virtually all airmen could tell within the first few minutes of the film that McKenna, to use the words he used of the Ombudsman, "had his own agenda", and that it had two objectives. One was to denigrate the airmen themselves under the guise of pitying them, and to use them as stalking horses for his other objective, which was to denigrate Harris and the other senior commanders who directed the bombing campaign. Attempting to drive wedges between fighting men and their senior commanders is a characteristic of the radical academic left, of which McKenna revealed himself to be a member (therefore explaining his affinity with Dyson). McKenna and the others of that ilk, whose motivation seems only to be envy coupled with a sense of inferiority, have no conception of the lasting bond of admiration and even affection which bind great military leaders to their men. I have been told that the ovations given to Harris at Bomber Command reunions were unforgettable.

Another characteristic of the radical academic left which McKenna displayed was purporting to express extreme sympathy for the suffering of an enemy nation's people in order to inculcate a sense of guilt in the people of one's own nation in the hope and expectation that they will transfer the blame to their military leaders. It is part of that tactic to refrain from drawing attention to the usually much greater suffering inflicted on one's own or other peoples by that enemy nation for which its people are ultimately responsible. The whole tactic is deceitful of course, but integrity disappears at the extreme ends of the political spectrum, invariably being subordinated to a 'cause', as witness Zundel and McKenna.

In attempting to deflect the storm of criticism over the film McKenna has consistently declared that no one has been able to point out a single inaccuracy. This brings Goebbels's famous theory instantly to mind: tell a big enough lie often enough and enough people will believe it. The theory worked on Patrick Watson (president of the CBC when the film was produced) and on Pierre Berton (perhaps the strongest journalist supporter of the film), because both have repeated McKenna's declaration that no one has been able to point to a single inaccuracy. One must assume that neither of them had discovered or been informed of the three striking instances of deceit that I pointed to in the early part of this letter. No excuse for those instances could ever be accepted by an honourable person who has become aware of them, whether CBC offical, journalist or otherwise, and no such person could ever stand up for the film or promote or acquiesce in its further showing or distribution in any form.

The CBC's admirable journalistic policies are anathema to the radical academic left, a faction which I and many others feel has gained far too much influence in the corporation. Edmund Burke once said: *"It is a general popular error to imagine the loudest complainers for the public to be the most anxious for its welfare."* John Crispo, a CBC director, put his finger on the matter with great perception when he spoke up about the Gemini award (for best documentary) to McKenna and others who made *The Valour and the Horror* series. He said:

The... award... is a disgrace and a travesty... made less in honour than in spite and ignorance... I concluded that The Valour and the Horror *represented one of the most flagrant forms of revisionist history I was ever likely to view. Especially in the case of the Bomber Command episode...* [The crisis] *following the release of the Ombudsman's report and the CBC board's decision to uphold it, is a manufactured crisis... ...created by the supporters of the series and their friends at the CBC and elsewhere who, in a few cases knowingly, but in most cases trustingly and in ignorance, helped those supporters to turn their petulance at the series being criticized into a phoney issue of free speech... At CBC... various employees parroted their evident bias, much of it based on lack of knowledge, in solidarity with* The Valour and the Horror *and those who supported it. Editors and writers in some of the country's major newspapers did likewise and the result was a mockery of the ideals of balanced and fair, let alone thorough, journalism... ...Regrettably... massive numbers of our own producers and journalists joined this cabal or conspiracy...* [The CBC's board's] *handling of this trying case will decide the future of media accountability at the CBC and whether the corporation is run just for the benefit of its staff and their friends or truly in the public interest.... The CBC is a public trust, largely funded by public money, and none of us – producers, journalists, management or board members – should ever let ourselves forget it.*

One hears more and more people say that the CBC's days are numbered and should be. I feel that if the CBC is to be so largely at the sway of its employees and others who are members of the radical academic left or largely under its influence, it would be in the national interest to dissolve it. I'm sure the great majority of Canadians are not interested in subsidizing the attempts of that faction to deceive them and their posterity. The CBC has produced or shared in the production of some superb films, such as *Love and Hate* and *The Boys of St. Vincent's*. I don't know whether the Canadian market place is sufficiently developed to sustain the talents of directors and writers of films like those two, but if it is, Canadians can be assured of more great films. If it isn't, its only a matter of time until it is.

To ensure the CBC's future, I feel that the first signal step should be the severance of all relations between the corporation and Brian McKenna, on the ground of his gross contempt for the corporation's journalistic policies and standards.

Yours sincerely, R.I.A.Smith

Copies were sent at the same time to Ms. Guylaine Saucier, chairwoman, CBC board of directors, and to Mr. John Crispo, CBC director.

Aside from his detailed and specific knowledge, that really was Rod Smith the barrister in full flow, presenting an immaculately researched case for consideration.

The Hedley Everard Obituary

Group Captain Hedley Everard, who had shared in the shooting down of the first Me 262 jet fighter on 5 October 1944, and who had subsequently taken over command of 401 Squadron on the conclusion of Rod's operational tour, died on 19 February 1999. While the formal notice of his death which appeared in *The Globe and Mail*, correctly noted *"He also shared in the destruction of the world's first operational jet fighter, a German ME262, in 1944,"* the *National Post* for Saturday, 6 March 1999 published a full-page obituary, carrying the headline: *"Ace was first Commonwealth pilot to shoot down a jet fighter,"* and carrying a description of the combat which made it appear that Everard had made the initial attack on the Luftwaffe aircraft. To be fair, it did then continue, *"Group Captain Everard's Canadian mates, who had caught up to the action by now, were also pouring fire into the disabled fighter in a series of rapid passes. As the last Spitfire attacked, the German pilot jumped from his cockpit, but his parachute failed to open."* This part of the obituary concluded with the words: *"An American Mustang had downed another 262 a few days earlier. And while the 401 Squadron now shared the honours that went to Canada, Group Captain Everard himself was credited with drawing 'first blood' on the historic kill."*

This publication provided Rod with some undoubted soul-searching, for to issue a correction might be seen as attacking the memory of a fellow fighter pilot and fellow Canadian. In the event the ever-precise Rod felt obliged to set the record straight, and on 12 March 1999 wrote to the newspaper accordingly:

Mr. Kenneth Whyte, Editor-in-Chief
National Post

Dear Sir,
Re: <u>Group Captain Hedley Everard's Obituary</u>
(by your Richard Foot)

Your Richard Foot's obituary of Group Captain Hedley Everard on page A14 of your Saturday, March 6 edition was not only highly inaccurate, it was demeaning of the parts played by some of his fellow squadron pilots in the action referred to in its heading, which reads:

Ace was first Commonwealth pilot
To shoot down a jet fighter

[Rod then set out the offending passage]

The heading clearly implies that Everard (a flight lieutenant then) shot down the jet fighter all by himself. But the text portion shows that at least one other member of the squadron must have hit the jet as well, thus evidencing journalistic deceit in the heading.

As for Everard to have been *"credited with drawing first blood"*, that is wholly incorrect. 401's John MacKay (a flying officer then) hit the jet first. That fact should not be covered up, because very many RCAF and RAF fighter pilots are aware of the 'historic kill'.

I was the commanding officer of 401 Squadron at the time, and I was leading its normal twelve airborne Spitfires on patrol at 13,000 feet over Holland's famous Nijmegen Bridge over the Rhine on the day of the action, October 5, 1944. After a while our ground radar controller warned us of an approaching enemy aircraft. A short time later, I (not Everard as Foot says) spotted the jet and reported it to the other pilots. It was a little below us, coming on very fast. I and three or four other pilots (Everard and MacKay included) swung out to the right to give ourselves room to swing back in behind it so that we could shoot at it as it passed by, before its very high speed would take it out of our range.

When I swung back in behind it I found that one pilot had not swung far enough out to the right to allow himself sufficient space to get in behind it, so he was not quite in a position to shoot at it. I thought it was MacKay, but I found out about 45 years later it was Everard! Unfortunately, he had come between me and the jet, spoiling my shot as well as his own, because I could not shoot for fear of hitting him.

Everard then told MacKay, who was his wingman and who had swung out far enough to the right, to attack. When MacKay opened fire several strikes from his cannons appeared on one of the jet's wing roots. One or two were close alongside the nascelle of one of its two engines. A thin stream of strange-looking whitish vapour issued out from that area. (Jets used kerosene, not gasoline, so I am sure it was vaporizing kerosene that issued out because the stream was not very long, leaving no lasting trail of smoke as gasoline would have done).

The jet began diving and rolling, with all of us streaming after it, and MacKay could not keep his gunsight on it for long. It pulled out of its dive at about 3000 feet. The whitish trail ceased issuing out, even though two or three pilots, Everard included, had kept firing. I and another 401 pilot, Tex Davenport, had pulled out of our dives about half way down because we had nearly collided with each other. When the jet pulled out of its dive it astonished us all by zooming almost vertically back up again, very fast, to where Davenport and I were. I was the closer to it, so I pulled up behind it and opened fire, one or two of my strikes being close alongside the same engine nacelle that one or two of McKay's strikes had been alongside. A plume of flame began to issue from that area and grow longer. The jet fell away from its climb and crashed into a field on the south-west edge of Nijmegen; its pilot bailed out too low and was killed.

A few days later our gun camera films came back developed. MacKay's film clearly showed that he was the one who had drawn 'first blood', and that the whitish trail had begun issuing out while he was firing. My film was 'whited out' for the first few seconds because the jet in its zoom had got at too close an angle between me and the sun, but as it fell away the film cleared and showed the plume of flame. Davenport's film showed the flame too but it also showed he was far out of range, and that my Spitfire was more than halfway between him and the jet while he was firing. (I wondered whether he cared less for my safety than I had cared for Everard's!) Everard's film showed nothing memorable, except that he had also fired from far out of range, as did the film of 'Sinc' Sinclair, the fifth pilot who fired.

While I remember very clearly that MacKay's film and mine were the only two that showed damage actually being inflicted, I also noticed that the flame appearing in my film was issuing from the area alongside the engine nacelle where one or two of MacKay's strikes had caused the trail of whitish vapour to issue from. That made me wonder whether the flame could possibly have been a delayed after-effect of those one or two strikes of his, even though the whitish trail had disappeared nearly half a minute before the flame appeared. If it was an after-effect (and jet engines run very hot), MacKay's first blood was the last as well. But we shall never know.

Frank Wootton, a fine aviation artist, and a photo of whose painting depicting the action accompanied the obituary, placed the jet much too low, with a long stream of black smoke issuing from an engine nacelle. He had obviously been misinformed.

If Everard's obituary had been written by a friend or relative, it would of course be understood not to have been made under oath, and I would not have written this letter. The actual author, Richard Foot, is held out by *National Post* to be on its staff. I cannot let pass the demeaning by a national newspaper of John MacKay's key part in the 'historic kill'. (And may I be forgiven for saying I believe my own part was not wholly insignificant either.)

National Post has quickly gained a reputation for accuracy in reporting, and for the quality of its journalists. But Foot's research for the obituary in question obviously fell far below that standard. His only source seems to have been *A Mouse in My Pocket*, a book written and published by Everard himself in 1988. It is the most emotional and error-filled fighter pilot's memoir I have ever seen. Foot seems to have failed even to obtain copies of the combat reports all of us wrote after we landed, though they are easily obtainable from the Public Records Office in Britain and perhaps Ottawa.

It was normal for most such reports, written right after landing, to contain inaccuracies; and where several pilots were involved, to be inconsistent and even out of sequence. They are usually the key source, though, next to gun camera film. Everard said in his report that the *"streamer of white smoke"* came from the jet while he was firing. MacKay said in his report: *"...Everard was slightly out of position (for shooting) and told me to go in to attack."* (As stated above, MacKay's film clearly showed that the whitish stream issued out while he was firing.) MacKay said later in his report that: *"...Squadron Leader Smith came in to attack. The starbaord engine nascelle burst into flames..."* (Everard's report began by saying and therefore confirming that it was I who spotted the jet first, not him as he claimed. I labour the spotting aspect because, as every fighter pilot knows, early spotting was usually a vital part of every successful air combat.)

In 1989 an English aviation historian. John Foreman, who was writing a book on the history of the Me 262 jet fighter, asked me to write a personal account of 401 Squadron's shooting down the one in question, which I did. I later sent to MacKay copies of my account and of Everard's account of the same incident in his *A Mouse in My Pocket*. MacKay had become reclusive but he let me know he was much put out by Everard's account. He said I had a remarkable memory.

He corrected an impression I had long been under; in my account to Foreman I had said it was MacKay who had spoiled my shot by getting in between me and the jet at the beginning, but MacKay told me it had been Everard. I reviewed the combat reports and realized he was right. It was too late, though, to correct my account for Foreman's book, which came out in 1990. (I do not mean to imply that Everard had kept this from me. I had never brought the matter up with either him or MacKay, so he probably just assumed I had been aware of it.)

To conclude, I noticed that at the beginning of the text of Everard's obituary Foot described him as *"one of Canada's most successful wartime flying aces"* (an ace being a rather journalistic term for a fighter pilot who is credited with five or more enemy aircraft destroyed). Everard was credited with five destroyed (plus one-fifth of the jet). This was a very good 'score', as it is arguable that the majority of fighter pilots were not even credited with one (though I am convinced that a number of them would rate among the finest of fighter pilots, strange as that may seem). However,

Canada's *"most successful wartime flying aces"*, in the public perception of those words, were credited with a lot more than five and one-fifth. (My own humble thirteen and one-fifth would not stack up well if I were foolish enough to throw them into the ring.)

Sincerely, R.I.A.Smith

So that was Rod the correspondent. Every point carefully thought out, researched and ultimately proveable. Coupled with that was a terrier-like determination to continue arguing each issue to the point where he felt an entirely rational outcome had been achieved. This, of course, required the demolition of any preconceived notions, conspiracy-theories or emotional assessments until fact and reason prevailed. Here was the advocate, the trained engineer and the historian all merged together to create a formidable proponent of his chosen point.

In his correspondence with Roland Beamont, one can sense poor Bee gradually becoming more irritated by this persistent demolisher of myths, as a consequence of which he began to retreat towards more irrational, emotional responses. This is precisely the result the experienced barrister will endeavour to achieve against the other side's witnesses in court. Truly, Rod was a master of his art.

PART THREE

ROD IN RETIREMENT

Rod and the Ladies

Having taken on the (welcome) task of seeking to complete
Rod's autobiography, one subject has to an extent defeated
me. Rod never married, but throughout his life a succession of
ladies seem never to have been too far away. But what was his
relationship with them? The rather prurient modern mind,
'trained' by the intrusive personal probing of the press and
television, demands 'the facts', but in this case close
questioning of the family – particularly his sister Wendy, failed
to give many clues. Wendy was instrumental in putting me in
touch with some of the ladies in question – virtually all of
whom seem still to be around and contactable. But I fear as a
historian rather than a hard-nosed journalist, I baulked at
pressing them for answers to any questions beyond which they
were readily willing to give.

One of the earliest was Billy Mills (below) – obviously
known to Rod during
the war years and
of whom photographs
in military uniform
remain amongst Rod's
collection. There was
also Patricia Johnson,
who later told Wendy
that Rod had 'loved
her too much'. Did
that signify that at
some stage Rod had
been hurt and dis-
appointed to a degree
that closed him to a
permanent 'one-to-
one' relationship?

There was Judy

196

McLennan (known to Rod as Jude – but mentioned in his Will officially as Elizabeth Tyler McLennan) – who knew Rod since first meeting him in Vancouver in 1956, and who described him as a dear and constant friend. Others too were generous in their memories of a man whose friendship and affection they clearly had the happiest of feelings for. One of these was Margarete Zillich, who – as most people do – remembers Rod most fondly:

In his Last Will Rod referred to several special women in his life. I am one of these women and am forever thankful that Rod was a part of my life for so many years.

I first met Rod at a law firm in Vancouver in the mid 1960s but didn't date him until the early 1970s. I found him handsome, dashing, smart, funny and just nice to be around. We started out as friends and always remained special friends other than for that short magical trip to Europe in 1984 which we later referred to as our honeymoon.

Both Rod and I were quite content being single even though we enjoyed the company of the opposite sex. In between other romantic entanglements we would enjoy each other's company. In particular, I have fond memories of Rod cooking me dinner at his lovely apartment overlooking Vancouver's Stanley Park. The menu was predictable – fried chicken or lamb chops with a baked potato and some sort of fresh vegetable. After dinner we often walked to a nearby movie theatre or rented a movie to watch at home. On some winter weekends we would travel on his much loved boat up Howe Sound enjoying the latest offering from the Metropolitan Opera on radio. If Rod had social commitments in town I was happy to accompany him as he had so many fascinating friends.

In early May of 1984 I happened to be between jobs and thus able to accept Rod's invitation to travel to Europe with him. While there we attended some official functions related to Rod's wartime service and met with long time friends such as Johnnie Johnson and his lovely wife Janet. We made a short side trip to Malta which was an emotional time for Rod as it recalled the loss of his brother who is memorialized at their war memorial. One night after dinner at our hotel the band struck up 'Canadian Sunset' and dedicated the dance to us – pretty special!

Back in England we visited more friends of Rod's before taking the Hovercraft across to France. We took the train to Paris where we met with long time friends from Ontario. In Paris we picked up a car and now our private holiday truly got under way. Due to Rod's determination and excellent navigational skills we soon left Paris behind us and reached Chartres our destination for the day.

Years later we would often marvel at how special our one night in Chartres had been – a miracle of sorts. The following morning over breakfast we wrote some long overdue postcards and I never forgot the following comment Rod made on a card to his best friend in Toronto: "If I had known that honeymoons were so special I would have gone on one a long time ago." The remainder of our trip through France and southern Germany became what we would always refer to as our honeymoon.

Back home in Vancouver we were never quite able to recapture what had made Chartres so special but our friendship continued to deepen and go from strength to strength until I met my husband Dave in 1987. After Dave and I moved to Okanagan Rod and I would speak on the phone now and then and exchange Christmas and birthday cards. I was deeply saddened when Wendy called me to tell me about Rod's death.

I once asked Rod why he never married. He thought about this for some time before answering. In essence he told me that he felt that marriage meant total commitment to one's spouse. In other words his wife would have to take precedence over anyone else in his life. At the same time he felt that he could not abandon family members and friends for the sake of marriage. Supreme loyalty was at the top of Rod's code of honour and I think that this is the reason why he remained a bachelor. In the end Rod preferred to love many rather than just one and I don't think he lost one friend because he decided to be an honourable gentleman.

One of Rod's greatest female friends was Robin Fleming. She recalls of him:

I met Rod in late summer of 1990. My father and Rod had served in the RCAF in WWII and later met while studying at McGill. Rod became a lawyer but Dad volunteered as a fighter pilot in Korea; later he became chief test pilot on the Canadair CF-104. He and Rod had remained friends. When he visited me in 1990, he wound up staying with Rod. My father over previous years had become an alcoholic. What struck me most about Rod was his kindness and loyalty to an old friend and as I eventually realized, to all close acquaintances. We formed a lasting friendship. I was even more in awe of his erudition and incredible memory. He never ceased to amaze me with recollections of dialogues with friends, quotations from books read and his knowledge of music, especially opera. I learned much from him about my Dad that cast him in a much more favourable light than my mother did. My parents divorced when I was very young so this information was important to me. He asked my father, Bruce, as he saw him depart off to Korea, if he was afraid and anxious about going, leaving his wife and young family. To this Dad swept his arm over the persons seated at the airport gate and responded that he did not want to be ordinary. *That* struck a chord with Rod.

Rod and I took long brisk walks together through Stanley Park, with me listening to narratives of his flying experiences and his career as a lawyer. I had frequent invitations to his other home, the Vancouver Club, with introductions to interesting people and others he enjoyed entertaining at the club.

It was evident that Rod was leagues ahead in his repertoire of reading. Occasionally we could reach a mutual level and review a book common to both of us. We dissected characters in films. His most favourite film, *High Noon*, surprised me, but of course it was understandable of him – the story of a man (Gary Cooper) who knew 'he had to do his duty'. And the televised serial, Evelyn Waugh's *Brideshead Revisited*, absolutely enthralled Rod, leading to my observation that he held an analytical interest in those born with a silver spoon. He was fascinated by the lives of people who made scads of money and yet it wasn't money he aspired to for himself, although he echoed every so often "...what one really needs in life is food, shelter and money, money, money!" His attention to others in need or to ailing friends was unwavering and he was truly a gentleman in every sense of the term.

Bertrand Russell was to him the ultimate writer. Rod was most impressed that Russell wrote his own biography at the age of 90. This inspired him to work on his own book, which he seemed to abandon following the death of his dear friend, Johnnie Johnson.

He was attentive and a good listener to others, but he could trip you up on the accuracy of a point without being insulting. While at his apartment, one could enjoy a most sparkling and stimulating conversation, but if one spoke of a subject matter lacking in fact or the slightest amount of credability, Rod quietly leaned over his chair and pulled some type of reference dictionary lying dormant in a drawer beside his chair. He would slide this onto his lap, still listening to the guest who still held the floor, and correct the errant in such a point-of-fact manner. If unable to research the answer at that time, he had no qualms about continuing with his mission by giving a call on the phone the next day to give the goods to set one straight on the facts. And yet he could be absentminded on domestic matters to the point of being such a 'darling'. I rescued his kitchen appliances by changing the fuses in the fusebox. Often while driving with him he would make a complete stop in an intersection with a green light; when I asked why he did this he would say he was just being cautious, to which I could not help but comment "Oh fearless fighter pilot!"

In May 1994 he wanted to plan and join his friends at Normandy's 50th Anniversary (of D-Day). I offered to fly him over in return for allowing me to tag along with the elite – later dubbed by me as the 'Rat Pack'. And so it was, we headed to London where he would be re-united with his friends. The tone was set while crossing 'the pond'. Rod and I were upgraded into

Executive Class following much persuasion on my part to Air Canada with accolades of this hero and the tribute due at Normandy. When asked by a flight director – a personal friend of mine – for his order from the bar, he requested his favourite, "a dry Bombay Martini, no vermouth, with an ever so light shaved piece of lemon rind, translucent like an onion, just use a potato peeler, please." It was then evident we were heading for a wonderful time.

While in London we planted ourselves into the RAF Club. This was where Rod stayed following his final tour of duty on Malta in 1942. He recalled then this hotel had strict water rationing. He had been deprived of any type of fresh water bathing facilities on Malta; a real bath before him with warm water was almost too much to bear. Hotel guests were permitted to fill $1/4$ of the tub daily. Rod claimed to have shed so much packed Maltese dust and dirt that the water very quickly turned black. After draining the tub he didn't hesitate in breaking club rules. He ran himself a second bath to give himself a better rinse. Then while luxuriating in the shallow water, he suddenly and uncontrollably burst into tears and wept, as if all the washed off grime and unfamilar comfort brought forth his realization and sorrow for all those who did not come out of Malta with him. His brother Jerry was one of them.

For two days in London, Rod re-united with remarkable friends; my first privileged encounter with most of them. A delightful lunch, accompanied by Dan Browne, Larry Robillard (former friends of my father's) at the home of Jill and Laddie Lucas, Laddie sharing photos and leafing through *Wings of War*. Dinner with Jeffrey and Clara Quill back at the RAF Club, and others. One such interesting person, Nancy Wake, known as the 'White Mouse', was a heroine of the French Resistance. I really had no idea of the significant background of all these persons. I suppose Rod told me, but now it was made real by their presence.

One of the things that struck me about these icons of aviation was how gracious and self-effacing they were.

Dan, Rod, Larry and I were driven to Portsmouth by Keith McNair, son of 'Buck'McNair. I was requested by Larry to turn off the audio taping I was starting regarding the recollections among the fellows. We met up with Johnnie Johnson and Janet. My initial impression of Johnnie was that of a professional hunter.

We took the Britannia Ferry to Ouistreham. Dozens of young adults were boarding in various World War II uniforms, extremely detailed; the girls' hairdos were swept into 1940s fashion and they were wearing seamed nylons. The crossing was delayed that night until after 11 pm, and Rod and his group exhausted me as they set to party into all hours of the night. This, by the way, continued each night in Normandy, and I – the youngest – was unable to maintain the pace. The excitement of being with each other was fuelled by their adrenaline.

Jean Pierre Benemou, then curator and director of the Bayeux Museum, loaned us his summer home on the Normandy beach at Ouistreham. This served as the base for the guys as they attended functions starting at Bayeux Cathedral, Bayeux Memorial Museum, a splendid low Spitfire flypast at Croix-sur-Mer and the commemoration of the D-Day landings at the Commonwealth Cemetery. We were impressed with Johnnie for preparing for his speeches by taking French lessons in the previous months. Larry too, presented speeches in French.

On a free afternoon, the six of us returned two days later to St Croix with a wine and cheese picnic packed in the back of Johnnie's Land Rover. This was intended as a quiet time away from the crowd. However, a young English teacher and his wife drove up holding a copy of *Full Circle*, making inquiries about the memorial, wondering if this was where the great Johnnie Johnson flew. Imagine his sheer delight when we invited him to meet and enjoy a glass of wine with the man himself.

Dan Browne surprised us by being an excellent and informative guide to Rod and me at the American cemeteries at Utah and Omaha beaches. He was precise in his descriptions of the attacks. People of Normandy, encompassed us at some of the memorial sights and listened intently without understanding English, but they knew all too well the battles. Here among them was one of those heroes.

Larry was far more reflective, spending hours sitting in front of the cottage on Normandy beach, looking out to sea.

During an afternoon, as Rod and I returned from grocery shopping, we passed a nice-looking small hotel a few blocks from our host's home. We both slowed down before it, and looked at one another. We had the same idea. The cottage we had been staying at had only two bathrooms. Johnnie, important guest of honour, had the ensuite while the rest of us shared a shower stall in the cellar. It had a showerhead which dribbled cold water.

We agreed and entered the premises. We asked the woman at reception, using our awful French, if we could have a room for only an hour. Then her husband arrived behind the desk. By moving our arms in brushing strokes, we indicated we wanted to simply take a warm bath. As we presented ourselves, more family appeared behind the desk, including two young teenage daughters. We had to forge on with our lame French. But we did get a key for a room and some subtle expressions of doubt. Without any change of clothes, we entered the room and took our turns bathing in the tub, the other enjoying a glimpse of television. An hour later we checked out with very wet hair and got a polite adieu from our patrons. It all seemed very civilized to us at the time. Later, after sharing this experience with the others, we did not hear the same politeness we had from that patron.

During those days, amongst the thousands who came to the 50th D-Day celebration, Johnnie, Larry, Rod and Dan were revered and hosted by Normandy's citizens and dignitaries, and an appearance by Princess Margaret. Once they entered a restaurant or event, people stood up and sang to them or saluted – all very moving. After the rock star agenda, the guys returned to the beach house. Relieved, ties loosened, jackets and medals removed (incidentally, Rod scoffed at wearing medals), G and T's and Martinis christened the cocktail hour. Laughter, kibitzing, fraternizing took hold of the night. Others were on the periphery – this was their time and it was glorious.

So it was with Rod I had such memorable times. And who could be so fortunate to have been in the midst of heroes. Rod, all his life had a yearning to understand and I was in awe of his knowledge. A kind of Renaissance man, but also a man who simply loved to come over, be pampered with a home-cooked Sunday dinner, listen to good music, and recite A.E.Houseman, Tennyson and Shakespeare, feeling the glowing affection of such a friend as me, who enjoyed making fun of him when he was being so clever. He was a masterpiece.

Joane Humphrey provides a vignette entitled 'Dinner at Rod's':

"Look at this," he says, delightedly. Rod is pointing to a small stand set beside his chair in the living room. Made of pale wood, its base supports a slim dowel topped with a rimmed circular plate. As ever, snuggled on his lap is Boofuls, the adored, adoring love-bug of a Siamese cat that came into his life when both were well into their senior years.

"Boofuls. Boofuls, bootiful Boofuls," Rod begins to croon. Their noses rapturously press together; his patrician... hers dark and furry.

"Oo is so bootiful, aren't oo, Boofuls?"

While wishing for the millionth time that the cat's name weren't 'Boofuls', I am staring quizzically at the odd little stand. "I designed that stand myself and had it made," he is saying, animated. He's as pleased as Punch.

"Fabulous!" I marvel. "A perfect design!" I don't reveal that I haven't one clue of what use that design could possibly serve.

He rises suddenly and I trail after him into the kitchen where he opens the freezer door, removes a martini glass, one of many lined up with military precision, and carries it back to the living room. Proudly he places the glass neatly into the rimmed wooden plate.

"Perfect!" he says. "A perfect fit. This way Boofuls and I can sit here watching TV and I can still reach my martini with no trouble at all."

We sit companionably talking and watching television. He's set the channel to a local community station that's showing a looped video of a cosy fire burning in a fireplace. Onscreen, flames are licking up, logs snapping and crackling. "Its here that the log to the upper left breaks," he says. It does.

Suddenly, a sharp 'ping' from the kitchen.

"The timer! Potatoes!" he shouts, springing up again, disentangling himself from both Boofuls and his now poured martini. Quickly the potatoes are whisked off the stove, neatly drained, and covered with a lid.

Later, another 'ping' sends us hurtling to the kitchen. Chicken. Then a third 'ping' signals that the broccoli is cooked. Between pings I've helped him set the table and watched as he's lit the candles in an exquisite Georgian candelabra. He has beautiful hands. Looking at him I think again of how, as the years have passed, he looks more and more like a particularly distinguished Roman emperor. One you'd like.

"You're so handsome, Rod," I say.

"Stop that! You're going to make me blush."

He removes warm plates from the oven; artfully arranges the food on them. At the table he pours the wine.

The music of Mozart that I'd first heard when I arrived continues to fill the air. Only a short distance away the waters of Burrard Inlet sparkle in the moonlight.

"Your very good health," he says, his glass raised. There's an infinite sweetness about him, in his face, his being. A boyish innocence. Is that a funny thing for me to say about this brilliant, learned man who'd been so dramatically, so heroically, so tragically part of that gruesome war? That's what it was, though. Innocence.

After dinner we look through his telescope, which is always set up by a large window in the living room. Forty years before, when I was twenty-three, we'd first met. He lived in a rented apartment then, and horrified me by describing with unfettered joy how, peering through his telescope, he loved watching women undressing near the windows of their West End apartments.

"How *disgusting*!" I had said.

Now, though, quickly shaking off that memory of youthful prurience (he was only in his early forties then) I'm fascinated as he describes, with his usual knowledge and enthusiasm, the stars that he's pointing out to me from that selfsame telescope. From there a line of poetry comes to one of us and if we can't remember the whole poem (usual for me; unusual for him) he dashes to his book shelves, retrieves one of his many poetry books and quickly finds the verses. Then, in his lovely voice, he reads aloud.

By one of those strange quirks of fate, for years now we've lived only three blocks from each other; he walks me home and outside my building we part with a loving hug.

Not long after, the phone rings.

"Oh, Joane! Rod here! On the way back I remembered something...." And off we go again, talking about the poem, or the historical anecdote he was relating to me; and he's reciting from memory what Plato or Churchill or Galileo or Baby Peggy or Ivan The Terrible had said about something that was pertinent to what we'd been discussing. But at the end of the conversation his voice takes on a certain cautionary note.

"Joane..."

My God, I think, what have I done now?

"Joane, sometimes when I'm walking down the alley I notice that you're not always using your wheel locking device on the Golden Tank." *(My Volvo.)*

"Cross my heart I'll remember,"I say. "Good night dearest Rod. Thank you for a beautiful evening. Such a beautiful evening."

"Good night, dearest Joane. Sleep well."

Ah, yes! Boofuls, the Siamese cat, and for years Rod's adored companion. Boofuls, it seems, was not a lady cat! Rod wrote to Johnnie Johnson about the arrival of this new resident:

I may be undergoing a major change of life. I expect a closet boyfriend will be moving in with me in early September; a Siamese cat named 'Suckypuss'. A woman friend I met a couple of years ago named Sandralee Jackson, a fifty year old who is lots of fun and who divorced her RCN Commodore husband some years before that, suffered Suckypuss, a stray at that time, to work his way by degrees into her affections and take over her ground floor apartment, not long after I met her. She says she chose that name because he accomplished all this by sucking up to her. I became emotionally involved (with Suckypuss) after a while. She says she has two neutered males on her hands but I point out that Suckypuss is the only one who has actually had an operation. Now Sandralee is going to marry a consulting mining engineer barely into his sixties who has three dogs and two cats. She and I are afraid Suckypuss may decide to take a hike in that milieu. Suckypuss has always been an only child (she tracked down his former owner – who said to keep him – when the vet found registration numbers in his ear). He is now five years old. The closet aspect arises because the rules of the condominium forbid pets, but Sandralee and I have decided to take a chance on transferring his domicile here. So, though I may have lost the girl, I am not to be denied her pussy. I'm really looking forward to it.

A Sad Ending

During the last two decades of the twentieth century Rod frequently attended symposia – mainly in the USA – where fighter pilots of note were invited to join the panel, speak about their experiences, answer questions – and always, sign books. A number of these events were organised by Virginia Bader, an American lady deeply involved in the preparation and sale of posters depicting various aviation scenes of note. These became very collectable during this period their value (to their collectors at least) being considerably enhanced by the inclusion thereon of as many relevant autographs as possible.

During some of these events, Rod was to meet many fellow pilots of note, including Adolf Galland, Guenther Rall, Chuck Yeager, and others. Between events probably his two closest friends of the genre remained Johnnie Johnson and Laddie Lucas. Sadly, both developed cancer-related illnesses, Laddie passing away first, followed not very long afterwards by Johnnie. These deaths hit Rod hard, but on 21 June 2001 he wrote to Guenther Rall:

Dear Guenther,
It was good to see you again, at Johnnie Johnson's memorial service. Though we spoke on the telephone some months ago when you were visiting Lute and Carol Eldridge, I hadn't seen you since Virginia Bader's "travelling road show" in California in 1989.

During the service for Johnnie I could not suppress a feeling that we are more or less at the end of an era. Our ranks are thinning out, though you look very well and I have little to complain about. You and I are the only survivors from Virginia's 1989 show.

We must keep going one day at a time, though. I want to outlive my beloved cat at the least; he is going on fourteen and would think I had abandoned him if I died before he did anywhere but at home!

I still enjoy reading and researching the historical and technical aspects of World War II in the air, and writing about them. I miss the cruising and fishing I used to do up and down our coast here, though.

Yours ever,

Despite the sentiments recorded here, following the loss of Johnnie, the heart seemed to go out of Rod's work on his autobiography, which virtually ground to a halt. Rod's serious side was normally complemented by a happy and cheerful disposition, but a note of despondency crept in as more friends 'dropped off the perch'.

Robin Fleming once told Rod that he was a hypochondriac. His response was, "Well, even hypochondriacs get sick." In the early 1990s he was about to be operated on for a left temporal lobe brain tumour when, three days before the operation was to take place, it was discovered by a radiologist to be a blood clot which doctors thought could have resulted from hitting the water with great force when he baled out of his Spitfire over the Mediterranean in 1942. It was a tremendous relief as the so-called 'tumour' was fairly deep-seated. The downside was that he was diagnosed with a condition called Cerebral Amyloid Angiopathy (CAA) which he was told would gradually result in a deterioration of the lining of the arteries of the brain. Robin was with him when he asked the doctor how long he would have to finish his book, and was told he would begin to feel the effects of the disease within three years. Except for some worrying episodes of extremely high blood pressure which he may have perceived to have been related, for the time being life was good again. But the diagnosis hung in the air and Rod called his condition Damocletian.

Over the years his family in Toronto had become familiar with Rod's periodic declarations of the intention to take his own life if faced with a disabling illness that might force him into a care facility, which he perceived as a burden to others. Robin, who cared deeply for him, says that she once responded to similar statements by telling him that she would take care of him, to which she says he responded, "No, no. I am determined. I will choose the way I go when the time comes." He asked her to respect his desire to make such a decision. He didn't want the manner of his leaving to be out of his hands.

In due course other health problems, albeit non-life threatening, followed, but although he was in the process of recuperating from a non-cancerous prostate operation, and seemed to want to recover, he was discouraged by discomfort caused by something not quite right with the operation. This appears to have been the resurgence of an old problem, for in a letter to me, written as far back as January 1989, he had said: "...I went into hospital as planned, for the old man's operation... I had a few little setbacks, but nothing serious, and when I got out I had to lie down for a month, except for some walking and meals. The op was successful (I am peeing like a horse again instead of a mouse) but I have fallen far behind in everything." He had been due to discuss this subsequent problem with the surgeon on the very day on which he died, but must have decided not to keep the appointment.

At age 80, on 16 April 2002, Rod followed through on his promise to chart the course of his demise when he launched himself from the balcony of his beautiful Vancouver apartment, high above the city's streets – and so, tragically, died a man who may clearly be called a most gentle hero. In the words of a close friend and colleague, "He took his last flight." The following was part of his file of treasured poetry and quotations:

> Duty is heavier than the grandest mountain
> Death is lighter than a feather*

Ironically, a cerebral autopsy performed after his death showed that he had not in fact had CAA, but only the normal changes in the brain of a man of his age.

---

* Japanese proverb – according to 'W.L. Wolper Presents'.

RECORDS OF SERVICE

Wg Cdr R.I.A.Smith, DFC & Bar

17 November 1940 – 9 January 1941	2 EFTS, Fort William
11 January 1941 – 7 March 1941	2 SFTS, Uplands

Transit to United Kingdom

12 May 1941 – 23 June 1941	58 OTU,Grangemouth
1 June 1941 – 1 June 1942	412 Squadron, Digby
7 July 1942 – 15 July 1942	HMS *Eagle*, transit to Malta
15 July 1942 – 11 December 1942	126 Squadron, Luqa, Malta

Transit to United Kingdom

7 January 1943 – 27 February 1943	53 OTU, Llandow
(13 January 1943 – 24 February 1943)	attached 3 FIS, Hullavington
27 February 1943 – 29 September 1943	55 OTU, Annan
October 1943 – January 1944	Home leave, Canada
6 January 1944 – 24 March 1944	401 Squadron, Biggin Hill
24 March 1944 – 19 September 1944	412 Squadron, Biggin Hill and various bases in France and Belgium
20 September 1944 – 4 December 1944	401 Squadron, Brussels/Evere
November 1946 – November 1949	401 Fighter Squadron (Aux) Westmount, PQ
September 1949 – November 1950	400 Fighter Squadron (Aux), Toronto
November 1950 – September 1952	411 Fighter Squadron (Aux), Toronto
September 1952 – End of Service	14 OP Wing (Aux), Toronto

Plt Off J.A.Smith

13 January 1941 – 21 February 1941	1 ITS, Toronto
21 February 1941 – 20 April 1941	10 EFTS, Mount Hope, Ontario
3 May 1941 – 14 July 1941	9 SFTS, Summerside, Prince Edward Island

Transit to United Kingdom

5 September 1941 – 21 October 1941	57 OTU, Hawarden
21 October 1941 – 31 April 1942	152 Squadron, Swanton Morley, Coltishall, Eglinton
	USS *Wasp*, transit to Malta
20 May 1942 – 30 June 1942	601 Squadron, Luqa, Malta
1 July 1942 – 10 August 1942	126 Squadron, Luqa, Malta
10 August 1942	Missing in Action

CLAIMS IN AERIAL COMBAT

Squadron Leader R.I.A.Smith

1942							
18 Jul		Ju88 Probable	Spitfire V	BP952	'F'	N Malta	126 Sqn
24 Jul	1/2	Ju88 (a)	"		'O'	Malta	"
28 Jul		Ju88 (b)	"		'C'	Kalafrana	"
13 Aug		S-79 (c)	"	AB465		over convoy	"
11 Oct		Ju88 (d)	"	EP330		Grand Harbour	"
13 Oct		Bf109 (e)	"	EP573		Sliema Bay	"
14 Oct		Ju88 Damaged	"	BR471		N St Paul's Bay	"
25 Oct		Bf109 (f)	"	BR311	'L'	Malta	"
1944							
7 Jul		FW190	Spitfire IXb	ML113		Argentan area	412 Sqn
26 Sep	2	Bf109s	"	MJ461		5-10m E Nijmegen	"
27 Sep	2	Bf109s	"			E and NE Nijmegen	"
29 Sep	2	Bf109s	"	MJ448	YO-W	10m SE Nijmegen	401 Sqn
5 Oct	1/5	Me262 (g)	"	MK577		5m NE Nijmegen	"

TOTAL: 13 and 1 shared destroyed, 1 shared probable, 1 damaged.

(a) M7+KH of KGr806; (b) 3Z+HP of II/KG77; (c) S-79sil of 132° Gruppo Aut AS; (d) B3+YL of I/KG54; (e) Actually an MC202 of 352ª Squadriglia, 20° Gruppo, 51° Stormo CT; Mar Maurizio Iannucci; (f) 'Weisse 16' of I/SchG 2; Uffz Willi Diepenseifen; (g) 9K+BL of I/KG(J)51; Hpt Hans-Christoph Buttmann.

Pilot Officer J.A.Smith

1942							
15 Jun		Ju87 Probable	Spitfire V	175	Z	S Pantelleria	601 Sqn
"		Bf109 Damaged	"		"	over convoy	"
"		Ju88 Damaged	"	BR381		over convoy	"
10 Jul		Ju88	"	BP952	F	Malta	126 Sqn
12 Jul		Ju88	"	BR242	A	"	"
18 Jul		Bf109 Damaged	"	BR176	Q	"	"
24 Jul	1/2	Ju88 Probable	"	BR242	A	"	"
26 Jul		Ju88 Damaged	"	BP952	F	30m N Malta	"
28 Jul	1/5	Ju88	"	BR242	A	Malta	"

TOTAL: 3 and 1 shared destroyed, 1 and 1 shared probable, 4 damaged.

INDEX